W9-BVT-715

American Heart
Association®

Learn and Live ℠

American Heart Association

Low-Salt
cookbook

3RD EDITION

Also by the American Heart Association

American Heart Association No-Fad Diet

The New American Heart Association Cookbook, 7th Edition

American Heart Association Low-Fat, Low-Cholesterol Cookbook, 3rd Edition

American Heart Association Low-Calorie Cookbook

American Heart Association Quick & Easy Cookbook

American Heart Association Meals in Minutes

American Heart Association One-Dish Meals

American Heart Association Low-Fat & Luscious Desserts

American Heart Association to Your Health! A Guide to Heart-Smart Living

American Heart Association Fitting in Fitness

American Heart Association
Learn and Live℠

American Heart Association

Low-Salt
cookbook

A Complete Guide to Reducing
Sodium and Fat in Your Diet

3RD EDITION

Clarkson Potter/Publishers
New York

Published in the United States by Clarkson Potter/Publishers, an imprint of the Crown Publishing Group, a division of Random House, Inc., New York.
www.crownpublishing.com
www.clarksonpotter.com

Clarkson N. Potter is a trademark and Potter and colophon are registered trademarks of Random House, Inc.

Originally published in different form by Times Books, New York, in 1990. Revised editions were subsequently published by Clarkson Potter, an imprint of the Crown Publishing Group, a division of Random House, Inc., New York, in 2001 and 2006.

Your contribution to the American Heart Association supports research that helps make publications like this possible. For more information, call 1-800-AHA-USA (1-800-242-8721) or contact us online at americanheart.org.

Library of Congress Cataloging-in-Publication Data
The American Heart Association low-salt cookbook : a complete guide to reducing sodium and fat in your diet / American Heart Association.—3rd ed.
    Includes index.
    1. Salt-free diet—Recipes.   I. American Heart Association.
RM237.8   .S73   2001
641.5'632—dc21 00-061184

ISBN 978-1-4000-9762-3

Printed in the United States of America

Design by Laura Palese
Illustrations by Liv Hansen

10   9   8   7

Third Edition

Front cover: Sirloin with Tomato, Olive, and Feta Topping (page 144)
Photograph by Ben Fink

Contents

Acknowledgments

American Heart Association Consumer Publications

Director: Linda S. Ball

Managing Editor: Deborah Ann Renza

Senior Editor: Janice Roth Moss

Science Editor: Jacqueline Fornerod Haigney

Assistant Editor: Roberta Westcott Sullivan

Senior Marketing Manager: Bharati Gaitonde

Recipe Developers for This and Previous Editions

Carol Ritchie

Nancy S. Hughes

Ruth Mossok Johnston

Frank Criscuolo

Sarah Fritschner

Christy Rost

Nutrition Analyst

Tammi Hancock, RD

Preface

Good food is one of life's great pleasures. It's reassuring to know that you don't need to give up that pleasure to give up the high level of sodium that has become part of the American diet. This book will show you how to prepare one delicious dish after another—all without the extra sodium that can adversely affect your health. Once you begin to experiment with the delicious recipes that follow, we think you will abandon your salt shaker!

Several recent studies have shown the effectiveness of the eating plan called Dietary Approaches to Stop Hypertension (DASH). The DASH diet was developed by the National Heart, Lung, and Blood Institute. The extensive research of the NHLBI showed that a diet low in saturated fat and cholesterol with an emphasis on fruits and vegetables, whole grains, and low-fat dairy products actually lowered blood pressure. The DASH diet will help you whether you are trying to lower your blood pressure now or prevent it from rising in the future.

To keep this book useful and relevant—and to take best advantage of the latest research—the American Heart Association has combined the recommendations of the DASH diet with our own science information to bring you this updated edition. When we first published *American Heart Association Low-Salt Cookbook* in 1990, we knew there was a correlation between sodium intake, high blood pressure, and heart disease. With the continuing advances in science, our understanding of that correlation keeps growing. We now know that watching your sodium intake is one of the best ways to take care of your heart and your health.

This book will show you how to do that with flavor and style. Not only is a low-salt diet good for you, it can be delicious, too. With these 200 tasty recipes—including more than 50 brand-new ones—cooking without salt is even easier and more enticing than before. Try a few of our kitchen-tested dishes to see why the *American Heart Association Low-Salt Cookbook* remains one of our longtime favorites.

Welcome to a Low-Salt Diet

Perhaps you've been told by your healthcare provider to switch to a low-salt diet. Maybe you know that consuming less salt can help you stay healthy. Whatever the reason, if you're looking for some help in reducing the amount of salt you eat each day, this book is a great place to start.

So What's the Big Deal About Salt?

Salt, or sodium chloride, is the most common source of the mineral sodium in your diet. The body needs some sodium to function properly, but most Americans eat about ten times more than they need. The American Heart Association currently recommends that if you are healthy, you should consume no more than 2,300 milligrams each day—that's just about 1 teaspoon of table salt. For optimum benefit, your goal should be even lower. Some people—African Americans, middle-aged and older adults, and people with high blood pressure—need less than 1,500 mg per day.

If you stop to think about it, you might be surprised at how much sodium you are actually eating. About 15 percent of the sodium in the average American diet comes from natural sources in foods and water. The rest comes from the salt that's added during food processing (about 67 percent) and at the stove and the dining table (about 18 percent).

The American Heart Association has good reason to be concerned about salt and sodium: A strong correlation exists between high sodium consumption and high blood pressure, especially in certain "salt-sensitive" people. (Unfortunately, there is no test to determine who is salt-sensitive.) High blood pressure leads to increased risks to your health, such as heart disease, heart failure, stroke, and kidney problems. Too much sodium in your system causes your body to retain water, which puts an extra burden on your heart and blood vessels. Reducing your sodium consumption will help reduce your blood pressure and therefore reduce your risk.

WHAT IS HIGH BLOOD PRESSURE?

Blood pressure is the force that blood exerts against the inside of artery walls. It is measured at two different points: when the heart beats (systolic) and when the heart relaxes between beats (diastolic). Blood pressure devices record these pressures in millimeters of mercury (abbreviated as mm Hg), and the resulting values are written as systolic over diastolic (for example, 120/80 mm Hg).

High blood pressure, also called hypertension, is one of the most common health problems in the United States. About 72 million U.S. adults have high blood pressure, and about one third don't even know it. That is largely because high blood pressure usually has no symptoms, so the only way to identify it is to have it checked regularly. Unfortunately, many of the people who are aware of their high blood pressure don't have it under control. Many factors contribute to this, but denial and lack of adherence to a prescribed diet and/or drug regimen are typical.

The relationship of high blood pressure to cardiovascular disease is direct: The higher the blood pressure, the greater the risk. Blood pressure that measures over 140/90 mm Hg on two separate occasions is classified as hypertension. Normal blood pressure is defined as systolic pressure less than 120 mm Hg and diastolic less than 80 mm Hg. Slightly elevated blood pressures that fall between these levels are considered to be approaching unhealthful limits. If you know your blood pressure is in this range (called prehypertension), you can take action to reduce it *before* it rises to critical levels.

BLOOD PRESSURE LEVEL	SYSTOLIC (mm Hg)		DIASTOLIC (mm Hg)
Normal	less than 120	and	less than 80
Prehypertension	120 to 139	or	80 to 89
Hypertension	140 or greater	or	90 or greater

For adults 18 years or older. These levels apply only to people who are not taking medication for high blood pressure and who do not have a short-term serious illness.

Source: *The Seventh Report of the Joint National Committee on Prevention, Detection, Evaluation, and Treatment of High Blood Pressure.* NIH Publication No. 03-5230, National High Blood Pressure Education Program, May 2003.

MANAGING YOUR BLOOD PRESSURE

The first step in managing your blood pressure is to make changes in your diet and lifestyle. (See pages xiv–xviii for more complete information.) If you're like many other people, you can control your high blood pressure by eating healthfully—which includes reducing the amount of sodium in your diet—and increasing your level of physical activity. These actions can also help prevent high blood pressure. If you take care of yourself and are persistent, even small steps will bring big health benefits in the long run.

Steps to a More Healthful Blood Pressure

- Change your diet:
    - *Follow the DASH eating plan (see page xiv).*
    - *Restrict your sodium intake.*
    - *Consume adequate amounts of potassium and calcium.*
- Reach and maintain a healthful body weight.
- Be physically active on a regular basis.
- Limit your alcohol intake.
- Stop smoking.
- Establish a good relationship with your healthcare providers and follow their advice. Have your blood pressure checked regularly and take medications as prescribed.

If you have high blood pressure and your healthcare provider feels you should do more to reduce it, you may also need medications. Once you start taking drugs to control your blood pressure, however, you will probably need to continue for the rest of your life. Be sure to continue to follow the diet and lifestyle recommendations above. Research shows that making these changes while adhering to an appropriate drug regimen is the best combination to keep your blood pumping at more healthful levels for good.

MAKE THE CHANGE

Whether your blood pressure is high now or you want to help keep it from rising in the future, this book gives you the know-how to change your eating habits for good. You'll be able to prepare delicious meals that focus on fresh and flavorful ingredients, as well as take advantage of all the low-sodium products now available. With so many fabulous tastes and textures waiting for you, there's no reason to think of low salt as low flavor. As you sit down to your meals, take the time to savor your food and stop to think . . .

It's time to shake the habit, not the salt shaker.

Lifestyle Changes to Prevent and Manage High Blood Pressure

You may think that using less salt on your foods is enough to make a big difference in your blood pressure. Cutting back on sodium is important, of course. For the most success, however, you should change your diet and your lifestyle as well.

CHANGE YOUR DIET

Several studies have established that you can lower your blood pressure—even if it's not especially high—by following an eating plan called the Dietary Approaches to Stop Hypertension (DASH). If you follow the DASH eating plan *and* reduce the amount of salt you add to your food, you will get the best results. The DASH diet is also an important addition to any regimen of medication to lower blood pressure.

The DASH eating plan, developed by the National Heart, Lung, and Blood Institute, is low in saturated fat and cholesterol and emphasizes fruits and vegetables. The DASH eating plan also includes low-fat dairy products, whole grains, fish, poultry, and nuts. It is particularly rich in potassium and calcium, which are thought to be important in lowering blood pressure. (See Appendix E, page 311, for a list of potassium-rich foods.)

The DASH diet recommends the following number of servings for each important food group, based on consumption of about 2,000 calories a day. The number of servings that is right for you will vary depending on your caloric needs.

FOOD GROUP	SERVINGS	SERVING SIZES	EXAMPLES AND NOTES
Grains*	6 to 8 per day	1 slice bread 1 oz. dry cereal† ½ cup cooked rice, pasta, or cereal	Whole-wheat bread and pasta, English muffin, pita bread, bagel, cereals, grits, oatmeal, crackers, unsalted pretzels, popcorn
Vegetables	4 to 5 per day	1 cup raw leafy vegetable ½ cup cut-up raw or cooked vegetable ½ cup vegetable juice	Broccoli, carrots, collard greens, green beans, kale, lima beans, potatoes, spinach, squash, sweet potatoes, tomatoes
Fruits	4 to 5 per day	1 medium fruit ¼ cup dried fruit ½ cup fresh, frozen, or canned fruit ½ cup fruit juice	Apples, apricots, bananas, dates, grapes, oranges, grapefruit, grapefruit juice, mangoes, melons, peaches, pineapples, raisins, strawberries, tangerines
Fat-free or low-fat milk and milk products	2 to 3 per day	1 cup milk or yogurt 1½ oz. cheese	Fat-free or low-fat (1%) milk or buttermilk; fat-free, low-fat, or reduced-fat cheese; fat-free or low-fat regular or frozen yogurt
Lean meats, poultry, and fish	2 or less per day	3 oz. cooked meats, poultry, or fish 1 egg‡	Select only lean; trim away visible fats; broil, roast, or poach; remove skin from poultry
Nuts, seeds, and legumes	4 to 5 per week	⅓ cup or 1½ oz. nuts 2 Tbsp. peanut butter 2 Tbsp. or ½ oz. seeds ½ cup cooked legumes	Almonds, hazelnuts, mixed nuts, peanuts, walnuts, sunflower seeds, peanut butter, kidney beans, lentils, split peas
Fats and oils§	2 to 3 per day	1 tsp. soft margarine 1 tsp. vegetable oil 1 Tbsp. low-fat mayonnaise 2 Tbsp. light salad dressing	Soft margarine, vegetable oil (such as canola, corn, olive, or safflower), low-fat mayonnaise, light salad dressing
Sweets and added sugars	5 or less per week	1 Tbsp. sugar 1 Tbsp. jelly or jam ½ cup sorbet or gelatin 1 cup lemonade	Fruit-flavored gelatin, fruit punch, hard candy, jelly, maple syrup, sorbet and ices, sugar

* Whole grains are recommended for most grain servings as a good source of fiber and nutrients.

† Serving sizes vary between ½ to 1¼ cups, depending on cereal type. Check product Nutrition Facts label.

‡ Since eggs are high in cholesterol, limit egg yolk intake to no more than 4 per week; 2 egg whites have the same protein content as 1 oz. of meat.

§ Fat content changes serving amount for fats and oils. For example, 1 Tbsp. regular salad dressing equals one serving; 1 Tbsp. low-fat dressing equals one-half serving; 1 Tbsp. fat-free dressing equals zero servings.

Source: U.S. Department of Health and Human Services; National Institutes of Health. NIH publication No. 06-4082; April 2006.

If you find that your usual eating habits are different from these recommendations, relax. You don't have to make every change at once. Take your time and gradually increase your intake of fruits, vegetables, and whole grains. You'll give your body a chance to adapt to the changes in your diet, and you'll be more likely to stick with them for good.

Practical Tips to Help You Eat Smart

- Introduce changes at your own pace. If you now eat one or two vegetables a day, try to add a serving at dinner every day for a week. The next week, add a serving at lunch as well.
- Increase the proportion of vegetables to meat in your meals. For example, include extra vegetables in stir-fries and casseroles or add grated vegetables to ground beef before shaping it into hamburgers and meat loaf.
- Include two or more meat-free meals each week.
- Replace high-calorie snacks with luscious fruits to cut calories and to add to your fruit servings each day. For example, substitute a pear for cookies or cake. To supplement fresh produce, select unsweetened frozen fruits or those canned in their own juice.
- Carry dried fruits with you for a quick pick-me-up.
- To increase the dairy in your diet, substitute fat-free or low-fat milk for sodas and sweetened teas or choose ½ cup of fat-free or low-fat frozen yogurt instead of a candy bar.
- Rinse salty processed foods, such as capers and canned beans, to reduce the sodium.

Keep a food diary of your current eating habits. Write down what you eat, how the food was prepared, and whether you added table salt. You may find some interesting surprises and insights. As you adopt the DASH plan, continue to use your food diary to keep track of the number of servings from each food group you are consuming. Your diary pages will give you a good idea of how effectively you are following the DASH plan.

For more information on the DASH eating plan, ask your healthcare provider or visit the NHLBI online at nhlbi.nih.gov.

REACH AND MAINTAIN A HEALTHFUL WEIGHT

If you are overweight or obese, losing weight can help you lower your blood pressure and blood cholesterol levels. Although the DASH eating plan is not a weight-loss diet, it emphasizes many of the foods, such as fruits and vegetables, that are high in nutrition and low in calories.

Despite the claims of fad diets, the key to losing weight is logical and simple: Eat fewer calories and increase your physical activity. You can eat smaller portions, substitute lower-calorie foods for high-calorie ones, follow a set weight-loss diet plan, or combine these techniques. You can find ways to add more activity to your life. Even if you don't reach your target weight, a loss of just 10 pounds can reduce your blood pressure by as much as 5 to 10 mm Hg.

Typically, most men will lose weight if they eat between 1,600 and 2,000 calories each day; most women will lose weight by eating between 1,200 and 1,600 calories a day. To maintain weight, usually men can eat 2,000 to 2,500 calories daily, and women from 1,600 to 2,000 calories. In general, if you cut out about 500 to 1,000 calories each day, you'll lose about 1 to 2 pounds per week. We recommend that you aim to lose no more than 2 pounds per week. It's the safe approach, and if you stick to that guideline, you'll be more likely to keep the pounds off for the long term.

GET ACTIVE

A healthful lifestyle is essential for controlling blood pressure. Being physically active on a regular basis is a major part of maintaining your energy and overall health. We recommend at least 30 minutes of physical activity on most, if not all, days of the week. Daily physical activity can lower your blood pressure, help blood-pressure medications work more effectively, and decrease your risk for heart disease and stroke. Even 10 to 15 minutes of brisk walking each day will bring health benefits. Thirty minutes a day of regular aerobic activity can reduce your blood pressure by 4 to 9 mm Hg.

LIMIT YOUR ALCOHOL INTAKE AND STOP SMOKING

Research shows that people who drink too much tend to have high blood pressure. What's too much? We recommend that men drink no more than two drinks per day and women no more than one drink per day. Alcohol is also a major source of calories and can contribute to weight gain, which in turn can increase blood pressure.

1 drink = 12 ounces beer, 4 ounces wine, or 1.5 ounces hard liquor

The health risks of using tobacco products and exposure to second-hand smoke are well-known and extensively documented. For example, smoking increases the risk of coronary heart disease and stroke. The risk is even greater when combined with other risk factors, such as high blood pressure. Smoking increases blood pressure, decreases exercise tolerance, and increases the tendency of blood to clot. If you smoke now, find a way to quit. Family and friends, support groups, and your healthcare professional can help you find a program that will work for you. Regardless of how long you have been a smoker, your risk of heart disease and stroke will begin to drop dramatically as soon as you beat the habit.

GIVE YOURSELF CREDIT

Changing long-held habits is difficult. Once you commit to taking care of yourself, set goals that are realistic. Go slowly, be persistent, and remember that the benefits to your health and well-being are worth the effort.

A diagnosis of high blood pressure can be scary or confusing. It causes some people to feel powerless and to decide there's nothing they can do to change their situation. Others don't really see how blood pressure affects their lives, so they do little or nothing to control it. You are reading this book, however, so you already understand that you can take the critical steps to manage your blood pressure levels and make a difference in the quality of your life. Each step you take—such as following a more healthful eating plan, reducing the sodium in your diet, and being active—will benefit your heart and your overall health.

How to Use These Recipes

We have analyzed each recipe in this cookbook to help you keep track of your sodium, saturated fat, cholesterol, and calorie intake. Also listed are total fat, monounsaturated fat, polyunsaturated fat, protein, carbohydrate, fiber, calcium, and potassium values. Except for the fats, these values are rounded to the nearest whole number; fat values are rounded to the nearest 0.5 gram. Values for saturated, monounsaturated, and polyunsaturated fats may not add up to the total fat value in the recipe because of the rounding and because total fat also includes other fatty substances and glycerol.

We have made every effort to check the accuracy of the nutrition analyses. Because of the many variables involved, however, the values should be considered approximate.

- Each analysis is based on a single serving unless otherwise indicated and includes all the ingredients listed. The analyses do not include optional ingredients or accompaniments, however, unless noted in the analysis.

- When figuring portions, remember that the measured amounts given for serving sizes are approximate.

- When a recipe lists ingredient options, such as ½ cup fat-free or low-fat Cheddar cheese, we analyzed the first one.

- Ingredients with a range—for example, a 2½- to 3-pound chicken—were analyzed using the average of the range.

- Meats were analyzed as cooked and lean, with all visible fat discarded. Values for ground beef are based on meat that is 90 percent fat free.

- If meat, poultry, or seafood is marinated and the marinade is discarded, we calculated only the amount of marinade absorbed. For marinated vegetables and basting liquids, we calculated the total amount of the marinade in our analyses.

- If a recipe calls for stick margarine, we used corn oil stick margarine in our analyses. (When selecting a stick margarine, choose one that lists liquid vegetable oil as the first ingredient.) We used the lowest-fat margarine possible in each recipe.

- If a recipe calls for alcohol, we estimated that most of the alcohol calories evaporate during the cooking process.

- Products in the marketplace come and go quickly, and the labeling changes as well. To avoid confusion, we use the terms "fat-free" for products labeled either "fat-free" or "nonfat." We use "low-fat" instead of specifying whether the product is labeled "low-fat," "reduced-fat," or a certain percentage less fat.
- We use the abbreviations "g" for gram and "mg" for milligram.

KEEPING THE SODIUM LOW

All the recipes were analyzed using unsalted or low-sodium ingredients, such as no-salt-added tomato sauce and light soy sauce, when possible. If this book provides a recipe for a common ingredient—for example, chicken broth—we used the data for our own version in the analysis. If the sodium in the products you use differs from these amounts, you'll need to adjust the analyses accordingly. Some of our recipes contain salt. Using no-salt-added foods and adding a small amount of salt for flavor usually results in a lower total sodium content than using commercial foods processed with salt. To keep the sodium level even lower, you can omit the salt from these dishes.

INGREDIENT EQUIVALENTS

To help you know how much of a particular ingredient to buy for a recipe, we have included a list of common equivalents (Appendix E, page 314). For less common ingredients, we have provided estimated guidelines in parentheses. We used the specific amount listed in the recipe, not the estimate, for the nutrition analysis in all cases.

SPECIAL DIET INSTRUCTIONS

Your doctor or dietitian may have given you an instruction sheet for a low-sodium diet. In that case, check it against the ingredients in these recipes. If there is a difference, follow your instruction sheet. If, for example, your instructions specify only unsalted bread, use that in place of the regular bread listed in our recipes. Such substitutions will result in slightly different values from those listed in our nutrition analysis for that particular recipe.

MEET THE CHALLENGE

One of the greatest challenges in cutting down on salt is that so many commercial products—such as bread, soups, and condiments—contain high amounts of sodium. This cookbook includes a variety of recipes for lower-sodium versions that you can make at home so you can continue to enjoy these foods.

Although specific ingredients are listed for each recipe, feel free to experiment or substitute—as long as your ingredient substitutions do not add sodium, saturated or trans fat, or cholesterol. Interchanging herbs, spices, spirits, vinegars, and vegetables will give you variety and can customize the recipe to your taste while not substantially changing the nutritional value of the dish.

Whether you choose fresh or dried herbs or fresh, bottled, or frozen citrus juices, the nutrition analysis will remain the same, but fresh will usually taste best, especially in uncooked dishes. Similarly, we just list pepper, but we encourage you to use different peppercorns, including freshly ground, as you prefer.

Finally, as you go into the kitchen, check the index for Cook's Tips on unfamiliar ingredients and cooking techniques. Above all, remember the cardinal rule of low-salt cooking and eating: Be adventurous and have fun!

American Heart Association

Low-Salt
cookbook

3RD EDITION

Recipes

Potato-Skin Nachos ▫

Red Bell Pepper Crostini ▫

Mushrooms Stuffed with Sherried Chicken ▫

Melon-Berry Kebabs ▫

Spinach-Artichoke Hummus ▫

Smoked Turkey Spread ▫

Appetizers and Snacks

▫ Black Bean Dip

▫ Horseradish and Dill Sour Cream Dip

▫ Waldorf Dip

▫ Hot and Smoky Chipotle-Garlic Dip

▫ Party Mix

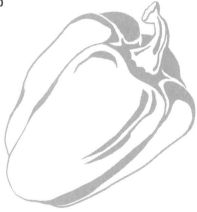

Potato-Skin Nachos

Serves 4; 1 cup per serving

Using potatoes instead of tortilla chips as the base for this south-of-the-border favorite helps you control your sodium intake.

1 pound whole fingerling potatoes or small red potatoes, cut into wedges
  Vegetable oil spray (olive oil spray preferred)
1 teaspoon Chili Powder (page 226) or commercial no-salt-added chili powder

Bean Topping

1 teaspoon olive oil
1 small onion, chopped
2 medium garlic cloves, minced
1 cup canned no-salt-added fat-free refried beans or 1 cup pureed canned no-salt-added pinto beans, rinsed and drained before pureeing
1 teaspoon Chili Powder (page 226) or commercial no-salt-added chili powder
1 teaspoon very low sodium beef bouillon granules
1/8 teaspoon pepper

Tomato Salsa

2 medium Italian plum tomatoes, chopped (about 1 cup)
1/2 medium bell pepper, any color, chopped
1/4 cup chopped red onion
1 tablespoon snipped fresh cilantro or parsley
1 tablespoon chopped fresh jalapeño (optional; wear plastic gloves while handling)

■ ■ ■

1/2 cup fat-free or reduced-fat shredded Cheddar cheese
2 tablespoons sliced black olives, drained
2 tablespoons fat-free or light sour cream

Preheat the oven to 375°F.

Put the potatoes on a nonstick baking sheet. Lightly spray the potatoes with olive oil spray. Sprinkle the potatoes with 1 teaspoon Chili Powder.

Bake for 30 minutes, or until the potatoes are tender when pierced with a fork.

Meanwhile, for the bean topping, heat a medium skillet over medium heat. Add the oil and swirl to coat the bottom. Cook the onion and garlic for 3 to 4 minutes, or until the onion is soft, stirring occasionally.

Stir in the remaining topping ingredients. Cook for 1 minute, or until warmed through, stirring occasionally. Spread the mixture in a large, shallow serving bowl. Let cool for 5 to 10 minutes.

Meanwhile, in a medium bowl, stir together the salsa ingredients.

Arrange the potatoes on a serving plate. Spread the bean topping over the potatoes. Spoon the salsa over the topping. Sprinkle with the cheese and olives. Top with the sour cream.

Handling Hot Chile Peppers

Hot chile peppers, such as jalapeño, Anaheim, serrano, and poblano, contain oils that can burn your skin, lips, and eyes. Wear plastic gloves or wash your hands thoroughly with warm, soapy water immediately after handling hot peppers.

PER SERVING
CALORIES 224
TOTAL FAT 3 g
    Saturated 0.5 g
    Polyunsaturated 1 g
    Monounsaturated 1.5 g
CHOLESTEROL 4 mg
SODIUM 186 mg
CARBOHYDRATES 41 g
    Fiber 9 g
    Sugars 8 g
PROTEIN 13 g
CALCIUM 197 mg
POTASSIUM 1166 mg
DIETARY EXCHANGES
    2 starch
    2 vegetable
    1 very lean meat

Red Bell Pepper Crostini

Serves 8; 2 crostini per serving

Arrange these triangular crostini, or "little toasts," in a pinwheel design for a spectacular presentation.

- 2   ounces low-fat or fat-free cream cheese
- 1   tablespoon chopped fresh basil leaves or 1 teaspoon dried, crumbled
- 1   tablespoon fat-free milk
- 1   medium garlic clove, minced
- ¼   teaspoon red hot-pepper sauce
- ½   cup roasted red bell peppers, bottled in water
- 16   slices low-sodium melba toast
- 3   tablespoons chopped fresh basil or parsley leaves

In a small mixing bowl, stir together the cream cheese, 1 tablespoon basil, milk, garlic, and hot-pepper sauce. Using an electric mixer, beat on medium until smooth.

Rinse, drain, and chop the roasted peppers.

At serving time, spoon ½ teaspoon cream cheese mixture onto each toast slice. Sprinkle with the roasted peppers and the remaining basil.

 Cook's TIP

You can prepare this appetizer up to 24 hours in advance and assemble it at serving time. Refrigerate the cream cheese mixture and the roasted bell peppers in separate airtight containers. Store the toasts in an airtight container at room temperature.

Roasting Bell Peppers

To roast your own peppers, preheat the broiler. Spray a broiling pan and rack with vegetable oil spray, preferably olive oil spray. Put the desired number of whole bell peppers on the rack; you'll need 2 medium red bell peppers for this recipe. Broil the peppers 3 to 4 inches from the heat until they are almost completely black, turning them to char evenly. Transfer the peppers to an airtight plastic bag and seal it, or put the peppers in a large bowl and cover it with plastic wrap. When the peppers are cool, in 20 to 30 minutes, slice them in half lengthwise and remove the stems, seeds, and veins. Gently peel the skin, using your fingers or rubbing the peppers between paper towels, or scrape the skin off with a knife. Discard the skin. If you wish, rinse the peppers to remove some of the bits of charred skin that remain. Chop the peppers.

For this recipe, stir 2 tablespoons cider vinegar into the peppers, and add ⅛ teaspoon salt when you prepare the cream cheese mixture.

PER SERVING
CALORIES 58
TOTAL FAT 1.5 g
    Saturated 1 g
    Polyunsaturated 0 g
    Monounsaturated 0.5 g
CHOLESTEROL 4 mg
SODIUM 40 mg
CARBOHYDRATES 9 g
    Fiber 1 g
    Sugars 0 g
PROTEIN 2 g
CALCIUM 22 mg
POTASSIUM 40 mg
DIETARY EXCHANGES
    ½ starch

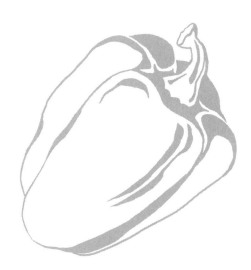

Mushrooms Stuffed with Sherried Chicken

Serves 8; 2 mushrooms per serving

This ever-popular appetizer will immediately break the ice at your party.

16	medium button mushrooms (about 1 pound)
	Vegetable oil spray
1	small onion, chopped
½	cup diced cooked chicken breast without skin, cooked without salt
1	slice light bread, torn into small pieces
2	tablespoons dry sherry
¼	teaspoon dried marjoram, crumbled
⅛	teaspoon pepper
⅛	teaspoon dried oregano, crumbled
2	teaspoons light tub margarine, melted

Preheat the broiler.

Finely chop the mushroom stems. Put the mushroom caps with the round side up on a baking sheet.

Heat a medium skillet over medium-high heat. Remove the skillet from the heat and lightly spray with vegetable oil spray (being careful not to spray near a gas flame). Cook the mushroom stems and onion for 2 to 3 minutes, or until the onion is just tender, stirring occasionally.

Stir in the remaining ingredients except the margarine.

Brush the mushroom caps with half the margarine.

Broil the mushrooms about 4 inches from the heat for 2 minutes. Remove from the broiler. Turn the mushrooms over and fill with the chicken mixture. Brush with the remaining margarine. Broil for 3 minutes, or until the mushrooms are tender and lightly browned on top.

PER SERVING
CALORIES 46
TOTAL FAT 1 g
  Saturated 0 g
  Polyunsaturated 0 g
  Monounsaturated 0.5 g
CHOLESTEROL 7 mg
SODIUM 28 mg
CARBOHYDRATES 5 g
  Fiber 1 g
  Sugars 1 g
PROTEIN 5 g
CALCIUM 9 mg
POTASSIUM 254 mg
DIETARY EXCHANGES
  1 vegetable
  ½ very lean meat

Melon-Berry Kebabs

Serves 4; 1 kebab per serving

Attractive, fragrant, and so tasty, these kebabs are a great way to fit more servings of fruit into your life.

2	tablespoons fresh lemon juice
½	teaspoon grated lemon zest
1	tablespoon sugar
1½	teaspoons grated peeled gingerroot
2	tablespoons chopped fresh mint leaves
12	1-inch watermelon or honeydew cubes (about 4 ounces)
8	whole strawberries

Pour the lemon juice into a small microwaveable bowl. Microwave on 100 percent power (high) for 15 seconds, or until hot. Stir in the lemon zest, sugar, and gingerroot. Set aside to cool.

Stir the mint into the lemon juice mixture, mashing the mint with a spoon to release the flavor.

In a shallow dish, such as a pie pan, gently stir together all the ingredients to coat the fruit completely.

Using 3 watermelon cubes and 2 strawberries per skewer, alternate the fruit as you thread it on four 6-inch bamboo skewers.

PER SERVING
CALORIES 32
TOTAL FAT 0 g
Saturated 0 g
Polyunsaturated 0 g
Monounsaturated 0 g
CHOLESTEROL 0 mg
SODIUM 2 mg
CARBOHYDRATES 8 g
Fiber 1 g
Sugars 6 g
PROTEIN 1 g
CALCIUM 14 mg
POTASSIUM 82 mg
DIETARY EXCHANGES
½ fruit

 Cook's TIP

You may want to add a whole mint leaf at the base of each kebab. The dark green provides a nice color contrast, and the mint keeps your fingers from touching the sticky fruit.

Spinach-Artichoke Hummus

Serves 16; 2 tablespoons per serving

Creamy texture, pretty green color, and assertive taste—this dip has it all.

2	ounces fresh spinach leaves (about 2 cups)
1	cup canned no-salt-added chick-peas, rinsed and drained
4	medium canned artichoke hearts, rinsed, squeezed dry, and quartered
¼	cup Chicken Broth (page 19), commercial fat-free, low-sodium chicken broth, or water
2	tablespoons shredded or grated Parmesan cheese
2	tablespoons tahini
½	teaspoon grated lemon zest
2	tablespoons fresh lemon juice
1	to 2 medium garlic cloves, minced
¼	teaspoon pepper
⅛	teaspoon salt

In a food processor or blender, process all the ingredients until the desired consistency. Serve at room temperature or cover and refrigerate until needed.

Tahini

Tahini is a thick paste made from ground sesame seeds. Look for it in the condiment or specialty gourmet sections in the grocery store. Add small amounts to enhance salad dressings, marinades, soups, and stuffings.

PER SERVING
CALORIES 51
TOTAL FAT 1.5 g
    Saturated 0.5 g
    Polyunsaturated 0.5 g
    Monounsaturated 0.5 g
CHOLESTEROL 0 mg
SODIUM 63 mg
CARBOHYDRATES 7 g
    Fiber 2 g
    Sugars 1 g
PROTEIN 3 g
CALCIUM 20 mg
POTASSIUM 65 mg
DIETARY EXCHANGES
    ½ starch

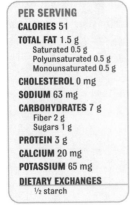

Smoked Turkey Spread

Serve this spread as a topping for cucumber slices, celery sticks, or bell pepper wedges, or use it on low-sodium crackers.

1	tablespoon plus 1½ teaspoons light stick margarine
¾	cup chopped sweet onion (Vidalia preferred)
5	ounces low-sodium, low-fat turkey (deli type), thinly sliced
1½	cups fat-free or low-fat cottage cheese
2	tablespoons tarragon vinegar
1½	teaspoons dried tarragon, crumbled
½	teaspoon no-salt-added liquid smoke
1	teaspoon very low sodium chicken bouillon granules or condensed low-sodium chicken soup base
	White pepper to taste

Heat a large skillet over medium-high heat. Add the margarine. When it has melted, swirl to coat the bottom. Cook the onion for 2 to 3 minutes, or until soft, stirring occasionally.

In a food processor or blender, process all the ingredients until smooth. Transfer the mixture to a glass serving bowl or dish. Cover with plastic wrap and refrigerate for 4 hours, or until firm.

PER SERVING

CALORIES 33
TOTAL FAT 0.5 g
    Saturated 0 g
    Polyunsaturated 0 g
    Monounsaturated 0 g
CHOLESTEROL 5 mg
SODIUM 142 mg
CARBOHYDRATES 2 g
    Fiber 0 g
    Sugars 1 g
PROTEIN 5 g
CALCIUM 23 mg
POTASSIUM 73 mg
DIETARY EXCHANGES
    1 very lean meat

Black Bean Dip

Serves 20; about 2 tablespoons per serving

Spread this smooth, spicy dip on crisp baked tortilla chips, or serve it with your favorite raw vegetables.

2	teaspoons canola or corn oil
¾	cup chopped onion
4	oil-packed sun-dried tomatoes, drained and coarsely chopped
2	large garlic cloves, chopped
2	15-ounce cans no-salt-added black beans, rinsed and drained
2	tablespoons fresh lime juice
2	tablespoons water
1½	teaspoons sugar
1	tablespoon snipped fresh cilantro or 1 teaspoon dried, crumbled
1	teaspoon ground coriander
1	teaspoon ground cumin
¼	teaspoon cayenne, or to taste
¼	cup sliced green onions (green part only)
¼	cup fat-free or light sour cream

Heat a large nonstick skillet over medium heat. Add the oil and swirl to coat the bottom. Cook the onion, tomatoes, and garlic for 3 to 5 minutes, or until the onion is soft, stirring constantly. Set aside to cool slightly.

In a food processor or blender, process the beans, lime juice, water, sugar, cilantro, coriander, cumin, cayenne, and onion mixture until smooth. Transfer the dip to a serving bowl. Refrigerate, covered, for at least 3 hours.

To serve, sprinkle with the green onions. Top with decorative dollops of sour cream.

Variation

For a zippy flavor addition, stir in some Roasted Tomato Chipotle Salsa (page 220).

PER SERVING
CALORIES 51
TOTAL FAT 0.5 g
  Saturated 0 g
  Polyunsaturated 0 g
  Monounsaturated 0.5 g
CHOLESTEROL 1 mg
SODIUM 5 mg
CARBOHYDRATES 9 g
  Fiber 2 g
  Sugars 2 g
PROTEIN 3 g
CALCIUM 21 mg
POTASSIUM 184 mg
DIETARY EXCHANGES
  ½ starch

Horseradish and Dill Sour Cream Dip

Serves 4; 2 tablespoons per serving

Adding horseradish to sour cream and dill gives you a dip with zip!

⅓ cup fat-free or light sour cream

2 tablespoons fat-free milk

2 teaspoons prepared white horseradish

1 teaspoon dried dillweed, crumbled

⅛ teaspoon salt

In a small bowl, whisk together all the ingredients. Cover and refrigerate until needed.

PER SERVING
CALORIES 28
TOTAL FAT 0 g
　　Saturated 0 g
　　Polyunsaturated 0 g
　　Monounsaturated 0 g
CHOLESTEROL 4 mg
SODIUM 101 mg
CARBOHYDRATES 5 g
　　Fiber 0 g
　　Sugars 2 g
PROTEIN 2 g
CALCIUM 42 mg
POTASSIUM 73 mg
DIETARY EXCHANGES
　　½ other carbohydrate

Waldorf Dip

For a double dose of spice, serve this "scent-sational" dip with crisp gingersnaps. The combination is perfect as a slightly sweet appetizer or a bite of quick dessert.

8	ounces fat-free or low-fat plain yogurt
1	medium apple, such as Granny Smith, Gala, or Fuji, peeled and finely chopped
1	medium rib of celery, finely chopped
¼	cup chopped walnuts, dry-roasted
1	tablespoon honey
1	teaspoon grated lemon zest
1	tablespoon fresh lemon juice
¼	teaspoon ground cinnamon
⅛	teaspoon ground nutmeg

In a medium bowl, stir together all the ingredients.

 Cook's TIP

You can cover the dip and refrigerate it for up to three days. If the mixture becomes slightly watery, stir it before serving.

PER SERVING
CALORIES 29
TOTAL FAT 1.5 g
    Saturated 0 g
    Polyunsaturated 1 g
    Monounsaturated 0 g
CHOLESTEROL 0 mg
SODIUM 13 mg
CARBOHYDRATES 4 g
    Fiber 0 g
    Sugars 3 g
PROTEIN 1 g
CALCIUM 32 mg
POTASSIUM 60 mg
DIETARY EXCHANGES
    Free

Hot and Smoky Chipotle-Garlic Dip

Serves 8; 2 tablespoons per serving

Without the milk, this spicy mixture is delicious on cucumber rounds or baked tortillas. Use the milk for a thinner dip to serve with vegetables.

- 2/3 cup fat-free or light sour cream
- 3 tablespoons fat-free or light mayonnaise
- 2 tablespoons fat-free milk (optional)
- 2 tablespoons fresh lemon juice
- 1 chipotle pepper, canned in adobo sauce
- 1 medium garlic clove, minced
- 1/8 teaspoon salt
- Fresh cilantro sprigs (optional)

In a food processor or blender, process all the ingredients except the cilantro until smooth.

To serve, transfer the dip to a serving bowl. Garnish with the cilantro.

Cook's TIP

Chipotle Peppers

These dried, smoked jalapeños provide a unique, smoky heat. You can find cans of these flavorful chiles, frequently in adobo sauce, in major supermarkets in the international or ethnic section. (Adobo sauce, also known as adobo paste, is a rather spicy mixture of chiles, vinegar, garlic, and herbs.) Chipotles are also sold dried in packages. To rehydrate the packaged type, wear plastic gloves and place the desired number of chiles in a bowl of boiling water. Let sit for 20 minutes. Drain and use as directed above. You can use the soaking water to spice up soup or beans.

PER SERVING
CALORIES 44
TOTAL FAT 1 g
  Saturated 0 g
  Polyunsaturated 0 g
  Monounsaturated 0 g
CHOLESTEROL 5 mg
SODIUM 152 mg
CARBOHYDRATES 6 g
  Fiber 0 g
  Sugars 2 g
PROTEIN 2 g
CALCIUM 33 mg
POTASSIUM 54 mg
DIETARY EXCHANGES
  1/2 other carbohydrate

Party Mix

Serves 12; ¼ cup per serving

This crunchy dish is great to serve instead of high-sodium potato chips.

1¼   cups corn cereal squares

¾   cup bite-size shredded wheat cereal squares

½   cup thin unsalted pretzel sticks

2   low-sodium bagel chips, broken into ½-inch pieces (about ½ cup)

¼   cup unsalted peanuts

1   tablespoon plus 1½ teaspoons low-sodium Worcestershire sauce

1   tablespoon Hot Mustard (page 221) or commercial honey mustard

2   teaspoons toasted sesame oil

½   teaspoon garlic powder

½   teaspoon ground cumin

⅛   teaspoon cayenne

     Vegetable oil spray

¼   teaspoon salt

Preheat the oven to 400°F.

In a large bowl, stir together the cereal squares, pretzels, bagel chips, and peanuts.

In a small bowl, stir together the Worcestershire sauce, mustard, oil, garlic powder, cumin, and cayenne. Stir into the cereal mixture. Spread in a single layer in a rimmed baking sheet.

Bake for 4 minutes, stirring halfway through. Place the baking sheet on a cooling rack.

Lightly spray the mixture with vegetable oil spray. Sprinkle with the salt. Let cool on the cooling rack for 10 minutes (the mixture will become crisp).

PER SERVING
CALORIES 62
TOTAL FAT 2.5 g
Saturated 0.5 g
Polyunsaturated 1 g
Monounsaturated 1 g
CHOLESTEROL 0 mg
SODIUM 104 mg
CARBOHYDRATES 8 g
Fiber 1 g
Sugars 1 g
PROTEIN 2 g
CALCIUM 18 mg
POTASSIUM 47 mg
DIETARY EXCHANGES
½ starch
½ fat

Beef Broth

Chicken Broth

Vegetable Broth

Black Bean Soup

Cream of Cauliflower Soup

Creamy Carrot Soup

Corn and Green Chile Soup

Onion Soup with Cheesy Pita Crisps

Lentil Soup with Lemon

Soups

- Fresh Basil, Spinach, and Tomato Soup
- Curried Split Pea Soup
- Gazpacho
- Minestrone
- New England Fish Chowder with Thyme
- Soup to Go
- Turkey Vegetable Soup
- Vegetable Beef Soup
- Lima Bean and Turkey Sausage Soup

Beef Broth

Beef broth is good on its own and is useful for adding flavor to many other dishes. Roasting the bones adds both flavor and color to the broth. Keep some in the freezer so you'll have it handy whenever you need it (see Cook's Tip on Broth, page 19).

4   pounds beef or veal bones (preferably shank or knuckle bones)

3   quarts water

1   medium onion, coarsely chopped

8   fresh parsley sprigs

1   teaspoon dried thyme, crumbled

5   or 6 peppercorns

2   whole cloves

1   bay leaf

Preheat the oven to 400°F.

Put the bones in a roasting pan.

Bake for 25 to 30 minutes, turning once. Using tongs, transfer the bones to a stockpot or Dutch oven.

Add the remaining ingredients. Bring to a boil over high heat. Reduce the heat and simmer for 4 to 6 hours; don't boil. Skim the fat off the top. Strain the broth into a covered container. Discard the bones, onion, and seasonings. Refrigerate the broth, covered, for 1 to 2 hours, or until the fat hardens on the surface. Discard the hardened fat before reheating the soup.

PER SERVING

CALORIES 8

TOTAL FAT 0 g
   Saturated 0 g
   Polyunsaturated 0 g
   Monounsaturated 0 g

CHOLESTEROL 0 mg

SODIUM 23 mg

CARBOHYDRATES 0 g
   Fiber 0 g
   Sugars 0 g

PROTEIN 2 g

CALCIUM 8 mg

POTASSIUM 75 mg

DIETARY EXCHANGES
   Free

Chicken Broth

Serves 12; ¾ cup per serving

With this big batch of broth, you'll have plenty to serve as an appetizer and to freeze for later use in a variety of recipes. Save the cooked chicken for Chicken Salad (page 56) or Chicken Enchiladas (pages 122–123).

3   pounds skinless chicken, all visible fat discarded

2   to 3 pounds chicken bones (optional)

3   quarts cold water

2   large carrots, chopped

2   medium ribs of celery, sliced

1   medium onion, chopped

5   or 6 whole peppercorns

1   bay leaf

1   teaspoon dried thyme, crumbled

¼   teaspoon pepper

In a stockpot or Dutch oven, stir together all the ingredients. Bring to a boil over high heat. Reduce the heat and simmer for 1 to 2 hours if not using the extra bones or 3 to 4 hours with the extra bones.

Skim the froth off the top. Remove the chicken and reserve for another use. Strain the broth into a covered container. Discard the vegetables. Refrigerate the broth, covered, for 1 to 2 hours, or until the fat hardens on the surface. Discard the hardened fat before reheating the soup.

Cook's TIP

Broth

Freeze leftover broth in ice cube trays for future use. Put 1 tablespoon of broth in each compartment of the tray, then freeze. Remove the broth cubes from the tray and store them in an airtight freezer bag. Then the broth is ready to use—a tablespoon at a time whenever you need it. In some recipes, you can toss in the still-frozen cubes. For dishes such as casseroles, thaw the cubes in the refrigerator for several hours or in the microwave.

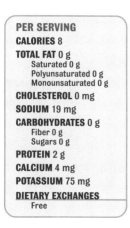

PER SERVING
CALORIES 8
TOTAL FAT 0 g
    Saturated 0 g
    Polyunsaturated 0 g
    Monounsaturated 0 g
CHOLESTEROL 0 mg
SODIUM 19 mg
CARBOHYDRATES 0 g
    Fiber 0 g
    Sugars 0 g
PROTEIN 2 g
CALCIUM 4 mg
POTASSIUM 75 mg
DIETARY EXCHANGES
    Free

Vegetable Broth

Serves 13; ¾ cup per serving

You can use this tasty, so-easy-to-make broth in place of beef or chicken broth for a wonderful flavor change.

    4   cups trimmings, such as carrots, celery, tomatoes, onions, spinach, and leeks
    6   cups water
    ⅛   to ¼ teaspoon pepper

In a stockpot or Dutch oven, stir together all the ingredients. Bring to a simmer over medium-high heat. Reduce the heat and simmer, covered, for 1 hour. Strain the broth into a covered container. Discard the trimmings.

 Cook's TIP

Keep a large airtight plastic bag in the freezer and add vegetable trimmings as you get them. When it's time to make this broth, your veggies will be waiting.

PER SERVING
CALORIES 12
TOTAL FAT 0 g
   Saturated 0 g
   Polyunsaturated 0 g
   Monounsaturated 0 g
CHOLESTEROL 0 mg
SODIUM 35 mg
CARBOHYDRATES 2 g
   Fiber 0 g
   Sugars 0 g
PROTEIN 2 g
CALCIUM 5 mg
POTASSIUM 41 mg
DIETARY EXCHANGES
   Free

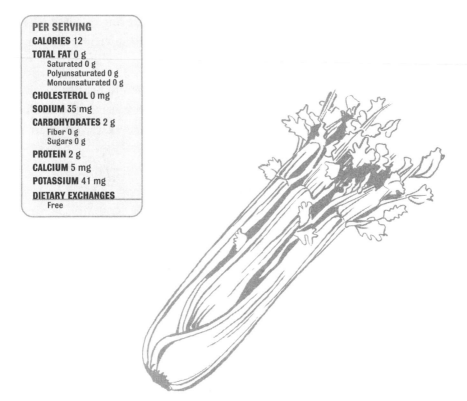

Black Bean Soup

Serves 10; 1 cup per serving

Interesting and flavorful, this soup is perfect as a first course with baked tortilla strips or sesame seed crisps. It also pairs well with a deep green salad and warm bread for a simple, hearty meal.

1	tablespoon olive oil
3	to 4 medium onions, chopped
3	medium ribs of celery, diced
5	large garlic cloves, chopped
3	15-ounce cans no-salt-added black beans, undrained
4	cups Chicken Broth (page 19) or commercial fat-free, low-sodium chicken broth
	28-ounce can no-salt-added stewed tomatoes, undrained
1	tablespoon ground cumin
1½	teaspoons dried cilantro, crumbled
⅛	to ¼ teaspoon cayenne
½	cup fat-free or light sour cream, beaten with a fork until smooth

Heat a stockpot or Dutch oven over medium-high heat. Add the oil and swirl to coat the bottom. Cook the onions for 2 to 3 minutes, or until soft, stirring occasionally. Reduce the heat to medium.

Add the celery and garlic. Cook for 4 minutes, stirring frequently.

Meanwhile, drain the beans, reserving 1 cup liquid. Rinse and drain the beans. Add the beans and reserved liquid to the stockpot.

PER SERVING
CALORIES 151
TOTAL FAT 1.5 g
  Saturated 0 g
  Polyunsaturated 0 g
  Monounsaturated 1 g
CHOLESTEROL 2 mg
SODIUM 42 mg
CARBOHYDRATES 30 g
  Fiber 9 g
  Sugars 9 g
PROTEIN 8 g
CALCIUM 113 mg
POTASSIUM 662 mg
DIETARY EXCHANGES
  1 starch
  3 vegetable
  1 very lean meat

Stir in the remaining ingredients except the sour cream. Increase the heat to high and bring to a boil. Reduce the heat and simmer, covered, for 25 minutes (no stirring needed). Remove from the heat.

Working in batches, process the soup in a food processor or blender until smooth.

To serve, ladle the soup into bowls. Garnish each serving with a dollop of sour cream.

If the liquid drained from the beans doesn't measure 1 cup, add enough water to make up the difference.

Cream of Cauliflower Soup

Serves 4; 1 cup per serving

Every spoonful of this soup is filled with aromatic vegetables, fragrant nutmeg, and Parmesan cheese. Good to the last drop!

1	teaspoon olive oil
1	medium rib of celery, chopped
½	medium onion, chopped
2	medium garlic cloves, minced
1	pound coarsely chopped cauliflower florets (about 4 cups)
2½	cups Chicken Broth (page 19) or commercial fat-free, low-sodium chicken broth
¼	teaspoon pepper
½	cup fat-free half-and-half
3	tablespoons all-purpose flour
⅛	teaspoon ground nutmeg
3	tablespoons shredded or grated Parmesan cheese

Heat a medium saucepan over medium heat. Add the oil and swirl to coat the bottom. Cook the celery, onion, and garlic for 3 to 4 minutes, or until the celery is tender-crisp and the onion is soft, stirring occasionally.

Stir in the cauliflower. Cook for 2 to 3 minutes, or until it is tender-crisp, stirring occasionally.

Stir in the broth and pepper. Increase the heat to medium-high and bring to a simmer. Reduce the heat and simmer, covered, for 10 to 15 minutes, or until the vegetables are tender.

Using a handheld immersion blender, blend the mixture in the saucepan until smooth. If you prefer, you can let the mixture cool slightly and process it in a food processor or blender until smooth, then return it to the pan.

In a small bowl, whisk together the half-and-half, flour, and nutmeg. Stir into the vegetable mixture. Bring to a simmer over medium-high heat. Reduce the heat and simmer for 2 to 3 minutes, or until thickened, stirring constantly and lowering the heat if the mixture splatters.

Add the Parmesan. Stir until melted, about 30 seconds.

Immersion Blenders

An immersion blender is a handheld implement that you immerse in the pan or bowl of food you want to blend. Try it for blending fruit smoothies and frothing warm fat-free milk for cappuccino or lattes.

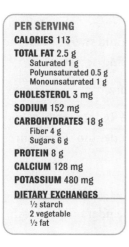

PER SERVING
CALORIES 113
TOTAL FAT 2.5 g
    Saturated 1 g
    Polyunsaturated 0.5 g
    Monounsaturated 1 g
CHOLESTEROL 3 mg
SODIUM 152 mg
CARBOHYDRATES 18 g
    Fiber 4 g
    Sugars 6 g
PROTEIN 8 g
CALCIUM 128 mg
POTASSIUM 480 mg
DIETARY EXCHANGES
    1/2 starch
    2 vegetable
    1/2 fat

Creamy Carrot Soup

Serves 5; 1 cup per serving

Beautiful in color, this soup is creamy without using dairy products. Serve it hot in the winter and chilled in the summer.

1 tablespoon olive oil

2 cups thinly sliced Vidalia or other sweet onions (about 2 large)

3 cups thickly sliced carrots

4 cups Chicken Broth (page 19) or commercial fat-free, low-sodium chicken broth
Dash of cayenne

2 teaspoons unsalted shelled pumpkin seeds or dry-roasted sunflower seeds (optional)
Chopped green onions (green part only; optional)

Heat a stockpot or Dutch oven over medium heat. Add the oil and swirl to coat the bottom. Cook the onions for 2 to 3 minutes, or until soft, stirring occasionally.

Stir in the carrots. Cook for 1 to 2 minutes, stirring occasionally.

Pour in the broth. Increase the heat to high and bring to a boil. Reduce the heat and simmer, uncovered, for 30 minutes, or until the carrots are tender (no stirring necessary). Remove from the heat.

Stir in the cayenne.

Working in batches, process the soup in a food processor or blender until smooth.

To serve, ladle the soup into bowls. Sprinkle with the seeds and green onions.

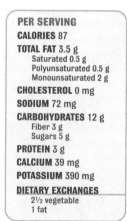

PER SERVING
CALORIES 87
TOTAL FAT 3.5 g
  Saturated 0.5 g
  Polyunsaturated 0.5 g
  Monounsaturated 2 g
CHOLESTEROL 0 mg
SODIUM 72 mg
CARBOHYDRATES 12 g
  Fiber 3 g
  Sugars 5 g
PROTEIN 3 g
CALCIUM 39 mg
POTASSIUM 390 mg
DIETARY EXCHANGES
  2½ vegetable
  1 fat

Cook's TIP

Dry-Roasting Seeds or Nuts

To dry-roast seeds or nuts, put them in a single layer in a small skillet. Cook over medium-high heat for 2 to 5 minutes, or until the seeds darken and begin to pop or until the nuts begin to brown, stirring frequently.

Corn and Green Chile Soup

Serves 4; heaping ¾ cup soup and 1 tablespoon cheese per serving

This chunky and spicy soup is ready in no time—with very little cleanup.

16 ounces frozen whole-kernel corn, thawed

12 ounces fat-free evaporated milk

4-ounce can chopped green chiles, rinsed and drained

¼ to ½ teaspoon ground cumin

¼ teaspoon pepper

⅛ teaspoon cayenne (optional)

½ medium red bell pepper, finely chopped (optional)

3 medium green onions, finely chopped

2 teaspoons light tub margarine

¼ cup shredded fat-free or reduced-fat sharp Cheddar cheese

In a medium saucepan, stir together the corn, milk, green chiles, cumin, pepper, and cayenne. Bring just to a simmer over medium heat, stirring frequently. Remove from the heat. Stir in the bell pepper, green onions, and margarine. To serve, ladle the soup into bowls. Sprinkle with the Cheddar.

 Cook's TIP

Thawing Frozen Vegetables

To thaw frozen vegetables quickly, put them in a colander and run them under cold water until thawed. Shake off the excess water and drain well.

PER SERVING

CALORIES 205

TOTAL FAT 2 g
  Saturated 0.5 g
  Polyunsaturated 0.5 g
  Monounsaturated 0.5 g

CHOLESTEROL 5 mg

SODIUM 299 mg

CARBOHYDRATES 37 g
  Fiber 5 g
  Sugars 16 g

PROTEIN 13 g

CALCIUM 389 mg

POTASSIUM 624 mg

DIETARY EXCHANGES
  1½ starch
  1 skim milk

Onion Soup with Cheesy Pita Crisps

Serves 4; 1 cup soup and 2 crisps per serving

Crisp pita wedges topped with melted cheese garnish a rich broth teeming with caramelized onions.

Soup

1½	teaspoons light stick margarine
1	teaspoon olive oil
2	medium onions, sliced
⅛	teaspoon sugar
3	tablespoons all-purpose flour
4	cups Beef Broth (page 18) or commercial fat-free, no-salt-added beef broth
2	tablespoons dry vermouth or dry white wine (regular or nonalcoholic)
⅛	teaspoon pepper

Cheesy Pita Crisps

	6-inch whole-wheat pita bread
	Vegetable oil spray
⅛	teaspoon garlic powder
¼	cup shredded low-fat Cheddar cheese
1	tablespoon plus 1 teaspoon shredded or grated Parmesan cheese

In a large saucepan, melt the margarine over medium-high heat. Add the oil and swirl to coat the bottom. Cook the onions for 2 to 3 minutes, or until soft, stirring occasionally.

Stir in the sugar. Cook for 7 to 10 minutes, or until the onions are a deep, golden brown, stirring occasionally.

Preheat the oven to 350°F.

Stir the flour into the onion mixture, combining thoroughly.

Stir in the broth, wine, and pepper. Increase the heat to high and bring to a boil. Reduce the heat to medium-low and cook for 15 to 20 minutes, or until the flavors have blended, stirring occasionally.

Meanwhile, cut the pita bread into 4 wedges. Separate each wedge into the top and bottom pieces (you will have 8 wedges total). Place the wedges on a baking sheet. Lightly spray the tops with vegetable oil spray. Sprinkle with the garlic powder, Cheddar, and Parmesan.

Bake for 8 to 10 minutes, or until the cheeses have melted.

To serve, ladle the soup into bowls. Float 2 pita crisps on each serving.

PER SERVING

CALORIES 142

TOTAL FAT 3 g
    Saturated 1 g
    Polyunsaturated 0.5 g
    Monounsaturated 1.5 g

CHOLESTEROL 3 mg

SODIUM 194 mg

CARBOHYDRATES 21 g
    Fiber 3 g
    Sugars 5 g

PROTEIN 8 g

CALCIUM 84 mg

POTASSIUM 266 mg

DIETARY EXCHANGES
    1 starch
    1 vegetable
    1 lean meat

Lentil Soup with Lemon

Serves 9; 1 cup per serving

Lentils and a potato provide wholesome fiber in this hearty main-dish soup. Serve it with Corn Muffins (pages 248–249) and a dessert of Spiced Fruit (page 281) for Sunday supper.

Vegetable oil spray (olive oil spray preferred)

1 teaspoon olive oil

1 small or medium onion, chopped

2 medium garlic cloves, minced

2 quarts Vegetable Broth (page 20), commercial low-sodium vegetable broth, or water

2 cups dried lentils (about 1 pound), sorted for stones and shriveled lentils, rinsed, and drained

1 medium potato, diced (about 1 cup)

½ teaspoon dried oregano, crumbled

¼ teaspoon salt

2 to 3 tablespoons fresh lemon juice

Pepper to taste

Heat a stockpot or Dutch oven over medium-high heat. Remove from the heat and lightly spray with vegetable oil spray (being careful not to spray near a gas flame). Add the oil, swirling to coat the bottom. Cook the onion and garlic for 2 to 3 minutes, or until the onion is soft, stirring occasionally.

Stir in the broth, lentils, potato, oregano, and salt. Reduce the heat and simmer, covered, for 45 minutes, or until the lentils are soft (no stirring needed).

Stir in the lemon juice and pepper.

PER SERVING
CALORIES 180
TOTAL FAT 1 g
   Saturated 0 g
   Polyunsaturated 0 g
   Monounsaturated 0.5 g
CHOLESTEROL 0 mg
SODIUM 111 mg
CARBOHYDRATES 31 g
   Fiber 14 g
   Sugars 3 g
PROTEIN 14 g
CALCIUM 35 mg
POTASSIUM 535 mg
DIETARY EXCHANGES
   2 starch
   1 very lean meat

Fresh Basil, Spinach, and Tomato Soup

Serves 4; ¾ cup per serving

Just a few minutes of standing time brings out the delectable flavor of the fresh basil in this easy-to-prepare soup.

2 cups Chicken Broth (page 19) or 14.5-ounce can fat-free, low-sodium chicken broth

1 teaspoon dried oregano, crumbled

1 medium garlic clove, minced

¼ teaspoon dried tarragon, crumbled

⅛ teaspoon crushed red pepper flakes (optional)

4 small tomatoes, diced

2 ounces spinach leaves, coarsely chopped (about 2 cups)

2 medium green onions, finely chopped

¼ cup chopped fresh basil leaves (about ⅓ ounce)

½ teaspoon olive oil (extra-virgin preferred)

¼ teaspoon salt

4 lemon slices (optional)

In a medium saucepan, stir together the broth, oregano, garlic, tarragon, and red pepper flakes. Bring to a boil over high heat. Reduce the heat and simmer for 5 minutes. Remove from the heat.

Stir in the remaining ingredients except the lemon. Let stand, covered, for 5 minutes to absorb flavors.

To serve, ladle the soup into bowls. Place a lemon slice in each bowl.

You'll get the very best flavor if you serve this soup right after the standing time.

PER SERVING
CALORIES 38
TOTAL FAT 1 g
  Saturated 0 g
  Polyunsaturated 0 g
  Monounsaturated 0.5 g
CHOLESTEROL 0 mg
SODIUM 176 mg
CARBOHYDRATES 6 g
  Fiber 2 g
  Sugars 3 g
PROTEIN 2 g
CALCIUM 37 mg
POTASSIUM 404 mg
DIETARY EXCHANGES
  1 vegetable

Curried Split Pea Soup

Serves 6; 1 cup per serving

With half a sandwich, this soup—unusual with curry and cumin—makes a filling lunch.

  6 cups Chicken Broth (page 19), Beef Broth (page 18), Vegetable Broth
     (page 20), commercial low-sodium broth, or water
  1 cup dried split peas (about ½ pound), sorted for stones and shriveled peas
     and rinsed
  2 medium carrots, chopped
  1 large onion, chopped
1½ teaspoons sugar
1½ teaspoons curry powder
  1 teaspoon ground cumin
 ⅛ teaspoon garlic powder
 ⅛ teaspoon cayenne
 ¾ teaspoon salt

In a Dutch oven or large saucepan, stir together all the ingredients except the salt.
Bring to a boil over high heat. Reduce the heat and simmer, covered, for 1 hour to
1 hour 30 minutes, or until the peas are tender (no stirring needed).

Whisk in the salt. Continue to whisk vigorously (but carefully) to thicken the soup
to the desired consistency by mashing the peas a bit.

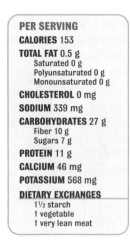

PER SERVING

CALORIES 153
TOTAL FAT 0.5 g
  Saturated 0 g
  Polyunsaturated 0 g
  Monounsaturated 0 g
CHOLESTEROL 0 mg
SODIUM 339 mg
CARBOHYDRATES 27 g
  Fiber 10 g
  Sugars 7 g
PROTEIN 11 g
CALCIUM 46 mg
POTASSIUM 568 mg
DIETARY EXCHANGES
  1½ starch
  1 vegetable
  1 very lean meat

Gazpacho

This no-cook soup will sustain you through the dog days of summer.

2	medium cucumbers
1	medium tomato
1	small green bell pepper
1	small zucchini
½	medium onion
3	or 4 green onions
4	cups reduced-sodium mixed-vegetable juice
¼	cup snipped fresh parsley or 1 tablespoon plus 1 teaspoon dried, crumbled
1	tablespoon fresh lemon juice (optional)
2	medium garlic cloves, minced
1	teaspoon low-sodium Worcestershire sauce
½	to 1 teaspoon pepper
1½	medium lemons, cut into 12 wedges (optional)

Finely chop the cucumbers, tomato, bell pepper, zucchini, onion, and green onions. Put in a large bowl.

Stir in the remaining ingredients except the lemons. Cover and refrigerate for at least 2 hours.

To serve, ladle the chilled soup into bowls or mugs. Garnish each serving with a wedge of lemon on the side.

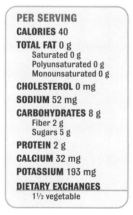

PER SERVING
CALORIES 40
TOTAL FAT 0 g
    Saturated 0 g
    Polyunsaturated 0 g
    Monounsaturated 0 g
CHOLESTEROL 0 mg
SODIUM 52 mg
CARBOHYDRATES 8 g
    Fiber 2 g
    Sugars 5 g
PROTEIN 2 g
CALCIUM 32 mg
POTASSIUM 193 mg
DIETARY EXCHANGES
    1½ vegetable

Minestrone

Serves 10; 1 cup per serving

Enjoy a bowl of this nourishing soup for lunch, and keep those mid-afternoon hunger pangs at bay.

Vegetable oil spray (olive oil spray preferred)
1½ teaspoons olive oil
1 small onion, chopped
1 medium carrot, thinly sliced
1 medium rib of celery, diced
1 to 2 medium garlic cloves, minced
6 cups Chicken Broth (page 19) or commercial fat-free, low-sodium chicken broth
1 cup canned no-salt-added diced tomatoes
1 cup cooked macaroni (cooked without salt or oil)
1 cup canned no-salt-added white beans, such as cannellini beans, rinsed and drained
½ teaspoon pepper
¼ cup shredded or grated Parmesan cheese

Heat a stockpot or Dutch oven over medium heat. Remove from the heat and spray with vegetable oil spray (being careful not to spray near a gas flame). Add the oil and swirl to coat the bottom. Cook the onion, carrot, celery, and garlic for 3 to 4 minutes, or until the onion is soft, stirring occasionally.

Stir in the remaining ingredients except the Parmesan. Bring to a simmer. Simmer, covered, for 5 minutes, or until heated through.

To serve, ladle the soup into bowls. Sprinkle with the Parmesan.

PER SERVING
CALORIES 76
TOTAL FAT 1.5 g
  Saturated 0.5 g
  Polyunsaturated 0 g
  Monounsaturated 0.5 g
CHOLESTEROL 1 mg
SODIUM 68 mg
CARBOHYDRATES 12 g
  Fiber 2 g
  Sugars 3 g
PROTEIN 5 g
CALCIUM 49 mg
POTASSIUM 212 mg
DIETARY EXCHANGES
  1 starch
  ½ very lean meat

New England Fish Chowder with Thyme

Serves 6; 1 cup per serving

This creamy chowder boasts chunks of potato and mild white fish. For a different twist, top it with crumbled low-sodium pretzels.

- 1 tablespoon light stick margarine
- 1 medium onion, chopped
- 3 cups low-sodium fish stock, Chicken Broth (page 19), or commercial fat-free, low-sodium chicken broth
- 2 medium potatoes, peeled and cut into ½-inch cubes (about 1½ cups)
- ¾ teaspoon dried thyme, crumbled
- ⅛ teaspoon pepper (white preferred)
- 1 pound fish fillets (haddock, cod, orange roughy, or other firm white fish)
- 1 cup fat-free evaporated milk
- ¼ cup all-purpose flour

In a large saucepan, melt the margarine over medium-high heat. Swirl to coat the bottom. Cook the onion for 2 to 3 minutes, or until soft, stirring occasionally.

Add the fish stock, potatoes, thyme, and pepper. Bring to a simmer. Reduce the heat to medium-low and cook, covered, for 20 to 25 minutes, or until the potatoes are tender.

Meanwhile, rinse the fish and pat dry with paper towels. Cut the fish into ½-inch cubes. Set aside.

In a small bowl, whisk together the evaporated milk and flour. Whisk into the stock mixture. Increase the heat to medium-high and cook for about 5 minutes, or until the mixture thickens, stirring occasionally. Reduce the heat to medium.

Stir in the fish. Cook for 6 to 7 minutes, or until the fish flakes easily when tested with a fork, stirring occasionally.

PER SERVING

CALORIES 175
TOTAL FAT 1.5 g
  Saturated 0.5 g
  Polyunsaturated 0.5 g
  Monounsaturated 0.5 g
CHOLESTEROL 45 mg
SODIUM 127 mg
CARBOHYDRATES 20 g
  Fiber 2 g
  Sugars 7 g
PROTEIN 21 g
CALCIUM 167 mg
POTASSIUM 715 mg
DIETARY EXCHANGES
  1 starch
  1 vegetable
  2½ very lean meat

Soup to Go

Here's the low-sodium answer to how to have a quick cup of soup. Keep this mixture on hand at work for an easy lunch, take it on a camping trip—in fact, you can use it wherever boiling water is available.

Basic Chicken Soup to Go

¼ cup instant brown rice or 2 tablespoons couscous, uncooked

¼ cup no-salt-added dried vegetables, such as carrots, tomatoes, peas, and corn

1½ teaspoons very low sodium chicken bouillon granules

½ teaspoon dried parsley, crumbled

½ teaspoon dried minced onion

⅛ teaspoon dried thyme, crumbled

⅛ teaspoon pepper

OR

Basic Beef Soup to Go

¼ cup instant brown rice or 2 tablespoons couscous, uncooked

¼ cup no-salt-added dried vegetables, such as carrots, tomatoes, peas, and corn

1½ teaspoons very low sodium beef bouillon granules

1 teaspoon dried shallots

½ teaspoon dried parsley, crumbled

⅛ teaspoon dried marjoram, crumbled

⅛ teaspoon pepper

■ ■ ■

1 cup boiling water

In a small airtight plastic bag or plastic container with a lid, stir together all the ingredients for the chicken or beef soup mix.

To prepare the soup, put the dry mixture in a soup bowl. Pour in the boiling water. Stir. Let stand for 1 to 2 minutes, or until the rice is tender.

Experiment with different dried-vegetable combinations and no-salt-added herb or seasoning combinations (¼ to ½ teaspoon), such as those on pages 223–225. Keep a small bottle of toasted sesame oil handy and pour a few drops on the chicken soup for an Asian flavor (similar to that of egg drop soup).

If you begin with new jars of herbs and bouillon granules, these soup mixtures will keep in an airtight container for up to a year. Be sure to keep them in a closed cabinet away from the light.

CHICKEN SOUP
PER SERVING
CALORIES 184
TOTAL FAT 1.5 g
   Saturated 0 g
   Polyunsaturated 0.5 g
   Monounsaturated 0.5 g
CHOLESTEROL 0 mg
SODIUM 43 mg
CARBOHYDRATES 38 g
   Fiber 3 g
   Sugars 0 g
PROTEIN 5 g
CALCIUM 39 mg
POTASSIUM 1190 mg
DIETARY EXCHANGES
   1½ starch
   3 vegetable

BEEF SOUP
PER SERVING
CALORIES 182
TOTAL FAT 1.5 g
   Saturated 0 g
   Polyunsaturated 0.5 g
   Monounsaturated 0.5 g
CHOLESTEROL 0 mg
SODIUM 50 mg
CARBOHYDRATES 37 g
   Fiber 3 g
   Sugars 2 g
PROTEIN 5 g
CALCIUM 38 mg
POTASSIUM 1140 mg
DIETARY EXCHANGES
   1½ starch
   3 vegetable

Turkey Vegetable Soup

Serves 9; 1 cup per serving

Here's a good way to use up that leftover holiday turkey.

Vegetable oil spray
1 teaspoon light stick margarine
1 medium onion, chopped
1/2 medium rib of celery, diced
6 cups Chicken Broth (page 19) or commercial fat-free, low-sodium chicken broth
1 cup canned no-salt-added diced tomatoes
1 cup chopped cooked turkey breast, cooked without salt, all visible fat and skin discarded
1/2 cup frozen green peas
1/2 cup frozen whole-kernel corn
1/2 teaspoon pepper
1/4 teaspoon red hot-pepper sauce

Heat a stockpot or Dutch oven over medium heat. Remove from the heat and spray with vegetable oil spray (being careful not to spray near a gas flame). Add the margarine. When it has melted, swirl to coat the bottom. Cook the onion and celery for 3 to 4 minutes, or until the onion is soft, stirring occasionally.

Stir in the remaining ingredients. Increase the heat to high and bring to a simmer. Reduce the heat and simmer, covered, for 20 minutes, or until the vegetables are tender.

PER SERVING
CALORIES 57
TOTAL FAT 0.5 g
　Saturated 0 g
　Polyunsaturated 0 g
　Monounsaturated 0 g
CHOLESTEROL 13 mg
SODIUM 52 mg
CARBOHYDRATES 6 g
　Fiber 1 g
　Sugars 3 g
PROTEIN 7 g
CALCIUM 18 mg
POTASSIUM 175 mg
DIETARY EXCHANGES
　1/2 starch
　1 very lean meat

Vegetable Beef Soup

Serves 6; 1 cup per serving

Here's a comforting and effortless way to work toward your daily vegetable servings.

Vegetable oil spray
1 medium onion, chopped
1 medium rib of celery, diced
1 medium carrot, sliced
1½ teaspoons chopped fresh oregano or ½ teaspoon dried oregano, crumbled
2 medium garlic cloves, minced
½ teaspoon dried thyme, crumbled
4 cups Beef Broth (page 18) or commercial fat-free, no-salt-added beef broth
1 cup chopped cooked lean roast beef, cooked without salt, all visible fat discarded
½ cup cut fresh or frozen green beans
1 medium tomato, chopped
Pepper to taste

Spray a Dutch oven or large saucepan with vegetable oil spray. Cook the onion, celery, carrot, oregano, garlic, and thyme over medium heat for 3 to 4 minutes, or until the onion is soft, stirring occasionally.

Stir in the remaining ingredients. Bring to a simmer. Reduce the heat and simmer, covered, for 30 minutes, or until the vegetables are tender.

Thickening Soup

To thicken and enrich most kinds of soup, either add some vegetables if none are called for or add more vegetables than the recipe specifies. Once they've cooked, remove some or all of the vegetables from the soup and process them in a food processor or blender, adding a little liquid if needed. Stir the processed vegetables back into the soup.

PER SERVING
CALORIES 71
TOTAL FAT 1 g
   Saturated 0.5 g
   Polyunsaturated 0 g
   Monounsaturated 0.5 g
CHOLESTEROL 16 mg
SODIUM 51 mg
CARBOHYDRATES 6 g
   Fiber 2 g
   Sugars 3 g
PROTEIN 9 g
CALCIUM 31 mg
POTASSIUM 340 mg
DIETARY EXCHANGES
   1 vegetable
   1 very lean meat

Lima Bean and Turkey Sausage Soup

Serves 9; 1 cup per serving

You may want to make some corn bread to dunk in this mildly smoky soup.

1	teaspoon olive oil
½	medium onion, chopped
1	medium rib of celery, cut crosswise into ½-inch slices
1	medium carrot, cut crosswise into ½-inch slices
6	cups Chicken Broth (page 19) or commercial fat-free, low-sodium chicken broth
1	pound frozen lima beans, thawed
4	ounces reduced-fat smoked turkey sausage, cut crosswise into ½-inch slices
2	tablespoons imitation bacon bits
1	teaspoon dried thyme, crumbled
1	teaspoon dried marjoram, crumbled
¼	teaspoon pepper
¼	teaspoon crushed red pepper flakes (optional)

Heat a large saucepan over medium heat. Add the oil and swirl to coat the bottom. Cook the onion, celery, and carrot for 3 to 4 minutes, or until the onion is soft.

Stir in the remaining ingredients. Increase the heat to medium high and bring to a simmer, stirring occasionally. Reduce the heat and simmer, covered, for 30 minutes, or until the lima beans and vegetables are tender (no stirring needed).

Slow-Cooker Method

Put all the ingredients in a slow cooker. Cook on high for 3 to 4 hours or on low for 8 to 10 hours.

PER SERVING

CALORIES 90
TOTAL FAT 1 g
   Saturated 0 g
   Polyunsaturated 0 g
   Monounsaturated 0.5 g
CHOLESTEROL 5 mg
SODIUM 283 mg
CARBOHYDRATES 14 g
   Fiber 3 g
   Sugars 2 g
PROTEIN 7 g
CALCIUM 29 mg
POTASSIUM 156 mg
DIETARY EXCHANGES
   1 starch
   ½ very lean meat

Spring Greens with Fruit, Goat Cheese, and Cranberry-Orange Vinaigrette

Garden Coleslaw

Cucumber Raita

Tomato-Artichoke Toss

Balsamic-Marinated Vegetables

Sliced Mango with Creamy Orange Sauce

Granny Apple and Cranberry Salad

Summer Pasta Salad

Mediterranean Couscous
CILANTRO COUSCOUS

Southwestern Black-Eyed Pea Salad

Red-Potato Salad

Tropical Tuna Salad

Salads and Salad Dressings

Spicy Shrimp Salad

Asian Brown Rice and Vegetable Salad

Chicken Salad

Balsamic Vinaigrette

Cider Vinaigrette

ITALIAN DRESSING

RUSSIAN DRESSING

TOMATO FRENCH DRESSING

Ranch Dressing with Fresh Herbs

Creamy Black Pepper and Garlic Dressing

Thousand Island Dressing

Lemon and Poppy Seed Dressing

Orange-Yogurt Dressing

APRICOT-YOGURT DRESSING

Spring Greens with Fruit, Goat Cheese, and Cranberry-Orange Vinaigrette

Serves 4; 2 cups salad mixture and 2 tablespoons vinaigrette per serving

Use seasonal fruit so you can serve this salad with its mildly sweet and tart vinaigrette year-round.

5 ounces spring greens (about 6 cups packed)

1½ cups quartered strawberries or sliced apples

¼ cup thinly sliced red onion

Cranberry-Orange Vinaigrette

⅓ cup sweetened cranberry juice

2 tablespoons honey

1 tablespoon plus 1½ teaspoons balsamic vinegar

1 teaspoon grated orange zest

½ teaspoon ground cumin

½ teaspoon ground cinnamon

■ ■ ■

2 ounces chilled goat cheese, cut crosswise into 4 slices, then quartered

In a shallow serving bowl or on a serving platter, arrange the greens, strawberries, and onion.

In a small jar with a tight-fitting lid, combine the vinaigrette ingredients. Shake vigorously until well blended.

To serve, pour the vinaigrette over the salad. Arrange the goat cheese on the salad. Serve immediately.

PER SERVING	
CALORIES 118	
TOTAL FAT 3.5 g	
Saturated 2 g	
Polyunsaturated 0 g	
Monounsaturated 0.5 g	
CHOLESTEROL 7 mg	
SODIUM 65 mg	
CARBOHYDRATES 20 g	
Fiber 2 g	
Sugars 16 g	
PROTEIN 4 g	
CALCIUM 60 mg	
POTASSIUM 242 mg	
DIETARY EXCHANGES	
½ fruit	
1 other carbohydrate	
½ high-fat meat	

Garden Coleslaw

Serves 7; ½ cup per serving

Because it doesn't contain mayonnaise, this slaw is a good picnic dish. It keeps well in the refrigerator for several days, so you can make it in advance.

Slaw

10-ounce package shredded cabbage (8 to 9 cups)

½   cup chopped onion

½   large green bell pepper, sliced into thin strips

1   medium carrot, shredded

Dressing

3   to 4 tablespoons sugar

3   tablespoons white vinegar

2   tablespoons plus 1½ teaspoons water

1   tablespoon plus 1½ teaspoons canola or corn oil

Pepper to taste

In a large bowl, stir together the slaw ingredients.

In a small bowl, whisk together the dressing ingredients. Pour over the slaw. Toss thoroughly. Cover and refrigerate for at least 1 hour before serving, if possible, to let the flavors blend.

PER SERVING
CALORIES 73
TOTAL FAT 3 g
  Saturated 0 g
  Polyunsaturated 1 g
  Monounsaturated 2 g
CHOLESTEROL 0 mg
SODIUM 14 mg
CARBOHYDRATES 12 g
  Fiber 1 g
  Sugars 10 g
PROTEIN 1 g
CALCIUM 26 mg
POTASSIUM 164 mg
DIETARY EXCHANGES
  1 vegetable
  ½ other carbohydrate
  ½ fat

Cucumber Raita

Serves 10; ½ cup per serving

You can prepare this delightful Indian-inspired raita *(RI-tah)* up to two hours ahead of time. Try serving it with a spicy entrée for contrast or using it to top Poached Salmon (page 76).

3 cups fat-free or low-fat plain yogurt

2 medium cucumbers, peeled, seeded, and finely diced (about 2 cups)

2 green onions, finely chopped

⅛ teaspoon cayenne

In a medium bowl, whisk the yogurt until smooth.

Whisk in the remaining ingredients. Cover and refrigerate until ready to serve.

Cook's TIP

English Cucumbers

Long and slender, English (or hothouse) cucumbers have thin skin and are virtually seedless. You can substitute one of them for the two regular cucumbers in this recipe and skip the peeling and seeding steps. English cucumbers are tightly wrapped in plastic. They will keep longer if you remove the plastic before refrigerating the cucumbers.

PER SERVING

CALORIES 48

TOTAL FAT 0 g
  Saturated 0 g
  Polyunsaturated 0 g
  Monounsaturated 0 g

CHOLESTEROL 2 mg

SODIUM 58 mg

CARBOHYDRATES 7 g
  Fiber 1 g
  Sugars 6 g

PROTEIN 5 g

CALCIUM 152 mg

POTASSIUM 257 mg

DIETARY EXCHANGES
  ½ skim milk

Tomato-Artichoke Toss

Serves 6; 1/2 cup per serving

A sprinkling of crumbled feta tops this mix of fresh spinach, sweet grape tomatoes, artichokes, and basil.

7	ounces grape tomatoes, halved (about 1½ cups)
1	ounce fresh spinach leaves, coarsely chopped (about 1 cup)
½	14-ounce can quartered artichoke hearts, rinsed, drained, and coarsely chopped
¼	cup finely chopped red onion
¼	cup chopped fresh basil leaves (about ⅓ ounce)
2	tablespoons balsamic vinegar
½	teaspoon sugar
¼	teaspoon pepper
¼	teaspoon salt
⅛	teaspoon crushed red pepper flakes (optional)
1	ounce fat-free or reduced-fat feta cheese, rinsed and drained, crumbled

In a large bowl, toss together all the ingredients except the feta. Sprinkle with the feta.

PER SERVING
CALORIES 30
TOTAL FAT 0 g
   Saturated 0 g
   Polyunsaturated 0 g
   Monounsaturated 0 g
CHOLESTEROL 0 mg
SODIUM 233 mg
CARBOHYDRATES 6 g
   Fiber 1 g
   Sugars 3 g
PROTEIN 2 g
CALCIUM 12 mg
POTASSIUM 122 mg
DIETARY EXCHANGES
   1 vegetable

Balsamic-Marinated Vegetables

Serves 10; ½ cup per serving

This pretty, quick-to-prepare, and divine-tasting salad is perfect for potlucks and picnics. Vary the vegetables and dressings for different flavors.

1½ cups diced raw broccoli florets
1½ cups diced raw cauliflower florets
  1 medium zucchini, sliced (about 1 cup)
 12 baby carrots, sliced (about 1 cup)
  ½ cup matchstick-size slices yellow onion
  1 recipe Balsamic Vinaigrette (page 57) or 1 cup low-fat, low-sodium Italian dressing

In a large glass or ceramic bowl, stir together all the ingredients except the vinaigrette.

Pour in the vinaigrette, stirring well. Cover and refrigerate for 6 to 24 hours, stirring occasionally.

PER SERVING

CALORIES 50
TOTAL FAT 3 g
  Saturated 0 g
  Polyunsaturated 1 g
  Monounsaturated 1.5 g
CHOLESTEROL 0 mg
SODIUM 22 mg
CARBOHYDRATES 6 g
  Fiber 1 g
  Sugars 4 g
PROTEIN 1 g
CALCIUM 21 mg
POTASSIUM 184 mg
DIETARY EXCHANGES
  1 vegetable
  ½ fat

Sliced Mango with Creamy Orange Sauce

Serves 4; ½ cup mango slices, 2 tablespoons yogurt mixture,
and ½ tablespoon fruit-spread mixture per serving

This attractive dish is terrific as a salad or a dessert.

- ½ cup fat-free or low-fat vanilla yogurt
- 1 tablespoon confectioners' sugar
- 1 tablespoon frozen orange juice concentrate, thawed
- 2 tablespoons all-fruit seedless raspberry spread
- ¼ teaspoon ground cinnamon
- 1 medium mango, sliced, or 2 cups sliced nectarines or peeled peaches

In a small bowl, whisk together the yogurt, confectioners' sugar, and orange juice concentrate.

Put the fruit spread in a small microwaveable bowl. Warm on 100 percent power (high) for 10 seconds, or until partially melted. Stir in the cinnamon. Let stand to cool slightly.

On four small plates, decoratively fan the mango slices. Spoon the yogurt mixture in the center of each serving. Top each with a dollop of the fruit-spread mixture.

PER SERVING
CALORIES 96
TOTAL FAT 0 g
  Saturated 0 g
  Polyunsaturated 0 g
  Monounsaturated 0 g
CHOLESTEROL 1 mg
SODIUM 22 mg
CARBOHYDRATES 23 g
  Fiber 1 g
  Sugars 21 g
PROTEIN 2 g
CALCIUM 63 mg
POTASSIUM 181 mg
DIETARY EXCHANGES
  1 fruit
  ½ other carbohydrate

Granny Apple
and Cranberry Salad

Serves 6; ½ cup per serving

Refreshing and crunchy, this fruit salad makes a good brunch dish with Turkey Sausage Patties (page 128).

2	tablespoons chopped pecans
2	medium Granny Smith apples, cut in ¼-inch pieces (about 1½ cups)
½	cup sweetened dried cranberries
½	teaspoon grated orange zest
¼	cup fresh orange juice
¼	teaspoon ground cinnamon

Heat a small skillet over medium-high heat. Dry-roast the pecans for 2 to 5 minutes, or until just browned and fragrant, stirring frequently. Transfer to a medium bowl. Set aside to let cool.

Stir the remaining ingredients into the cooled pecans. Serve immediately for peak flavor.

Chop the apples up to 2 hours in advance. Stir in 1 to 2 teaspoons of fresh lemon juice to keep them from turning brown.

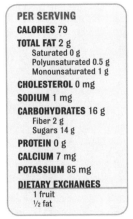

PER SERVING
CALORIES 79
TOTAL FAT 2 g
    Saturated 0 g
    Polyunsaturated 0.5 g
    Monounsaturated 1 g
CHOLESTEROL 0 mg
SODIUM 1 mg
CARBOHYDRATES 16 g
    Fiber 2 g
    Sugars 14 g
PROTEIN 0 g
CALCIUM 7 mg
POTASSIUM 85 mg
DIETARY EXCHANGES
    1 fruit
    ½ fat

Summer Pasta Salad

Serves 10; ½ cup per serving

Crisp, colorful vegetables highlight this salad, perfect for a summertime picnic for a group.

1½ cups dried rotini (about 4 ounces)

1½ cups broccoli florets

½ cup sliced carrots, sliced on diagonal

1 cup sliced yellow summer squash

Dressing

3 tablespoons chopped fresh basil leaves or 1 tablespoon dried, crumbled

3 tablespoons cider vinegar

1 tablespoon extra-virgin olive oil

2 medium garlic cloves, minced

¼ teaspoon pepper

■ ■ ■

2 tablespoons shredded or grated Parmesan cheese

⅛ teaspoon salt

In a stockpot or large saucepan, prepare the pasta using the package directions, omitting the salt and oil. When the pasta has cooked for 4 minutes, stir in the broccoli and carrots. Cook for 1 minute.

Stir in the squash. Cook for 30 seconds. Immediately drain in a colander and run under cold water to stop the cooking process and cool quickly. Set aside.

In a large bowl, whisk together the dressing ingredients.

To assemble, stir the pasta mixture into the dressing. Sprinkle with the Parmesan and salt. Toss gently. Refrigerate for 15 minutes to 4 hours before serving.

PER SERVING
CALORIES 72
TOTAL FAT 2 g
Saturated 0.5 g
Polyunsaturated 0.5 g
Monounsaturated 1 g
CHOLESTEROL 1 mg
SODIUM 55 mg
CARBOHYDRATES 12 g
Fiber 1 g
Sugars 1 g
PROTEIN 3 g
CALCIUM 27 mg
POTASSIUM 116 mg
DIETARY EXCHANGES
1 starch

Cook's TIP

Extra-Virgin Olive Oil

Extra-virgin olive oil is considered to be the fruitiest of all olive oils. It is available in a variety of shades, from crystalline to bright green. For a more intense olive flavor, choose an oil that is deeper in color.

Mediterranean Couscous

Couscous is a quick-cooking Moroccan staple made of coarsely ground wheat. You can serve it hot or cold.

⅓	cup uncooked couscous
	14.5-ounce can artichoke quarters, rinsed, drained, and chopped
4	ounces Italian plum tomatoes, chopped (about 1 cup)
½	medium cucumber, peeled and diced
2	tablespoons finely chopped red onion
2	tablespoons snipped fresh parsley
2	tablespoons fresh lemon juice
1	tablespoon chopped fresh oregano or 1 teaspoon dried, crumbled
1	tablespoon minced fresh mint leaves or 1 teaspoon dried, crumbled
1	ounce blue cheese, crumbled

Prepare the couscous using the package directions, omitting the salt. Fluff with a fork and set aside to cool.

Meanwhile, in a medium bowl, stir together the remaining ingredients except the blue cheese. Gently stir in the cooled couscous, then the blue cheese. Serve immediately for peak flavor.

PER SERVING
CALORIES 66
TOTAL FAT 1.5 g
    Saturated 1 g
    Polyunsaturated 0 g
    Monounsaturated 0.5 g
CHOLESTEROL 3 mg
SODIUM 160 mg
CARBOHYDRATES 11 g
    Fiber 1 g
    Sugars 1 g
PROTEIN 3 g
CALCIUM 34 mg
POTASSIUM 100 mg
DIETARY EXCHANGES
    ½ starch
    1 vegetable

Cilantro Couscous

1/3 cup uncooked couscous

14.5-ounce can artichoke quarters, rinsed, drained, and chopped

4 ounces Italian plum tomatoes, chopped (about 1 cup)

1/2 medium cucumber, peeled and diced

2.25-ounce can sliced black olives, rinsed and drained

2 tablespoons finely chopped radish

2 tablespoons snipped fresh parsley

2 tablespoons snipped fresh cilantro

2 tablespoons fresh lemon juice

2 to 3 drops red hot-pepper sauce (optional)

Prepare the couscous using the package directions, omitting the salt. Fluff with a fork and set aside to cool.

Meanwhile, in a medium bowl, stir together the remaining ingredients. Gently stir in the cooled couscous. Serve immediately for peak flavor.

PER SERVING

CALORIES 61

TOTAL FAT 1 g
  Saturated 0 g
  Polyunsaturated 0 g
  Monounsaturated 0.5 g

CHOLESTEROL 0 mg

SODIUM 177 mg

CARBOHYDRATES 11 g
  Fiber 2 g
  Sugars 1 g

PROTEIN 2 g

CALCIUM 16 mg

POTASSIUM 90 mg

DIETARY EXCHANGES
  1/2 starch
  1 vegetable

Southwestern Black-Eyed Pea Salad

Serves 10; ½ cup per serving

A popular dish in the Lone Star State, where it is called Texas Caviar, this flavorful salad is sure to become a favorite in your household, too. Even people who "don't like" black-eyed peas like them prepared this way.

2   tablespoons finely chopped fresh jalapeño, stem, ribs, and seeds discarded (wear plastic gloves while handling)

½   medium green bell pepper, diced

1   small white onion, diced

3   tablespoons red wine vinegar

1   tablespoon canola or corn oil

1   tablespoon water

1   medium garlic clove, minced

¼   teaspoon pepper

3   15.5-ounce cans no-salt-added black-eyed peas, rinsed and drained, or 3 10-ounce packages frozen black-eyed peas, cooked

In a medium bowl, stir together all the ingredients except the peas.

Stir in the peas. Cover and refrigerate for 2 to 24 hours before serving.

Cook's TIP

Canned Black-Eyed Peas

For more flavor, look for canned no-salt-added "fresh" black-eyed peas rather than canned "dried" peas.

PER SERVING
CALORIES 130
TOTAL FAT 1.5 g
   Saturated 0 g
   Polyunsaturated 0.5 g
   Monounsaturated 1 g
CHOLESTEROL 0 mg
SODIUM 1 mg
CARBOHYDRATES 22 g
   Fiber 5 g
   Sugars 4 g
PROTEIN 7 g
CALCIUM 42 mg
POTASSIUM 325 mg
DIETARY EXCHANGES
   1½ starch
   ½ very lean meat

Red-Potato Salad

Serves 9; 1/2 cup per serving

An ingredient key to great potato salad is the right amount of mustard. Since prepared mustard is usually high in sodium, we used our own recipe. If you prefer, you may use dry mustard instead.

1½ to 2 pounds red potatoes, cooked and diced (about 5 medium)

1 or 2 medium ribs of celery with leaves, chopped

6 medium radishes, sliced

2 medium green onions, sliced

Dressing

3 tablespoons fat-free or low-fat sour cream

2 tablespoons plus 1½ teaspoons vinegar

2 tablespoons fat-free or light mayonnaise

2 tablespoons fat-free or low-fat plain yogurt

1 tablespoon sugar

1 tablespoon Hot Mustard (page 221) or 1 teaspoon dry mustard

½ teaspoon celery seeds (optional)

¼ teaspoon pepper

¼ teaspoon turmeric

In a large bowl, stir together the potatoes, celery, radishes, and green onions.

In a small bowl, whisk together the dressing ingredients. Pour into the potato mixture, stirring gently to combine. Cover and refrigerate for about 2 hours before serving.

PER SERVING

CALORIES 85

TOTAL FAT 0 g
  Saturated 0 g
  Polyunsaturated 0 g
  Monounsaturated 0 g

CHOLESTEROL 1 mg

SODIUM 42 mg

CARBOHYDRATES 20 g
  Fiber 2 g
  Sugars 5 g

PROTEIN 3 g

CALCIUM 30 mg

POTASSIUM 498 mg

DIETARY EXCHANGES
  1½ starch

Tropical Tuna Salad

Serves 4; ¼ cup tuna salad and ¼ cup mango slices per serving

Mango, pineapple, and walnuts lift tuna salad to new heights.

Tuna Salad

6-ounce can low-sodium albacore tuna packed in water, rinsed, drained, and flaked

½   cup drained pineapple tidbits canned in their own juice

¼   medium carrot, shredded

2   tablespoons fat-free or light mayonnaise

2   tablespoons chopped walnuts, dry-roasted

½   teaspoon grated lemon zest

2   teaspoons fresh lemon juice

⅛   teaspoon pepper

■ ■ ■

1   medium mango, sliced, or 1 cup sliced bottled mango, drained

In a medium bowl, stir together all the tuna salad ingredients.

To serve, arrange the mango slices on salad plates. Using an ice-cream scoop or spoon, mound the tuna salad on the mango slices.

To complete the presentation of this salad, garnish with sprigs of fresh herbs. Some good choices are mint, basil, rosemary, thyme, tarragon, lemon balm, or lavender. You'll add a colorful and fragrant touch, as well as an edible garnish for enhanced flavor.

PER SERVING

CALORIES 136

TOTAL FAT 4 g
  Saturated 0.5 g
  Polyunsaturated 2.5 g
  Monounsaturated 0.5 g

CHOLESTEROL 18 mg

SODIUM 91 mg

CARBOHYDRATES 15 g
  Fiber 2 g
  Sugars 13 g

PROTEIN 11 g

CALCIUM 17 mg

POTASSIUM 222 mg

DIETARY EXCHANGES
  1½ lean meat
  1 fruit

Spicy Shrimp Salad

Serves 5; about ¾ cup per serving

Forget what you think about shrimp salad. This one is shrimp with dressing, not the other way around. It's fairly spicy, but you can vary the pepper and cayenne to suit your own palate.

½   cup fat-free or light mayonnaise

⅓   cup chopped red or green bell pepper

¼   cup chopped green onions

¼   cup snipped fresh parsley

2   tablespoons snipped fresh dillweed or 2 teaspoons dried, crumbled

2   tablespoons fresh lemon juice

1   medium garlic clove, minced

⅛   to ¼ teaspoon pepper

⅛   to ¼ teaspoon cayenne

12   ounces shelled cooked shrimp

In a medium bowl, stir together all the ingredients except the shrimp.

Gently stir in the shrimp, thoroughly coating with the dressing. Cover and refrigerate for 1 to 24 hours before serving.

PER SERVING

CALORIES 99

TOTAL FAT 1 g
   Saturated 0 g
   Polyunsaturated 0.5 g
   Monounsaturated 0 g

CHOLESTEROL 133 mg

SODIUM 356 mg

CARBOHYDRATES 5 g
   Fiber 1 g
   Sugars 4 g

PROTEIN 15 g

CALCIUM 34 mg

POTASSIUM 202 mg

DIETARY EXCHANGES
   ½ other carbohydrate
   2 very lean meat

Asian Brown Rice and Vegetable Salad

Serves 4; ½ cup rice, ½ cup spinach, ½ cup broccoli slaw, and 2 tablespoons dressing per serving

This rice- and vegetable-based main dish salad, topped with a sesame-wasabi dressing, is an interesting combination of colors, textures, aromas, and flavors.

1¼ cups water

2 tablespoons plain rice vinegar or white wine vinegar

1 tablespoon light brown sugar

1 teaspoon grated peeled gingerroot

1 cup uncooked instant brown rice

Sesame-Wasabi Dressing

⅓ cup Chicken Broth (page 19) or commercial fat-free, low-sodium chicken broth

1 tablespoon plain rice vinegar or white wine vinegar

2 teaspoons light soy sauce

1 teaspoon toasted sesame oil

½ teaspoon wasabi paste or ½ teaspoon rehydrated wasabi powder (see Cook's Tip on Wasabi, page 55)

■ ■ ■

2 ounces fresh spinach leaves (about 2 cups)

2 cups broccoli slaw or shredded cabbage coleslaw mix

2 tablespoons chopped walnuts, dry-roasted

In a medium saucepan, stir together the water, 2 tablespoons vinegar, brown sugar, and gingerroot. Bring to a simmer over medium-high heat, stirring occasionally.

Stir in the rice. Reduce the heat and simmer, covered, for 10 minutes. Remove the pan from the heat. Let stand, covered, for 5 minutes. Uncover and fluff the rice with a fork. Let the mixture cool in the pan, uncovered, for 5 to 10 minutes.

Meanwhile, in a small bowl, whisk together the dressing ingredients.

To assemble the salads, in each salad bowl make a single layer of spinach, followed in order by a layer of rice, broccoli slaw, and walnuts. Drizzle with the dressing.

Wasabi

Rehydrating wasabi powder is quite simple but a bit unusual. In a small bowl, stir together 1 tablespoon plus 1 teaspoon wasabi powder and 1 tablespoon lukewarm water. Turn the bowl upside down and let the mixture stand for about 1 minute to develop the flavor and the heat. The mixture should be thick enough that it will adhere to the upturned bowl. Add small amounts of wasabi paste or rehydrated wasabi powder to various dishes, such as salad dressings, marinades, and sauces, to enhance the flavor without adding sodium. Just proceed carefully—this Japanese horseradish is fiery! To store, transfer the rehydrated wasabi to an airtight container and refrigerate, covered, for up to one week.

PER SERVING

CALORIES 151

TOTAL FAT 4.5 g
   Saturated 0.5 g
   Polyunsaturated 2.5 g
   Monounsaturated 1 g

CHOLESTEROL 0 mg

SODIUM 110 mg

CARBOHYDRATES 24 g
   Fiber 3 g
   Sugars 4 g

PROTEIN 4 g

CALCIUM 23 mg

POTASSIUM 255 mg

DIETARY EXCHANGES
   1½ starch
   ½ fat

Chicken Salad

Celery and green onions give this versatile salad a crunch and a fresh taste that will make you want to use it however you can—to stuff a tomato, fill a sandwich, or provide protein on a salad plate.

> 15-ounce can no-salt-added chicken breast, canned in water, drained
> 1 medium rib of celery, finely chopped
> 4 medium green onions, chopped
> 1/2 cup fat-free or light mayonnaise
> 1/2 teaspoon Dijon mustard
> 1/4 teaspoon ground ginger
> 1/4 teaspoon pepper

Using your fingers or a fork, shred the chicken into a medium bowl.

Stir in the celery and green onions.

In a small bowl, whisk together the remaining ingredients. Pour over the chicken mixture. Stir until well combined. Serve immediately, or cover and refrigerate until needed.

Garnish this salad with halved seedless grapes, pineapple chunks, Sweet Bread-and-Butter Pickles (pages 230–231), or tomato wedges.

PER SERVING
CALORIES 126
TOTAL FAT 1.5 g
    Saturated 0 g
    Polyunsaturated 0.5 g
    Monounsaturated 0.5 g
CHOLESTEROL 38 mg
SODIUM 274 mg
CARBOHYDRATES 5 g
    Fiber 1 g
    Sugars 4 g
PROTEIN 18 g
CALCIUM 4 mg
POTASSIUM 213 mg
DIETARY EXCHANGES
    1/2 other carbohydrate
    2 1/2 very lean meat

Balsamic Vinaigrette

Serves 10; 2 tablespoons per serving

When tomatoes are at their peak, drizzle some with a little of this dressing for a salad that's simple perfection. It's also very good on cooked or chilled raw vegetables.

½ cup water

¼ cup plus 2 tablespoons balsamic vinegar

¼ cup finely snipped fresh parsley

2 tablespoons canola or corn oil

½ teaspoon pepper

In a jar with a tight-fitting lid, combine all the ingredients. Shake well. Refrigerate until needed.

This and other vinaigrette dressings make great marinades for beef, seafood, poultry, and vegetables to be grilled or broiled.

PER SERVING

CALORIES 34

TOTAL FAT 3 g
  Saturated 0 g
  Polyunsaturated 1 g
  Monounsaturated 1.5 g

CHOLESTEROL 0 mg

SODIUM 3 mg

CARBOHYDRATES 2 g
  Fiber 0 g
  Sugars 2 g

PROTEIN 0 g

CALCIUM 4 mg

POTASSIUM 16 mg

DIETARY EXCHANGES
  ½ fat

Cider Vinaigrette

Serves 8; 2 tablespoons per serving

Fresh lemon juice and garlic intensify the flavor of this dressing. With it and the variations below, you'll be able to complement many different types of salad.

⅓ cup cider vinegar

¼ cup fresh lemon juice

3 tablespoons water

2 tablespoons canola or corn oil

1 tablespoon plus 1½ teaspoons Dijon mustard

2½ teaspoons sugar

2 medium garlic cloves, minced

½ teaspoon pepper

In a jar with a tight-fitting lid, combine all the ingredients. Shake well. Refrigerate until needed.

For each variation below, follow the same instructions.

Italian Dressing

Serves 8; 2 tablespoons per serving

1 recipe Cider Vinaigrette

1 teaspoon dried basil, crumbled

1 teaspoon dried oregano, crumbled

CIDER VINAIGRETTE	ITALIAN DRESSING
PER SERVING	**PER SERVING**
CALORIES 45	**CALORIES** 46
TOTAL FAT 3.5 g	**TOTAL FAT** 3.5 g
Saturated 0.5 g	Saturated 0.5 g
Polyunsaturated 1 g	Polyunsaturated 1 g
Monounsaturated 2 g	Monounsaturated 2 g
CHOLESTEROL 0 mg	**CHOLESTEROL** 0 mg
SODIUM 58 mg	**SODIUM** 58 mg
CARBOHYDRATES 3 g	**CARBOHYDRATES** 4 g
Fiber 0 g	Fiber 0 g
Sugars 2 g	Sugars 2 g
PROTEIN 0 g	**PROTEIN** 0 g
CALCIUM 5 mg	**CALCIUM** 12 mg
POTASSIUM 29 mg	**POTASSIUM** 36 mg
DIETARY EXCHANGES	**DIETARY EXCHANGES**
1 fat	1 fat

Russian Dressing

Serves 10; 2 tablespoons per serving

1   recipe Cider Vinaigrette

2   tablespoons no-salt-added tomato paste

1   tablespoon finely chopped green bell pepper

¼   teaspoon Chili Powder (page 226) or commercial no-salt-added chili powder

⅛   teaspoon onion powder

      Dash of red hot-pepper sauce

Tomato French Dressing

Serves 10; 2 tablespoons per serving

1   recipe Cider Vinaigrette

3   tablespoons no-salt-added tomato paste

2   teaspoons sugar

1   tablespoon dried minced onion

RUSSIAN DRESSING
PER SERVING
CALORIES 39
TOTAL FAT 3 g
Saturated 0 g
Polyunsaturated 1 g
Monounsaturated 1.5 g
CHOLESTEROL 0 mg
SODIUM 50 mg
CARBOHYDRATES 3 g
Fiber 0 g
Sugars 2 g
PROTEIN 0 g
CALCIUM 6 mg
POTASSIUM 60 mg
DIETARY EXCHANGES
½ fat

TOMATO FRENCH DRESSING
PER SERVING
CALORIES 44
TOTAL FAT 3 g
Saturated 0 g
Polyunsaturated 1 g
Monounsaturated 1.5 g
CHOLESTEROL 0 mg
SODIUM 51 mg
CARBOHYDRATES 5 g
Fiber 0 g
Sugars 3 g
PROTEIN 1 g
CALCIUM 7 mg
POTASSIUM 79 mg
DIETARY EXCHANGES
½ other carbohydrate
½ fat

Ranch Dressing with Fresh Herbs

Serves 12; 2 tablespoons per serving

Fresh dillweed and parsley perk up this low-salt version of a classic.

- 1 cup fat-free or low-fat buttermilk
- ½ cup fat-free or light sour cream
- 1 tablespoon snipped fresh dillweed or 1 teaspoon dried, crumbled
- 1 tablespoon snipped fresh parsley or 1 teaspoon dried, crumbled
- 1 tablespoon Dijon mustard
- 2 teaspoons dried minced onion
- ¼ teaspoon garlic powder
- ⅛ to ¼ teaspoon pepper

In a jar with a tight-fitting lid, combine all the ingredients. Shake well. Refrigerate for at least 2 hours to allow the flavors to blend.

PER SERVING
CALORIES 23
TOTAL FAT 0.5 g
    Saturated 0 g
    Polyunsaturated 0 g
    Monounsaturated 0 g
CHOLESTEROL 3 mg
SODIUM 56 mg
CARBOHYDRATES 3 g
    Fiber 0 g
    Sugars 2 g
PROTEIN 2 g
CALCIUM 39 mg
POTASSIUM 63 mg
DIETARY EXCHANGES
    Free

Creamy Black Pepper and Garlic Dressing

Serves 8; 2 tablespoons per serving

The black pepper gives this dressing a surprising kick that contrasts with its creamy texture.

½ cup fat-free or light mayonnaise

½ cup fat-free milk

1 tablespoon plus 2 teaspoons cider vinegar

1 teaspoon black pepper

1 medium garlic clove, minced

In a small bowl, whisk together all the ingredients. Transfer to a jar with a tight-fitting lid. Refrigerate until needed.

PER SERVING
CALORIES 22
TOTAL FAT 0 g
  Saturated 0 g
  Polyunsaturated 0 g
  Monounsaturated 0 g
CHOLESTEROL 0 mg
SODIUM 133 mg
CARBOHYDRATES 3 g
  Fiber 0 g
  Sugars 3 g
PROTEIN 1 g
CALCIUM 18 mg
POTASSIUM 18 mg
DIETARY EXCHANGES
  Free

Thousand Island Dressing

Serves 10; 2 tablespoons per serving

Creamy and just a wee bit spicy, this classic dressing will perk up your salad creations.

½ cup fat-free or low-fat plain yogurt

½ cup Chili Sauce (page 218), or ½ cup Ketchup (page 219) or commercial no-salt-added ketchup plus dash of red hot-pepper sauce

2 tablespoons fat-free or light mayonnaise

White of 1 large hard-cooked egg, finely chopped

1 tablespoon finely chopped green bell pepper

1 tablespoon finely chopped celery

¼ teaspoon onion powder

Dash of pepper

In a small bowl, whisk together all the ingredients. Transfer to a jar with a tight-fitting lid. Refrigerate until needed.

PER SERVING

CALORIES 27

TOTAL FAT 0 g
  Saturated 0 g
  Polyunsaturated 0 g
  Monounsaturated 0 g

CHOLESTEROL 0 mg

SODIUM 46 mg

CARBOHYDRATES 5 g
  Fiber 0 g
  Sugars 3 g

PROTEIN 1 g

CALCIUM 29 mg

POTASSIUM 110 mg

DIETARY EXCHANGES
  1 vegetable

Lemon and Poppy Seed Dressing

Serves 8; 2 tablespoons per serving

Remember this dressing for your summertime luncheons. Its tangy-sweet flavor is an ideal accent for juicy chunks of cantaloupe and honeydew melon.

$\frac{1}{2}$ cup frozen lemonade concentrate, thawed and undiluted

$\frac{1}{3}$ cup honey

1 tablespoon plus 2 teaspoons canola or corn oil

1 teaspoon poppy seeds

In a small mixing bowl, whisk together all the ingredients. Transfer to a jar with a tight-fitting lid. Refrigerate until needed.

Cook's TIP

Poppy Seeds

Because they contain so much oil, poppy seeds tend to become rancid quickly. Store them in an airtight container in the refrigerator for up to six months.

PER SERVING

CALORIES 104

TOTAL FAT 3 g
  Saturated 0 g
  Polyunsaturated 1 g
  Monounsaturated 1.5 g

CHOLESTEROL 0 mg

SODIUM 1 mg

CARBOHYDRATES 20 g
  Fiber 0 g
  Sugars 20 g

PROTEIN 0 g

CALCIUM 7 mg

POTASSIUM 22 mg

DIETARY EXCHANGES
  1½ other carbohydrate
  ½ fat

Orange-Yogurt Dressing

Serves 10; 2 tablespoons per serving

This dressing is particularly delicious served over fresh melon or pineapple.

- 1   cup fat-free or low-fat plain yogurt
- ¼   cup orange juice
- 1   teaspoon honey

In a small bowl, whisk together all the ingredients until well blended. Transfer to a jar with a tight-fitting lid. Refrigerate until needed.

Apricot-Yogurt Dressing

Serves 10; 2 tablespoons per serving

- 1   cup fat-free or low-fat plain yogurt
- ¼   cup all-fruit apricot spread
- 2   teaspoons honey
- ½   teaspoon vanilla extract

In a small bowl, whisk together all the ingredients until well blended. Transfer to a jar with a tight-fitting lid. Refrigerate until needed.

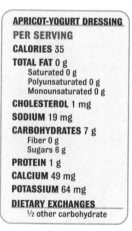

ORANGE-YOGURT DRESSING	APRICOT-YOGURT DRESSING
PER SERVING	**PER SERVING**
CALORIES 19	**CALORIES** 35
TOTAL FAT 0 g	**TOTAL FAT** 0 g
Saturated 0 g	Saturated 0 g
Polyunsaturated 0 g	Polyunsaturated 0 g
Monounsaturated 0 g	Monounsaturated 0 g
CHOLESTEROL 1 mg	**CHOLESTEROL** 1 mg
SODIUM 19 mg	**SODIUM** 19 mg
CARBOHYDRATES 3 g	**CARBOHYDRATES** 7 g
Fiber 0 g	Fiber 0 g
Sugars 3 g	Sugars 6 g
PROTEIN 1 g	**PROTEIN** 1 g
CALCIUM 50 mg	**CALCIUM** 49 mg
POTASSIUM 75 mg	**POTASSIUM** 64 mg
DIETARY EXCHANGES	**DIETARY EXCHANGES**
Free	½ other carbohydrate

Pan-Seared Fillets with Cilantro

Oven-Fried Fish

Spicy Baked Fish

Fish Steaks with Thyme

Oregano Snapper with Lemon

Mediterranean Fish Fillets

Halibut with Cilantro Pesto

Southern Fish Fillets

Pecan-Crusted Catfish with Zesty Tartar Sauce

Poached Salmon

Salmon with Mexican Rub and Chipotle Sour Cream

Grilled Salmon Fillet with Fresh Herbs

SALMON SALAD

Seafood

- Cajun Snapper
- Herbed Fillet of Sole
- Sole with Vegetables and Dijon Dill Sauce
- Tuna Penne Casserole
- Tuna Teriyaki Stir-Fry

- Scallops and Bok Choy with Balsamic Sauce
- Grilled Shrimp on Lemongrass Skewers
- Shrimp and Pasta with Spinach and Lemony Cream Sauce
- Risotto with Shrimp and Vegetables
- Spanish-Style Crab and Vegetable Tortilla

Pan-Seared Fillets with Cilantro

Serves 4; 3 ounces fish per serving

Quickly sear the fish fillets, then keep them moist by reducing the heat. Top them with a mild zing of jalapeño and a splash of fresh lime—that's dinner in a snap!

½	medium fresh jalapeño (cut lengthwise)
2	tablespoons snipped fresh cilantro
2	tablespoons light tub margarine
4	grouper or other mild fish fillets (about 4 ounces each)
½	teaspoon paprika
¼	teaspoon pepper
¼	teaspoon salt
	Vegetable oil spray
1	medium lime, quartered

Wearing plastic gloves, discard the stem, ribs, and seeds of the jalapeño. Mince the jalapeño. Put in a small bowl.

Stir in the cilantro and margarine. Set aside.

Rinse the fish and pat dry with paper towels. Sprinkle the fish on only one side with the paprika, pepper, and salt.

Heat a large nonstick skillet over medium-high heat. Remove from the heat and lightly spray with vegetable oil spray (being careful not to spray near a gas flame). Cook the fish for 2 minutes. Reduce the heat to medium. Turn the fish. Cook for 4 to 5 minutes, or until it flakes easily when tested with a fork.

PER SERVING
CALORIES 128
TOTAL FAT 3.5 g
    Saturated 0.5 g
    Polyunsaturated 1 g
    Monounsaturated 1.5 g
CHOLESTEROL 42 mg
SODIUM 251 mg
CARBOHYDRATES 1 g
    Fiber 0 g
    Sugars 0 g
PROTEIN 22 g
CALCIUM 34 mg
POTASSIUM 573 mg
DIETARY EXCHANGES
    3 very lean meat

To serve, transfer the fish to plates. Using the back of a spoon, spread the cilantro mixture over the fish. Squeeze the lime over the fish.

Oven-Fried Fish

The answer to your fried-fish cravings, this oven-fried version is golden brown and crisp, yet easy on your heart and oh so easy to clean up.

Vegetable oil spray
1 tablespoon plus 1½ teaspoons corn oil stick margarine, melted
1 tablespoon fresh lemon juice
½ teaspoon dried basil, crumbled
¼ teaspoon salt
¼ teaspoon pepper
¼ teaspoon paprika
⅛ teaspoon garlic powder
11 fat-free, low-sodium saltine crackers, crushed (about ½ cup)
4 flounder, sole, or cod fillets (about 4 ounces each)
1 medium lemon, quartered

Preheat the oven to 475°F. Lightly spray a nonstick baking sheet with vegetable oil spray.

In a medium shallow bowl, stir together the margarine, lemon juice, basil, salt, pepper, paprika, and garlic powder.

Put the cracker crumbs in a separate medium shallow bowl. Set the bowls and baking sheet in a row, assembly-line fashion.

Rinse the fish and pat dry with paper towels. Dip the fish in the margarine mixture, then roll it in the cracker crumbs, coating well. Arrange the fish in a single layer on the baking sheet. Spoon the remaining margarine mixture over the fish.

Bake for 15 minutes, or until the fish flakes easily when tested with a fork. Serve with the lemon wedges.

PER SERVING
CALORIES 165
TOTAL FAT 5.5 g
    Saturated 1 g
    Polyunsaturated 1.5 g
    Monounsaturated 2.5 g
CHOLESTEROL 53 mg
SODIUM 327 mg
CARBOHYDRATES 8 g
    Fiber 0 g
    Sugars 1 g
PROTEIN 20 g
CALCIUM 23 mg
POTASSIUM 312 mg
DIETARY EXCHANGES
    ½ starch
    3 lean meat

Spicy Baked Fish

Serves 4; 3 ounces fish per serving

A crust of whole-wheat crumbs and parsley with just a few drops of hot-pepper sauce provides a refreshing flavor change to baked fish.

2   slices light whole-wheat bread, coarsely torn
¼   cup snipped fresh parsley
½   teaspoon pepper
    Vegetable oil spray
2   tablespoons fat-free or light mayonnaise
1   tablespoon water
4   drops red hot-pepper sauce
4   fish fillets, such as cod, haddock, flounder, or sole (about 4 ounces each)
1   medium lemon, quartered (optional)

Preheat the oven to 350°F.

In a food processor or blender, process the bread until the crumbs are very fine. Sprinkle the crumbs on an ungreased baking sheet.

Bake for 5 to 7 minutes, or until lightly browned. Transfer to a medium shallow bowl.

Stir in the parsley and pepper.

Increase the oven temperature to 450°F. Spray the baking sheet with vegetable oil spray.

In another shallow bowl, whisk together the mayonnaise, water, and hot-pepper sauce. Set the bowls (this one first) and baking sheet in a row, assembly-line fashion.

Rinse the fish and pat dry with paper towels. Dip the fish in the mayonnaise mixture, then roll it in the bread crumbs. Arrange in a single layer on the baking sheet.

Bake for 17 to 18 minutes, or until the fish flakes easily when tested with a fork. Serve with the lemon wedges.

PER SERVING
CALORIES 112
TOTAL FAT 1 g
    Saturated 0 g
    Polyunsaturated 0 g
    Monounsaturated 0 g
CHOLESTEROL 43 mg
SODIUM 184 mg
CARBOHYDRATES 6 g
    Fiber 2 g
    Sugars 2 g
PROTEIN 19 g
CALCIUM 17 mg
POTASSIUM 220 mg
DIETARY EXCHANGES
    ½ starch
    3 very lean meat

Fish Steaks with Thyme

Serves 4; 3 ounces fish per serving

You'll have time to make a salad while the fish marinates.

  2 tablespoons fresh lemon juice
  1 tablespoon dried parsley, crumbled
  2 teaspoons olive oil
  1 teaspoon dried thyme, crumbled
  ½ teaspoon pepper
  4 fish steaks, such as tuna or shark (about 4 ounces each)
     Vegetable oil spray

In a small bowl, stir together the lemon juice, parsley, oil, thyme, and pepper.

Rinse the fish and pat dry with paper towels. Rub the fish with the lemon juice mixture. Cover and refrigerate for 30 to 60 minutes.

Lightly spray the grill rack with vegetable oil spray. Preheat the grill on medium high. Grill the fish at least 6 inches from the heat for 3 to 5 minutes on each side for tuna, or 4 to 5 minutes on each side for other fish, or until the fish flakes easily when tested with a fork.

Grilling Fish

For an attractive crosshatch pattern, grill the fish for about one-quarter of the total grilling time. Rotate the fish 90 degrees, and grill for about one-quarter of the total grilling time. Turn the fish over and repeat.

PER SERVING
CALORIES 147
TOTAL FAT 3.5 g
    Saturated 0.5 g
    Polyunsaturated 0.5 g
    Monounsaturated 2 g
CHOLESTEROL 51 mg
SODIUM 43 mg
CARBOHYDRATES 1 g
    Fiber 0 g
    Sugars 0 g
PROTEIN 27 g
CALCIUM 26 mg
POTASSIUM 527 mg
DIETARY EXCHANGES
    3 very lean meat

Oregano Snapper with Lemon

Serves 4; 3 ounces fish per serving

Sprinkle, bake, and serve—any easier and it wouldn't be called cooking!

Vegetable oil spray

4 mild white fish fillets, such as snapper or grouper (about 4 ounces each)

1 teaspoon dried oregano, crumbled

½ teaspoon ground cumin

¼ teaspoon salt

¼ teaspoon pepper

Paprika to taste

1 medium lemon, quartered

Preheat the oven to 350°F. Line a baking pan with aluminum foil. Lightly spray with vegetable oil spray.

Rinse the fish and pat dry with paper towels. Place the fish in a single layer in the baking pan.

Sprinkle the fish with the remaining ingredients except the lemon. Lightly spray with vegetable oil spray.

Bake for 10 to 12 minutes, or until the fish flakes easily when tested with a fork. Squeeze the lemon over the fish.

PER SERVING

CALORIES 114

TOTAL FAT 1.5 g
  Saturated 0.5 g
  Polyunsaturated 0.5 g
  Monounsaturated 0.5 g

CHOLESTEROL 40 mg

SODIUM 195 mg

CARBOHYDRATES 1 g
  Fiber 0 g
  Sugars 0 g

PROTEIN 23 g

CALCIUM 42 mg

POTASSIUM 471 mg

DIETARY EXCHANGES
  3 very lean meat

Mediterranean Fish Fillets

Serves 6; 3 ounces fish per serving

Drizzling fresh lemon juice directly on the fish provides a subtle flavor that will please your palate.

Vegetable oil spray (olive oil spray preferred)

6 cod fillets (about 4 ounces each)

Juice of 1 medium lemon

⅛ teaspoon pepper

2 large tomatoes, sliced ¼ inch thick (about 3 cups)

½ medium green bell pepper, finely chopped

2 tablespoons capers packed in balsamic vinegar, rinsed and drained

¼ cup plain dry bread crumbs

1 tablespoon olive oil

1½ teaspoons dried basil, crumbled

Preheat the oven to 350°F. Lightly spray a nonstick rimmed pan (such as a jelly-roll pan) with the vegetable oil spray.

Rinse the fish and pat dry with paper towels. Put the fish in a single layer in the pan. Drizzle with the lemon juice. Sprinkle with the pepper. Top with the tomato slices, bell pepper, and capers.

In a small bowl, stir together the bread crumbs, oil, and basil. Sprinkle over the fish.

Bake for 25 minutes, or until the fish flakes easily when tested with a fork.

PER SERVING
CALORIES 136
TOTAL FAT 3.5 g
  Saturated 0.5 g
  Polyunsaturated 0.5 g
  Monounsaturated 2 g
CHOLESTEROL 43 mg
SODIUM 176 mg
CARBOHYDRATES 7 g
  Fiber 1 g
  Sugars 2 g
PROTEIN 19 g
CALCIUM 36 mg
POTASSIUM 385 mg
DIETARY EXCHANGES
  ½ starch
  3 very lean meat

Halibut with Cilantro Pesto

Pesto made with cilantro, lime, and jalapeño turns simple grilled or broiled fish into a delicious entrée.

Vegetable oil spray

Cilantro Pesto

1 fresh medium jalapeño (optional)

½ cup loosely packed fresh cilantro, coarsely chopped

2 tablespoons finely chopped walnuts

2 tablespoons shredded or grated Parmesan cheese

1 teaspoon grated lime zest

1 tablespoon fresh lime juice

2 teaspoons olive oil

1 medium garlic clove, minced

■ ■ ■

4 halibut or salmon fillets (about 4 ounces each)

If using a grill, preheat on medium high. Wearing oven mitts, remove the grill rack and lightly spray with vegetable oil spray. If using a broiler, preheat the broiler and lightly spray the broiler pan with vegetable oil spray.

Wearing plastic gloves, slice the jalapeño in half lengthwise. Discard the seeds and ribs. Finely chop the jalapeño. Put in a small bowl.

Stir the remaining pesto ingredients into the jalapeño.

Rinse the fish and pat dry with paper towels. Brush half the pesto on one side of the fish. Place the fish with the pesto side up on the grill rack or in the broiler pan.

Cook about 6 inches from the heat for 4 minutes. Turn the fish and spread with the remaining pesto. Cook for 4 to 6 minutes, or until it flakes easily when tested with a fork. Watch carefully so the walnuts don't burn.

PER SERVING	
CALORIES	182
TOTAL FAT	8 g
Saturated	1.5 g
Polyunsaturated	3 g
Monounsaturated	3 g
CHOLESTEROL	38 mg
SODIUM	105 mg
CARBOHYDRATES	1 g
Fiber	0 g
Sugars	0 g
PROTEIN	25 g
CALCIUM	92 mg
POTASSIUM	548 mg
DIETARY EXCHANGES	
3 very lean meat	
1 fat	

Southern Fish Fillets

Try this entrée with Green Beans and Corn (page 191) and Drop Biscuits (page 255), which can bake at the same time as the fish.

Vegetable oil spray

4 fish fillets, such as orange roughy, perch, or crappie (about 4 ounces each)

½ teaspoon pepper

½ cup fat-free milk

4 drops red hot-pepper sauce

½ cup cornmeal

¼ cup minced fresh parsley

1 teaspoon dried tarragon, crumbled

¼ teaspoon cayenne

1 medium lemon, quartered (optional)

Preheat the oven to 450°F. Lightly spray a $13 \times 9 \times 2$-inch baking dish with vegetable oil spray.

Rinse the fish and pat dry with paper towels. Sprinkle the fish with the pepper.

In a shallow bowl, stir together the milk and hot-pepper sauce.

In a separate shallow bowl, stir together the remaining ingredients except the lemon wedges. Set the bowls and baking dish in a row, assembly-line fashion. Dip the fish in the milk mixture, then roll it in the cornmeal mixture. Place in a single layer in the baking dish.

Bake for 15 to 17 minutes, or until the fish flakes easily when tested with a fork. Serve with the lemon wedges.

PER SERVING
CALORIES 155
TOTAL FAT 1 g
   Saturated 0 g
   Polyunsaturated 0 g
   Monounsaturated 0.5 g
CHOLESTEROL 23 mg
SODIUM 91 mg
CARBOHYDRATES 17 g
   Fiber 1 g
   Sugars 2 g
PROTEIN 20 g
CALCIUM 77 mg
POTASSIUM 405 mg
DIETARY EXCHANGES
   1 starch
   3 very lean meat

Pecan-Crusted Catfish
with Zesty Tartar Sauce

Serves 4; 3 ounces fish and 2 tablespoons sauce per serving

Sour cream replaces mayonnaise as the base for the tartar sauce here. Serve this dish with chilled slices of melon on the side.

4   catfish fillets (about 4 ounces each)

2   tablespoons fat-free or low-fat buttermilk

2   slices light whole-wheat bread

2   medium green onions, thinly sliced

3   tablespoons chopped pecans

1/2   teaspoon salt-free lemon pepper, such as Lemon-Herb Seasoning (page 224)

Zesty Tartar Sauce

1/2   cup fat-free or light sour cream

2   tablespoons dill pickle relish

1   teaspoon grated lemon zest

1   teaspoon fresh lemon juice

1/2   teaspoon dried dillweed, crumbled

Rinse the fish and pat dry with paper towels. Put the fish in a large airtight plastic bag. Pour in the buttermilk. Seal the bag and turn to coat. Let stand at room temperature for 10 to 15 minutes, or refrigerate for up to 1 hour, turning occasionally.

Preheat the oven to 400°F.

In a food processor or blender, process the bread for 5 to 10 seconds to make soft bread crumbs. Pour the crumbs into a shallow bowl.

Stir in the green onions, pecans, and lemon pepper.

Drain the fish, discarding the buttermilk. Coat both sides of the fish with the bread-crumb mixture. Place in a single layer on a nonstick baking sheet. Sprinkle the excess bread-crumb mixture over the fish.

Bake for 10 to 12 minutes, or until the fish flakes easily when tested with a fork.

Meanwhile, in a small bowl, stir together the tartar sauce ingredients. Cover and refrigerate until ready to serve.

To serve, transfer the fish to a platter. Serve the sauce on the side.

PER SERVING
CALORIES 221
TOTAL FAT 7.5 g
    Saturated 1 g
    Polyunsaturated 2 g
    Monounsaturated 3.5 g
CHOLESTEROL 71 mg
SODIUM 224 mg
CARBOHYDRATES 16 g
    Fiber 3 g
    Sugars 6 g
PROTEIN 23 g
CALCIUM 75 mg
POTASSIUM 563 mg
DIETARY EXCHANGES
    1 starch
    3 lean meat

Poached Salmon

Serves 4; 3 ounces fish per serving

This fresh salmon is so quick and easy that it will become an on-the-go favorite. The hint of cloves gives it a distinctive flavor. For a change of taste, try topping it with Yogurt Dill Sauce (page 212).

1-pound salmon fillet (1 to 1½ inches thick) or 4 salmon steaks (about 4 ounces each)
¾ cup water
¾ cup dry white wine (regular or nonalcoholic)
1 medium onion, chopped
1 bay leaf
¼ teaspoon pepper
⅛ teaspoon ground cloves
⅛ teaspoon dried thyme, crumbled
1 medium lemon, quartered (optional)

Rinse the fish and pat dry with paper towels.

In a large skillet, stir together the remaining ingredients except the lemon wedges. Bring to a simmer over medium-high heat. Reduce the heat to medium-low and cook, partially covered, for 5 minutes.

Add the fish. If necessary, add water to barely cover. Simmer, covered, for 10 to 15 minutes, or until the fish flakes easily when tested with a fork. Using a slotted spatula or pancake turner, transfer the fish to plates. Serve with the lemon wedges.

Fresh Salmon

You may prefer salmon fillets to the steaks because fillets have very few, if any, bones. Salmon steaks, cut crosswise through the spine, contain many bones.

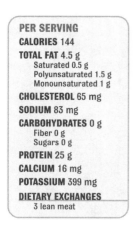

PER SERVING
CALORIES 144
TOTAL FAT 4.5 g
   Saturated 0.5 g
   Polyunsaturated 1.5 g
   Monounsaturated 1 g
CHOLESTEROL 65 mg
SODIUM 83 mg
CARBOHYDRATES 0 g
   Fiber 0 g
   Sugars 0 g
PROTEIN 25 g
CALCIUM 16 mg
POTASSIUM 399 mg
DIETARY EXCHANGES
   3 lean meat

Salmon with Mexican Rub and Chipotle Sour Cream

Serves 4; 3 ounces fish and 2 tablespoons sour cream mixture per serving

A mildly spicy, citrus-tinged sour cream sauce tops these baked salmon fillets. The ground chipotle adds just a hint of smokiness.

Vegetable oil spray

1 teaspoon Chili Powder (page 226) or commercial no-salt-added chili powder

½ teaspoon ground cumin

⅛ teaspoon salt

4 salmon fillets (about 4 ounces each)

Chipotle Sour Cream

½ cup fat-free or light sour cream

1 tablespoon fresh lime juice

¼ teaspoon ground cumin

¼ teaspoon ground chipotle or ⅛ to ¼ teaspoon cayenne

⅛ teaspoon salt

■ ■ ■

1 medium lemon or lime, quartered

Preheat the oven to 350°F. Line a baking sheet with aluminum foil. Lightly spray with vegetable oil spray.

In a small bowl, stir together the Chili Powder, cumin, and salt.

PER SERVING
CALORIES 183
TOTAL FAT 4.5 g
Saturated 0.5 g
Polyunsaturated 1.5 g
Monounsaturated 1 g
CHOLESTEROL 70 mg
SODIUM 254 mg
CARBOHYDRATES 7 g
Fiber 0 g
Sugars 2 g
PROTEIN 27 g
CALCIUM 63 mg
POTASSIUM 497 mg
DIETARY EXCHANGES
½ other carbohydrate
3 lean meat

Rinse the fish and pat dry with paper towels. Sprinkle the rub mixture over both sides of the fish. Using your fingertips, gently press the rub into the fish so it will adhere. Place the fish in a single layer on the baking sheet.

Bake for 20 minutes, or until the fish flakes easily when tested with a fork.

Meanwhile, in a small bowl, stir together the Chipotle Sour Cream ingredients.

To serve, transfer the fish to plates. Spoon the sour cream mixture to the side of the fish. Serve with the lemon wedges.

Grilled Salmon Fillet with Fresh Herbs

Serves 4; 3 ounces fish per serving

Fresh salmon with fresh herbs and lemon—a stellar combination. If you prefer your fish with sauce, this entrée is also great topped with Creamy Lime and Mustard Sauce (page 213).

Vegetable oil spray (olive oil spray preferred)
1-pound salmon fillet with skin (tail end preferred)
1 medium lemon, halved
1½ teaspoons snipped fresh dillweed or ½ teaspoon dried, crumbled
12 fresh thyme sprigs

Generously spray the grill rack with vegetable oil spray. Preheat the grill on medium high.

Rinse the fish and pat dry with paper towels. Place the fish with the skin side down on a shallow plate. Squeeze the juice from one lemon half over the fish. Sprinkle with the dillweed.

Slice the remaining lemon half. Lay the slices on the fish. Top with 8 thyme sprigs.

Grill with the skin side down for 20 minutes (no turning), or until the fish flakes easily when tested with a fork.

To serve, transfer the fish to plates. Garnish with the remaining thyme sprigs.

PER SERVING

CALORIES 147
TOTAL FAT 4.5 g
    Saturated 0.5 g
    Polyunsaturated 1.5 g
    Monounsaturated 1 g
CHOLESTEROL 65 mg
SODIUM 83 mg
CARBOHYDRATES 1 g
    Fiber 0 g
    Sugars 0 g
PROTEIN 25 g
CALCIUM 17 mg
POTASSIUM 414 mg
DIETARY EXCHANGES
    3 lean meat

Salmon Salad

Serves 1

Stir together 3 ounces grilled salmon, cut into bite-size pieces or shredded, with 2 tablespoons fat-free or light mayonnaise and ¼ cup thinly sliced celery.

PER SERVING

CALORIES 161

TOTAL FAT 4 g
   Saturated 0.5 g
   Polyunsaturated 1.5 g
   Monounsaturated 1 g

CHOLESTEROL 57 mg

SODIUM 347 mg

CARBOHYDRATES 5 g
   Fiber 1 g
   Sugars 4 g

PROTEIN 22 g

CALCIUM 27 mg

POTASSIUM 450 mg

DIETARY EXCHANGES
   ½ other carbohydrate
   3 lean meat

Cajun Snapper

Serves 4; 3 ounces fish per serving

A brightly colored, intensely flavored entrée, this fish is ready in less than 15 minutes.

Cajun Rub

2	teaspoons fresh lemon juice
1½	teaspoons low-sodium Worcestershire sauce
1	teaspoon paprika
¾	teaspoon chopped fresh thyme or ¼ teaspoon dried, crumbled
½	teaspoon red hot-pepper sauce
¼	teaspoon garlic powder
¼	teaspoon onion powder
¼	teaspoon salt

■ ■ ■

4	red snapper or other lean white fish fillets (about 4 ounces each)
	Vegetable oil spray
2	teaspoons olive oil
2	tablespoons water

In a small bowl, stir together the rub ingredients.

Rinse the fish and pat dry with paper towels. Spoon the rub onto one side of each fillet. Using the back of a spoon, spread the rub to cover that side.

Spray a large nonstick skillet with vegetable oil spray. Heat over medium-high heat. Add the oil and swirl to coat the bottom. Cook the fish with the coated side down for 4 minutes. Gently turn the fish and cook for 3 to 4 minutes, or until it flakes easily when tested with a fork. Transfer the fish to plates, reserving any pan residue.

Add the water to the skillet, scraping to dislodge any browned bits. Cook for 15 to 20 seconds, or until heated through. Spoon over the fish.

PER SERVING
CALORIES 133
TOTAL FAT 4 g
 Saturated 0.5 g
 Polyunsaturated 1 g
 Monounsaturated 2 g
CHOLESTEROL 40 mg
SODIUM 201 mg
CARBOHYDRATES 1 g
 Fiber 0 g
 Sugars 0 g
PROTEIN 23 g
CALCIUM 38 mg
POTASSIUM 466 mg
DIETARY EXCHANGES
 3 lean meat

Herbed Fillet of Sole

Serves 4; 3 ounces fish per serving

Fragrant herbs and tart lemon juice flavor this moist broiled sole. Also try the seasonings with flounder or orange roughy.

2   tablespoons light tub margarine
¼   cup fresh lemon juice (2 medium)
1   tablespoon dried parsley, crumbled
2   teaspoons dried chives, crumbled
½   teaspoon dried tarragon, crumbled
¼   teaspoon dry mustard
4   sole fillets (about 4 ounces each)

Preheat the broiler. Spread the margarine over the bottom of a 13 × 9 × 2-inch broilerproof baking dish.

In a small bowl, stir together the lemon juice, parsley, chives, tarragon, and dry mustard.

Rinse the fish and pat dry with paper towels. Place the fish in a single layer in the baking dish. Pour half the lemon juice mixture over the fish.

Broil about 4 inches from the heat for 4 minutes with the oven door partially open. Pour the remaining lemon juice mixture over the fish. Broil for 4 to 6 minutes, or until the fish flakes easily when tested with a fork.

Cook's TIP

Broiling

Leaving the oven door partially open when broiling keeps the oven from retaining heat, which can overcook the food.

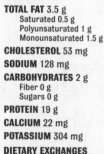

PER SERVING
CALORIES 118
TOTAL FAT 3.5 g
    Saturated 0.5 g
    Polyunsaturated 1 g
    Monounsaturated 1.5 g
CHOLESTEROL 53 mg
SODIUM 128 mg
CARBOHYDRATES 2 g
    Fiber 0 g
    Sugars 0 g
PROTEIN 19 g
CALCIUM 22 mg
POTASSIUM 304 mg
DIETARY EXCHANGES
    3 very lean meat

Sole with Vegetables and Dijon Dill Sauce

Serves 4; 3 ounces fish and ½ cup vegetables per serving

A citrusy aroma will fill your kitchen as this fish dish bakes. Carefully open the foil packets that are keeping the fish and vegetables moist, and you'll have a colorful surprise. Spoon on the sauce and enjoy!

4 sole fillets (about 4 ounces each)

1 teaspoon olive oil

2 medium leeks (white part only), thinly sliced (about ⅓ cup)

4 ounces golden Italian or button mushrooms, quartered

1 medium carrot, thinly sliced

½ medium red bell pepper, thinly sliced

1 cup fresh or frozen sugar snap peas, trimmed if fresh

½ teaspoon very low sodium chicken bouillon granules

Vegetable oil spray

1 small lemon, cut into 8 slices and seeded

1 small lime, cut into 8 slices and seeded

1 teaspoon dried marjoram or dried oregano, crumbled

¼ teaspoon pepper

Dijon Dill Sauce

½ cup fat-free or low-fat plain yogurt

1 tablespoon Dijon mustard

1 teaspoon snipped fresh dillweed or ¼ teaspoon dried, crumbled

½ teaspoon grated lemon zest

1 teaspoon fresh lemon juice

½ teaspoon sugar

Rinse the fish and pat dry with paper towels. Set aside.

Heat a large nonstick skillet over medium heat. Add the oil and swirl to coat the bottom. Cook the leeks, mushrooms, carrot, and bell pepper for 2 to 3 minutes, or until the carrot slices are tender-crisp, stirring occasionally.

Stir in the peas and chicken bouillon granules. Remove from the heat.

Preheat the oven to 400°F.

To assemble the packets, lightly spray four 12-inch-square pieces of aluminum foil with vegetable oil spray. Put 2 slices of lemon and 2 slices of lime in a single layer in the middle of each piece of foil. Place each fillet on the citrus slices. Sprinkle with the marjoram and pepper. Spoon about ½ cup vegetable mixture onto each fillet. Seal the foil tightly. Put the packets on a baking sheet.

Bake for 20 minutes, or until the fish flakes easily when tested with a fork. To prevent steam burns, open the packets carefully.

Meanwhile, in a small bowl, whisk together the sauce ingredients. (Sauce can be made ahead and refrigerated for up to four days.) If desired, heat the sauce in a small saucepan over low heat for 1 to 2 minutes, or until heated through, stirring occasionally. Or microwave the sauce in a microwaveable bowl covered with vented plastic wrap. Cook on 100 percent power (high) for 30 to 45 seconds, stirring once.

To serve, place each foil packet on a plate and open carefully. Spoon 2 tablespoons sauce over each serving.

PER SERVING
CALORIES 182
TOTAL FAT 3 g
    Saturated 0.5 g
    Polyunsaturated 1 g
    Monounsaturated 1 g
CHOLESTEROL 54 mg
SODIUM 205 mg
CARBOHYDRATES 16 g
    Fiber 3 g
    Sugars 8 g
PROTEIN 23 g
CALCIUM 136 mg
POTASSIUM 692 mg
DIETARY EXCHANGES
    3 vegetable
    3 very lean meat

Tuna Penne Casserole

Serves 5; 1 cup per serving

Curry powder provides a new twist to a familiar dish.

- 1 tablespoon cornstarch
- 3 tablespoons water
- 1⅓ cups dried penne or macaroni
- Vegetable oil spray
- 1 teaspoon canola or corn oil
- ¼ cup chopped onion
- 1½ cups fat-free milk
- 1 tablespoon finely snipped fresh parsley or 1 teaspoon dried parsley flakes, crumbled
- ½ to 1 teaspoon curry powder
- ¼ teaspoon salt
- ⅛ teaspoon pepper
- 6-ounce can low-sodium albacore tuna packed in water, rinsed, drained, and flaked
- ½ cup drained no-salt-added canned diced tomatoes
- 1 tablespoon corn oil stick margarine, melted (optional)
- ½ cup rice square cereal crumbs (optional)

Put the cornstarch in a small bowl. Add the water, whisking to dissolve. Set aside.

Prepare the pasta using the package directions, omitting the salt and oil. Drain well and set aside.

Meanwhile, lightly spray a large nonstick skillet with vegetable oil spray. Heat over medium-high heat. Add the oil and swirl to coat the bottom. Cook the onion for 2 to 3 minutes, or until soft, stirring occasionally.

Preheat the broiler.

Whisk the milk, parsley, curry powder, salt, and pepper into the onion. When the milk mixture is hot, gently whisk in the cornstarch mixture. Continue to whisk gently for 3 to 5 minutes, or until slightly thickened. Remove from the heat.

Stir the tuna, pasta, and tomatoes into the sauce.

In a small bowl, stir together the margarine and crumbs. Sprinkle over the casserole.

Broil for 5 minutes, or until the crumbs are lightly browned.

Cornstarch

Cornstarch needs gentle treatment. Too much heat or stirring will cause a cornstarch-thickened sauce to become thin.

PER SERVING

CALORIES 199

TOTAL FAT 2.5 g
   Saturated 0.5 g
   Polyunsaturated 1 g
   Monounsaturated 1 g

CHOLESTEROL 15 mg

SODIUM 185 mg

CARBOHYDRATES 29 g
   Fiber 1 g
   Sugars 5 g

PROTEIN 15 g

CALCIUM 94 mg

POTASSIUM 147 mg

DIETARY EXCHANGES
   2 starch
   1½ very lean meat

WITH OPTIONAL INGREDIENTS

PER SERVING

CALORIES 238

TOTAL FAT 5 g
   Saturated 1 g
   Polyunsaturated 1.5 g
   Monounsaturated 2 g

CHOLESTEROL 15 mg

SODIUM 259 mg

CARBOHYDRATES 33 g
   Fiber 1 g
   Sugars 6 g

PROTEIN 15 g

CALCIUM 111 mg

POTASSIUM 153 mg

DIETARY EXCHANGES
   2 starch
   1½ lean meat

Tuna Teriyaki Stir-Fry

Serves 4; 1 cup tuna and vegetable mixture and ½ cup rice per serving

Cubes of fresh albacore tuna are stir-fried with plump sugar snap peas and thin slices of carrots and red bell pepper, then glazed with a teriyaki sauce and served over brown rice. It's a one-dish meal that is perfect for the cook on the go!

1	cup uncooked instant brown rice

Teriyaki Glaze

¼	cup water
2½	tablespoons light teriyaki sauce
½	teaspoon cornstarch
½	teaspoon toasted sesame oil

■ ■ ■

4	albacore tuna steaks (about 4 ounces each)
1	teaspoon canola or corn oil
2	medium garlic cloves, minced
1	teaspoon grated peeled gingerroot
4	ounces sugar snap peas, trimmed
4	medium green onions, thinly sliced (green and white parts)
1	medium carrot, thinly sliced
½	medium red bell pepper, thinly sliced

Prepare the rice using the package directions, omitting the salt and margarine. Cover and keep warm.

Meanwhile, in a small bowl, whisk together the teriyaki glaze ingredients. Set aside.

Rinse the tuna and pat dry with paper towels. Cut the tuna into ¾-inch cubes.

Heat a wok or large nonstick skillet over medium-high heat. Add the oil and swirl to coat the bottom. Cook the tuna, garlic, and gingerroot for 3 to 4 minutes, or until the tuna is golden brown on the outside (it will still be slightly pink inside), stirring constantly.

Stir in the peas, green onions, carrot, and bell pepper. Cook for 2 to 3 minutes, or until the vegetables are tender-crisp, stirring constantly.

Make a well in the center. Pour in the teriyaki mixture. Simmer for 1 to 2 minutes, or until the mixture is thickened, stirring occasionally in the well only. Stir the tuna and vegetables into the thickened glaze. Cook for 1 minute, or until the mixture is heated through, stirring constantly.

To serve, spoon the rice into shallow bowls or onto plates. Ladle the tuna-vegetable mixture on top.

PER SERVING

CALORIES 345

TOTAL FAT 11 g
    Saturated 2.5 g
    Polyunsaturated 1 g
    Monounsaturated 1 g

CHOLESTEROL 43 mg

SODIUM 356 mg

CARBOHYDRATES 27 g
    Fiber 4 g
    Sugars 5 g

PROTEIN 32 g

CALCIUM 50 mg

POTASSIUM 726 mg

DIETARY EXCHANGES
    1½ starch
    1 vegetable
    3 lean meat

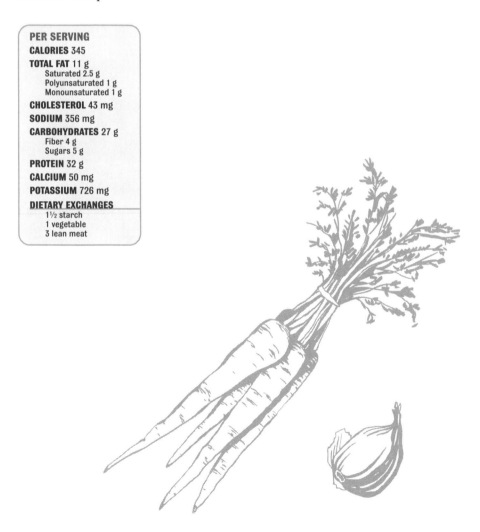

Scallops and Bok Choy with Balsamic Sauce

Serves 4; 3 ounces scallops per serving

On their own, scallops have a rich, sweet flavor. When topped with this bold balsamic sauce, they're transformed into an extraordinary dish fit for company. Serve the scallops over steamed rice for a delectable dinner.

4	stalks bok choy
2	medium green onions
1/2	cup bottled roasted red bell peppers, rinsed and drained
1	pound bay scallops
1	teaspoon olive oil
1/4	cup Chicken Broth (page 19) or commercial fat-free, low-sodium chicken broth
2	medium garlic cloves, minced
1/8	teaspoon pepper
2	tablespoons balsamic vinegar

Trim the ends off the bok choy. Cut the stalks and leaves crosswise into 1/2-inch slices. Cut the green onions into 1-inch pieces. Cut the roasted peppers into thin strips. Rinse the scallops and pat dry with paper towels.

Heat a large nonstick skillet over medium-high heat. Add the oil and swirl to coat the bottom. Let the oil get hot, then cook the scallops for 1 minute, stirring occasionally after 30 seconds. (If the scallops were frozen, they may need to cook for an additional 1 to 2 minutes to evaporate the extra liquid they release.)

Stir in the remaining ingredients except the vinegar. Cook, covered, for 1 to 2 minutes, or until the scallops are cooked through (white and opaque, not translucent, in the center), stirring occasionally. Watch carefully; scallops become rubbery when overcooked. Using a slotted spoon, transfer the scallops and vegetables to a serving platter. Cover with aluminum foil to keep warm.

Add the vinegar to the liquid in the skillet. Cook for 1 to 2 minutes, or until the liquid is reduced by half. Pour over the scallops.

Bok Choy

Look for bok choy, with its long white stalks and large dark green leaves, near the cabbage in the produce section. Slices of raw bok choy stalks add a pleasant crunch to salads. Both the stalks and the leaves are good in stir-fry dishes and soups.

Scallops

When scallops are called for, you can use either sea or bay scallops. Bay scallops (as many as 40 per pound) are milder—and more expensive—than sea scallops (12 to 15 per pound). To reduce cooking time or to substitute sea scallops for bay, cut the sea scallops in halves, quarters, or slices.

Because scallops are delicate, they need gentle handling. Overcooking scallops, even for an extra minute or two, can cause them to shrink and become tough and chewy. Dry them well before cooking, have the oil hot before adding the scallops, and don't overcrowd (no more than one layer, with some space between pieces). Otherwise, the scallops will steam and won't brown.

PER SERVING
CALORIES 128
TOTAL FAT 2 g
    Saturated 0 g
    Polyunsaturated 0.5 g
    Monounsaturated 1 g
CHOLESTEROL 37 mg
SODIUM 225 mg
CARBOHYDRATES 7 g
    Fiber 1 g
    Sugars 2 g
PROTEIN 20 g
CALCIUM 47 mg
POTASSIUM 454 mg
DIETARY EXCHANGES
    ½ other carbohydrate
    3 very lean meat

Grilled Shrimp
on Lemongrass Skewers

Serves 4; 1 skewer per serving

These lemon-flavored shrimp are delicious paired with Asian Fried Rice with Peas (page 204). Lemongrass skewers are more flexible than bamboo skewers, but they're strong enough to handle the job.

Marinade

1	stalk fresh lemongrass
½	cup mirin or sweet wine
2	tablespoons minced peeled gingerroot
2	tablespoons light soy sauce or reduced-sodium teriyaki sauce
2	tablespoons canola or corn oil
2	tablespoons fresh lemon juice
1	tablespoon finely snipped fresh cilantro
⅛	teaspoon crushed red pepper flakes

■ ■ ■

1	pound raw medium shrimp with shells
4	stalks fresh lemongrass, outer leaf of each discarded

Cut 1 stalk of lemongrass to separate the tender bottom part (4 to 6 inches) from the rest. Peel to the inside layers of the tender part, and discard the outer layers and the tough part of the stalk. Thinly slice the inner layers. Put the sliced lemongrass and the remaining marinade ingredients in a large airtight plastic bag.

Peel the shrimp, leaving the tails intact. Rinse and drain. Pat dry with paper towels. Add the shrimp to the marinade. Seal the bag and turn to coat. Refrigerate for 1 to 12 hours, turning the bag occasionally.

Preheat the grill on medium-high.

Peel the remaining 4 lemongrass stalks to the size of heavy-duty bamboo skewers. Thread the shrimp on each lemongrass stalk, with the tails facing in the same direction.

Grill the skewers for 5 minutes on each side, or until the shrimp turn pink. Don't overcook the shrimp, or they'll become tough.

Variations

Replace the shrimp with 1 pound scallops or 1 pound salmon, cubed, or use ⅓ pound each of shrimp, scallops, and salmon for a mixed seafood grill.

Lemongrass

An herb, lemongrass is somewhat like a green onion in structure. The fibrous outer leaves and tops are too tough to eat, but the lower white part is tender and edible. You can use the tops to impart a fragrant lemon flavor to marinades, soups, and sauces. When making chicken soup, tie 3 chopped lemongrass stalks in a small piece of cheesecloth and place it in the pot with the broth (about 8 cups of broth for 3 stalks of lemongrass). It is customary in Asian cooking to leave the cheesecloth bag in the soup and ladle around it while serving. When making sauce, place the lemongrass in cheesecloth as directed for soup. Simmer the lemongrass in the sauce for 5 to 10 minutes, then remove the bag. Finish the sauce as directed in your recipe.

Mirin

Mirin is a sweet Japanese rice wine. It's available in some supermarkets and most Asian markets. When shopping for mirin, be sure to purchase regular mirin, not cooking mirin, which has salt added.

PER SERVING

CALORIES 80

TOTAL FAT 1 g
  Saturated 0 g
  Polyunsaturated 0.5 g
  Monounsaturated 0 g

CHOLESTEROL 147 mg

SODIUM 364 mg

CARBOHYDRATES 1 g
  Fiber 0 g
  Sugars 16 g

PROTEIN 17 g

CALCIUM 31 mg

POTASSIUM 158 mg

DIETARY EXCHANGES
  2½ very lean meat

Shrimp and Pasta with Spinach and Lemony Cream Sauce

Serves 5; 1 cup per serving

The cream sauce for this dish is about the easiest and tastiest you'll ever make. Don't worry about leftovers. There won't be any!

1   pound raw medium shrimp with shells
⅓   cup sliced almonds
¼   cup dry white wine (regular or nonalcoholic)
    Vegetable oil spray
¼   teaspoon garlic powder
¼   teaspoon white pepper, or to taste
6   ounces dried vermicelli or other thin pasta
¾   cup fat-free or light sour cream
1   tablespoon light stick margarine
2   teaspoons fresh lemon juice
¼   teaspoon salt
1   tablespoon light stick margarine
4   ounces (about 4 cups) fresh whole baby spinach leaves or regular spinach leaves, stems discarded and leaves coarsely chopped
2   tablespoons finely chopped green onions

Peel the shrimp. Rinse and pat dry with paper towels. Set aside.

Heat a large nonstick skillet over medium-high heat. Dry-roast the almonds for 3 to 4 minutes, or until just beginning to lightly brown, stirring frequently. Transfer to a small bowl. Set aside.

In a small saucepan, bring the wine to a boil over high heat. Boil for about 1 minute, or until reduced to 2 tablespoons. Pour into a small bowl and let cool completely.

Meanwhile, lightly spray the same skillet with vegetable oil spray. Heat over medium heat. Put the shrimp in the skillet. Sprinkle the shrimp with the garlic powder and pepper. Cook for 8 to 10 minutes, or until opaque in the center, stirring frequently.

While the shrimp cook, prepare the pasta using the package directions, omitting the salt and oil. Drain well.

In the saucepan used for the wine, heat the sour cream and 1 tablespoon margarine over medium-low heat for 2 to 3 minutes, or until the margarine has melted and the mixture is heated through, stirring frequently. Remove from the heat.

Whisk the cooled wine, lemon juice, and salt into the sour cream mixture. Cover to keep warm.

When the shrimp is cooked, stir in 1 tablespoon margarine.

Add the spinach and stir until wilted, about 2 minutes.

To assemble, spread the pasta on plates, spoon the sauce over the pasta, and top with the shrimp mixture. Sprinkle with the green onions and almonds.

PER SERVING

CALORIES 300

TOTAL FAT 6.5 g
    Saturated 1 g
    Polyunsaturated 2 g
    Monounsaturated 3 g

CHOLESTEROL 124 mg

SODIUM 333 mg

CARBOHYDRATES 36 g
    Fiber 2 g
    Sugars 4 g

PROTEIN 21 g

CALCIUM 118 mg

POTASSIUM 444 mg

DIETARY EXCHANGES
    2½ starch
    2 lean meat

Risotto with Shrimp and Vegetables

Serves 5; 1 cup per serving

Arborio rice gives risotto its creamy texture, and onion, red bell pepper, and garlic give it plenty of taste in this attractive dish. The delicate crunch of snow peas and the burst of flavor from lemon zest add interesting surprises.

  1 pound raw large shrimp with shells
  1 small lemon
  1 teaspoon olive oil
½ medium onion, sliced
½ medium red bell pepper, chopped
  2 medium garlic cloves, minced
  1 cup uncooked arborio rice
1½ cups Chicken Broth (page 19) or commercial fat-free, low-sodium chicken broth
⅛ teaspoon pepper
  1 cup dry white wine (regular or nonalcoholic)
½ cup Chicken Broth (page 19) or commercial fat-free, low-sodium chicken broth
  6 ounces snow peas, trimmed and halved crosswise (about 2 cups)
½ cup water
  3 tablespoons shredded or grated Romano cheese
  1 tablespoon snipped fresh dillweed
  1 tablespoon thinly sliced green onions (green part only)

Peel and rinse the shrimp. Pat dry with paper towels. Set aside.

Using a vegetable peeler or sharp knife, remove the zest from the lemon. Cut the zest into very thin strips. Set aside.

Heat a medium saucepan over medium heat. Add the oil and swirl to coat the bottom. Cook the onion, bell pepper, and garlic for 2 to 3 minutes, or until tender-crisp, stirring frequently.

Stir in the rice. Cook for 5 minutes, stirring frequently.

Add 1½ cups broth and pepper. Increase the heat to high and bring to a boil, stirring occasionally. Reduce the heat and simmer for 5 minutes, stirring occasionally.

(The rice will be slightly plump, the liquid will not be entirely absorbed, and the mixture will have a thick, soupy or stewlike consistency.)

Stir in the wine and ½ cup broth. Increase the heat to high and bring to a simmer. Reduce the heat to medium high and cook for 8 to 10 minutes, stirring constantly (a small amount of liquid should remain).

Stir in the shrimp, peas, and water. Reduce the heat to medium and cook for 2 to 3 minutes, or until the liquid is almost absorbed, stirring constantly. The rice should be just tender and slightly creamy, and the shrimp should be pink.

Stir in the lemon zest and the remaining ingredients.

Risotto

For proper consistency, carefully regulate the cooking temperature so the risotto boils lightly, not vigorously. If the liquid is absorbed before the rice reaches the just-tender stage, gradually add more broth, wine, or water. Arborio rice is usually used in risottos, but you can substitute a medium-grain rice if you prefer. It won't be quite as creamy, however.

Shrimp

For a decorative look, leave the tails on the shrimp. When the shrimp cook, the tails become brilliant pink.

PER SERVING
CALORIES 200
TOTAL FAT 2 g
  Saturated 0.5 g
  Polyunsaturated 0.5 g
  Monounsaturated 1 g
CHOLESTEROL 119 mg
SODIUM 186 mg
CARBOHYDRATES 20 g
  Fiber 2 g
  Sugars 3 g
PROTEIN 17 g
CALCIUM 64 mg
POTASSIUM 276 mg
DIETARY EXCHANGES
  1½ starch
  2 very lean meat

Spanish-Style Crab and Vegetable Tortilla

Serves 4; 1 wedge per serving

In Mexico, a tortilla is a type of unleavened bread, but in Spain, a tortilla is an omelet, often served open-face.

1   cup frozen vegetables, such as artichoke hearts or asparagus (½ 10-ounce package), peas and carrots, or mixed vegetables

    Vegetable oil spray (olive oil spray preferred)

    Egg substitute equivalent to 6 eggs

4   ounces crab (fresh, frozen, or canned), all cartilage and shell discarded (about ¾ cup)

¼   teaspoon dried dillweed, crumbled

    Pepper to taste

If using artichoke hearts or asparagus, cut into bite-size pieces.

Lightly spray a medium skillet with vegetable oil spray. Heat over medium-low heat. Cook the vegetables for 3 minutes, stirring occasionally.

Stir in the remaining ingredients. Cook for 1 minute, constantly scrambling lightly with a fork. Cook, covered, for 11 to 14 minutes, or until the center of the tortilla is firm and doesn't run.

To serve, cut the tortilla into 4 wedges and place on plates.

PER SERVING

CALORIES 96
TOTAL FAT 0.5 g
    Saturated 0 g
    Polyunsaturated 0 g
    Monounsaturated 0 g
CHOLESTEROL 22 mg
SODIUM 317 mg
CARBOHYDRATES 6 g
    Fiber 3 g
    Sugars 2 g
PROTEIN 16 g
CALCIUM 48 mg
POTASSIUM 245 mg
DIETARY EXCHANGES
    1 vegetable
    2 very lean meat

Chicken Dijon

Oven-Fried Chicken

Chicken Cacciatore

Seared Chicken with Fresh Pineapple, Ginger, and Mint Salsa

Glazed Raspberry-Ginger Chicken

Blue Cheese and Basil Chicken

Chicken Marengo

Blackened Chicken with Mustard Aïoli

Lemon Chicken with Oregano

Blackberry and Balsamic Chicken

Chicken with Yogurt-Cilantro Sauce

Grilled Sesame Chicken

Chicken with Ginger and Snow Peas

Cumin-Lime Chicken

Poultry

Arroz con Pollo (Chicken with Rice)

Chicken Paprikash

Lettuce Wraps with Chicken and Vegetables

Chicken Primavera

Chicken Enchiladas

Roasted Lemon-Herb Turkey Breast

Tarragon Turkey Medallions
TARRAGON PORK MEDALLIONS

Turkey Tenderloin with Rosemary
PORK TENDERLOIN WITH ROSEMARY

Turkey Sausage Patties

Turkey Picadillo

Turkey Stew

Turkey and Broccoli Stir-Fry

New-Style Turkey Club Sandwich for One

Chicken Dijon

Serves 6; 3 ounces chicken, 1/3 cup vegetables, and 2 tablespoons sauce per serving

A smooth Dijon sauce enhances the combination of chicken breasts and colorful vegetables. Serve this dish with couscous and melon slices.

6   boneless, skinless chicken breast halves (about 4 ounces each), all visible fat discarded
1/4 teaspoon pepper
2   teaspoons olive oil
1/2 cup Chicken Broth (page 19) or commercial fat-free, low-sodium chicken broth
2   medium carrots, sliced
1   medium zucchini, sliced
1/2 medium red bell pepper, cut into strips
1   medium garlic clove, minced
1/2 cup fat-free milk
2   tablespoons all-purpose flour
2   tablespoons light tub margarine
1   to 2 teaspoons Dijon mustard
1   tablespoon snipped fresh parsley or 1 teaspoon dried, crumbled

Put a chicken breast half with the smooth side up between two pieces of plastic wrap. Using a tortilla press, the smooth side of a meat mallet, or a rolling pin, lightly flatten the chicken to 1/2-inch thickness, being careful not to tear the meat. Repeat with the remaining chicken. Sprinkle both sides of the chicken with the pepper.

Heat a large nonstick skillet over medium-high heat. Add the oil and swirl to coat the bottom. Cook the chicken for 2 to 3 minutes on each side, or until browned.

Stir in the broth, carrots, zucchini, bell pepper, and garlic. Cook, covered, for 5 to 8 minutes, or until the chicken is no longer pink in the center and the vegetables are tender, stirring occasionally. Using a slotted spoon, transfer the chicken and vegetables to a plate. Reserve the liquid. Cover the plate with aluminum foil to keep warm.

In a small bowl, whisk together the milk and flour. Add with the margarine and mustard to the liquid in the skillet. Bring to a simmer over medium-high heat, whisking occasionally. Cook for 2 to 3 minutes, or until thickened, whisking occasionally.

To serve, pour the sauce over the chicken and vegetables. Sprinkle with the parsley.

PER SERVING

CALORIES 190

TOTAL FAT 4.5 g
  Saturated 0.5 g
  Polyunsaturated 1 g
  Monounsaturated 2.5 g

CHOLESTEROL 66 mg

SODIUM 163 mg

CARBOHYDRATES 8 g
  Fiber 2 g
  Sugars 3 g

PROTEIN 28 g

CALCIUM 51 mg

POTASSIUM 493 mg

DIETARY EXCHANGES
  1½ vegetable
  3 lean meat

Oven-Fried Chicken

Serves 6

Serve this moist chicken in its crisp herb "crust" with Green Beans and Corn (page 191) and Garden Coleslaw (page 41).

Vegetable oil spray
½ cup fat-free or low-fat plain yogurt
2 medium garlic cloves, minced
2 cups light whole-wheat or plain dry bread crumbs
¼ cup minced fresh parsley
2 tablespoons shredded or grated Parmesan cheese
1 teaspoon dried basil, crumbled
1 teaspoon dried oregano, crumbled
¼ teaspoon pepper
2½- to 3-pound chicken, cut into serving pieces, skin and all visible fat discarded

Preheat the oven to 400°F. Lightly spray a $13 \times 9 \times 2$-inch baking pan with vegetable oil spray.

In a shallow bowl, stir together the yogurt and garlic.

In a separate shallow bowl, stir together the remaining ingredients except the chicken. Set the bowls and baking pan in a row, assembly-line fashion.

Dip each piece of chicken in the yogurt mixture, then roll the chicken in the bread crumb mixture and place it in the baking pan. Lightly spray the top of the chicken with vegetable oil spray.

Bake for 55 to 60 minutes, or until no longer pink in the center.

Whole-Wheat Bread Crumbs

To make your own whole-wheat bread crumbs, lightly toast slices of whole-wheat bread. Process the toast in a food processor or blender for 15 to 20 seconds, or until the desired texture.

PER SERVING
CALORIES 180
TOTAL FAT 3.5 g
  Saturated 1 g
  Polyunsaturated 0.5 g
  Monounsaturated 1 g
CHOLESTEROL 71 mg
SODIUM 240 mg
CARBOHYDRATES 12 g
  Fiber 4 g
  Sugars 3 g
PROTEIN 26 g
CALCIUM 86 mg
POTASSIUM 338 mg
DIETARY EXCHANGES
  1 starch
  3 very lean meat

Chicken Cacciatore

Serves 6; 3 ounces chicken per serving

Cacciatore *refers to a style of preparation that includes onions, tomatoes, herbs, often wine, and sometimes mushrooms. Serve this dish over rice or with polenta.* Buon appetito!

- 1 tablespoon canola or corn oil
- 1 medium garlic clove, minced
- 6 boneless, skinless chicken breast halves (about 4 ounces each), all visible fat discarded
- 1 medium onion, chopped
- 2 tablespoons chopped green bell pepper
- 4 medium tomatoes, peeled if desired and chopped
- ¼ cup dry white wine (regular or nonalcoholic)
- ¼ teaspoon dried rosemary leaves, crushed
- ¼ teaspoon dried basil, crumbled
- ⅛ teaspoon pepper
- 1 bay leaf
- 8 ounces button mushrooms, sliced

In a large nonstick skillet, heat the oil and garlic over medium-high heat. Swirl to coat the bottom. Brown the chicken on both sides. Transfer to a plate.

Reduce the heat to medium and cook the onion and green pepper for 2 to 3 minutes, or until the onion is soft, stirring occasionally.

Return the chicken to the skillet. Stir in the remaining ingredients except the mushrooms. Bring to a simmer. Reduce the heat and simmer, covered, for 20 minutes.

Stir in the mushrooms. Simmer, covered, for 10 minutes, or until the chicken is tender.

Remove the bay leaf before serving the chicken.

PER SERVING
CALORIES 190
TOTAL FAT 4 g
   Saturated 0.5 g
   Polyunsaturated 1 g
   Monounsaturated 2 g
CHOLESTEROL 66 mg
SODIUM 82 mg
CARBOHYDRATES 8 g
   Fiber 2 g
   Sugars 5 g
PROTEIN 29 g
CALCIUM 34 mg
POTASSIUM 702 mg
DIETARY EXCHANGES
   2 vegetable
   3 lean meat

Seared Chicken with Fresh Pineapple, Ginger, and Mint Salsa

Serves 4; 3 ounces chicken and ¼ cup salsa per serving

For a refreshing break from the usual vegetable salsa, toss together an aromatic blend of pineapple, grated ginger, mint, and a splash of fresh lemon.

Salsa

1 cup finely chopped fresh pineapple

3 tablespoons chopped fresh mint leaves or snipped fresh cilantro

2 tablespoons finely chopped red onion

1 tablespoon fresh lemon juice

¾ teaspoon grated peeled gingerroot

■ ■ ■

1 teaspoon Chili Powder (page 226) or commercial no-salt-added chili powder

½ teaspoon dried thyme, crumbled

¼ teaspoon ground allspice

¼ teaspoon pepper

¼ teaspoon salt

4 boneless, skinless chicken breast halves (about 4 ounces each), all visible fat discarded

Vegetable oil spray

In a small bowl, stir together the salsa ingredients. Set aside.

PER SERVING
CALORIES 152
TOTAL FAT 1.5 g
Saturated 0.5 g
Polyunsaturated 0.5 g
Monounsaturated 0.5 g
CHOLESTEROL 66 mg
SODIUM 222 mg
CARBOHYDRATES 7 g
Fiber 1 g
Sugars 4 g
PROTEIN 27 g
CALCIUM 35 mg
POTASSIUM 365 mg
DIETARY EXCHANGES
½ fruit
3 very lean meat

In another small bowl, stir together the Chili Powder, thyme, allspice, pepper, and salt. Sprinkle over both sides of the chicken.

Heat a large nonstick skillet over medium-high heat. Remove from the heat and lightly spray with vegetable oil spray (being careful not to spray near a gas flame). Cook the chicken for 4 minutes. Turn the chicken and lightly spray with vegetable oil spray. Cook for 2 minutes, or until no longer pink in the center.

To serve, transfer the chicken to plates. Serve with the salsa on the side.

Glazed Raspberry-Ginger Chicken

Serves 4; 3 ounces chicken and ¾ cup sweet potatoes per serving

A showpiece, this incredibly easy and elegant entrée is rich in color and in flavor.

Glaze

½ cup all-fruit seedless raspberry spread

2 to 3 tablespoons cider vinegar

1 teaspoon grated peeled gingerroot or ¼ teaspoon ground ginger

⅛ to ¼ teaspoon crushed red pepper flakes

¼ teaspoon salt

■ ■ ■

Vegetable oil spray

4 boneless, skinless chicken breast halves (about 4 ounces each), all visible fat discarded

1 pound sweet potatoes, peeled and cut crosswise into ½-inch slices

2 teaspoons sugar

⅛ teaspoon ground cinnamon

In a small bowl, whisk together the glaze ingredients.

Lightly spray a large nonstick skillet with vegetable oil spray. Heat over medium-high heat. Add the chicken and reduce the heat to medium. Cook for 6 minutes. Turn the chicken and top each piece with 1 tablespoon glaze (some will remain). Cook for 7 minutes, or until no longer pink in the center. Transfer to a plate.

Meanwhile, steam the potato slices for 10 to 12 minutes, or until tender. Arrange the potatoes on a serving plate. Cover with aluminum foil to keep warm.

Add the remaining glaze to the skillet. Bring to a boil over high heat. Boil for 2 minutes, or until the mixture begins to thicken slightly, scraping the skillet frequently.

Return the chicken to the skillet and cook for about 2 minutes, or until richly glazed and beginning to darken intensely, turning constantly with a fork and spoon. Arrange the chicken on the plate with the potatoes.

In a small bowl, stir together the sugar and cinnamon. Sprinkle over the potatoes.

PER SERVING

CALORIES 328

TOTAL FAT 1.5 g
  Saturated 0.5 g
  Polyunsaturated 0.5 g
  Monounsaturated 0.5 g

CHOLESTEROL 66 mg

SODIUM 259 mg

CARBOHYDRATES 52 g
  Fiber 4 g
  Sugars 25 g

PROTEIN 28 g

CALCIUM 32 mg

POTASSIUM 607 mg

DIETARY EXCHANGES
  2 starch
  1½ fruit
  3 very lean meat

Blue Cheese and Basil Chicken

Serves 4; 3 ounces chicken per serving

Full-flavored blue cheese gives a kick to this very simple-to-fix entrée.

1 teaspoon dried basil, crumbled

¼ teaspoon pepper

⅛ teaspoon salt

4 boneless, skinless chicken breast halves (about 4 ounces each), all visible fat discarded

Vegetable oil spray

1 ounce crumbled blue cheese

1 medium green onion, finely chopped

Sprinkle the basil, pepper, and salt over both sides of the chicken.

Heat a large skillet over medium heat. Remove from the heat and lightly spray with vegetable oil spray (being careful not to spray near a gas flame). Cook the chicken for 6 minutes on each side, or until no longer pink in the center. Remove the skillet from the heat.

Sprinkle the chicken with the blue cheese and green onion. Let stand, covered, until the blue cheese has melted slightly, 2 to 3 minutes.

PER SERVING

CALORIES 154

TOTAL FAT 3.5 g
   Saturated 1.5 g
   Polyunsaturated 0.5 g
   Monounsaturated 1 g

CHOLESTEROL 71 mg

SODIUM 247 mg

CARBOHYDRATES 1 g
   Fiber 0 g
   Sugars 0 g

PROTEIN 28 g

CALCIUM 58 mg

POTASSIUM 339 mg

DIETARY EXCHANGES
   3 ½ very lean meat

Chicken Marengo

Serves 6; 3 ounces chicken and ½ cup sauce per serving

This European dish stars chicken that is seared, then cooked in an herbed tomato and wine sauce, making it moist and tender. Add a bed of spinach pasta and a tossed salad for a tempting meal.

6   boneless, skinless chicken breast halves (about 4 ounces each), all visible fat discarded
½   teaspoon pepper
2   teaspoons olive oil
8   ounces button mushrooms, sliced
1   medium red onion, chopped
2   medium garlic cloves, minced
    14.5-ounce can diced no-salt-added tomatoes, undrained
½   cup marsala, dry white wine (regular or nonalcoholic), Chicken Broth (page 19), or commercial fat-free, low-sodium chicken broth
1   teaspoon sugar
1   teaspoon dried oregano, crumbled
½   teaspoon dried thyme, crumbled
¼   to ½ teaspoon crushed red pepper flakes (optional)

Season both sides of the chicken with the pepper.

Heat a large nonstick skillet over medium-high heat. Add the oil and swirl to coat the bottom. Cook the chicken for 2 to 3 minutes on each side, or until golden brown. Transfer to a plate.

PER SERVING
CALORIES 207
TOTAL FAT 3 g
Saturated 0.5 g
Polyunsaturated 0.5 g
Monounsaturated 1.5 g
CHOLESTEROL 66 mg
SODIUM 105 mg
CARBOHYDRATES 11 g
Fiber 2 g
Sugars 7 g
PROTEIN 28 g
CALCIUM 39 mg
POTASSIUM 473 mg
DIETARY EXCHANGES
2 vegetable
3 very lean meat

Add the mushrooms, onion, and garlic to the skillet. Reduce the heat to medium and cook for 3 to 4 minutes, or until soft, stirring occasionally.

Stir in the remaining ingredients. Return the chicken to the skillet. Spoon the sauce over the chicken. Increase the heat to medium high and bring to a simmer. Reduce the heat to medium-low. Cook, covered, for 25 to 30 minutes, or until the chicken is no longer pink in the center.

Blackened Chicken with Mustard Aïoli

Serves 4; 3 ounces chicken and 2 tablespoons sauce per serving

Aïoli *(ay-OH-lee)*, a mixture of garlic and mayonnaise, lends itself to a variety of interpretations. Here it gets a slightly sweet, slightly tangy lift from tarragon and Dijon mustard.

4   boneless, skinless chicken breast halves (about 4 ounces each), all visible fat discarded

1   teaspoon Creole Seasoning (page 227) or commercial salt-free Creole or Cajun seasoning blend
      Vegetable oil spray

Aïoli

¼   cup plus 2 tablespoons fat-free or light sour cream

2   tablespoons fat-free or light mayonnaise

2   teaspoons Dijon mustard

½   teaspoon dried tarragon, crumbled

½   medium garlic clove, minced

⅛   teaspoon salt

⅛   teaspoon red hot-pepper sauce

Sprinkle the chicken breasts on both sides with the seasoning blend.

PER SERVING
CALORIES 163
TOTAL FAT 1.5 g
Saturated 0.5 g
Polyunsaturated 0.5 g
Monounsaturated 0.5 g
CHOLESTEROL 70 mg
SODIUM 280 mg
CARBOHYDRATES 6 g
Fiber 0 g
Sugars 3 g
PROTEIN 28 g
CALCIUM 48 mg
POTASSIUM 358 mg
DIETARY EXCHANGES
½ other carbohydrate
3 very lean meat

Heat a large nonstick skillet over medium-high heat. Remove from the heat and lightly spray with vegetable oil spray (being careful not to spray near a gas flame). Cook the chicken for 4 minutes. Turn the chicken and lightly spray with vegetable oil spray. Cook for 2 to 3 minutes, or until no longer pink in the center.

Meanwhile, in a small bowl, stir together the aïoli ingredients.

To serve, transfer the chicken to plates. Serve the aïoli on the side.

Lemon Chicken with Oregano

Serves 4; 3 ounces chicken per serving

Serve this beautifully browned chicken over steamed rice with green beans on the side.

Vegetable oil spray

2 teaspoons canola or corn oil

½ teaspoon grated lemon zest

2 tablespoons fresh lemon juice

1 pound chicken breast tenders, all visible fat discarded

2 to 3 tablespoons chopped fresh oregano or 2 to 3 teaspoons dried, crumbled

1 medium garlic clove, minced

⅛ teaspoon pepper

¼ teaspoon paprika

2 tablespoons snipped fresh parsley

Lightly spray a large nonstick skillet with vegetable oil spray. Heat over medium-high heat. Add the oil, lemon zest, and lemon juice, swirling to coat the bottom.

Add the chicken, oregano, garlic, and pepper. Cook, covered, for 3 to 5 minutes, or until the chicken begins to turn white. Turn the chicken. Cook for 3 to 5 minutes, or until the entire surface is white. Pour the pan liquid into a small bowl to reserve.

Cook the chicken, uncovered, for 2 to 5 minutes on each side, or until lightly brown.

Sprinkle the paprika over the chicken. Pour the pan liquid into the skillet. Cook for 3 to 5 minutes, or until the chicken is no longer pink in the center, stirring frequently.

To serve, transfer the chicken to plates. Sprinkle with the parsley.

PER SERVING

CALORIES 152

TOTAL FAT 4 g
  Saturated 0.5 g
  Polyunsaturated 1 g
  Monounsaturated 1.5 g

CHOLESTEROL 66 mg

SODIUM 75 mg

CARBOHYDRATES 2 g
  Fiber 0 g
  Sugars 0 g

PROTEIN 26 g

CALCIUM 29 mg

POTASSIUM 329 mg

DIETARY EXCHANGES
  3 lean meat

Blackberry and Balsamic Chicken

Serves 4; 3 ounces chicken, ½ cup rice, and 2 heaping tablespoons sauce per serving

When the leaves start to change color, prepare this earthy dish of seared chicken breasts topped with a sauce made of blackberries, balsamic vinegar, and a hint of brown sugar and lemon zest.

½   6- to 7-ounce box quick-cooking white and wild rice, seasoning packet discarded

4   boneless, skinless chicken breast halves (about 4 ounces each) or 1 pound turkey breast cutlets, all visible fat discarded

1   teaspoon salt-free all-purpose seasoning blend, such as Herb Seasoning (page 223) or Savory Herb Blend (page 225)

1   teaspoon olive oil

1   cup frozen unsweetened blackberries, thawed, juice reserved

¼   cup Chicken Broth (page 19), commercial fat-free, low-sodium chicken broth, or water

1   tablespoon light brown sugar

1   tablespoon balsamic vinegar

1   teaspoon grated lemon zest

Prepare the rice using the package directions for half the box, omitting the salt and margarine. Cover and set aside.

Meanwhile, put the chicken with the smooth side up between two pieces of plastic wrap. Using a tortilla press, the smooth side of a meat mallet, or a rolling pin, lightly flatten the breasts to a thickness of ¼ inch, being careful not to tear the meat. Season both sides of the chicken with the seasoning blend. (If using turkey cutlets, there is no need to flatten first.)

Heat a large nonstick skillet over medium-high heat. Add the oil and swirl to coat the bottom. Cook the chicken for 5 to 6 minutes on each side, or until browned and no longer pink in the center. Transfer to a serving plate. Cover with aluminum foil to keep warm.

Put the remaining ingredients in the skillet and stir. Cook over medium heat for 3 to 4 minutes, or until warmed through, stirring occasionally. Stir in any juices from the chicken.

To serve, spoon the rice to the side of the chicken. Pour the sauce over all.

Variation

If you prefer a seedless sauce, use a rubber scraper to push the sauce through a fine-mesh sieve into a medium bowl. This will yield about ¼ cup sauce. If you would like ½ cup strained sauce total, start with 2 cups frozen blackberries (thawed with juice). The remaining ingredient amounts stay the same.

PER SERVING
CALORIES 265
TOTAL FAT 3 g
    Saturated 0.5 g
    Polyunsaturated 1 g
    Monounsaturated 1 g
CHOLESTEROL 60 mg
SODIUM 116 mg
CARBOHYDRATES 35 g
    Fiber 3 g
    Sugars 14 g
PROTEIN 25 g
CALCIUM 37 mg
POTASSIUM 411 mg
DIETARY EXCHANGES
    2 starch
    1 vegetable
    3 very lean meat

Chicken with Yogurt-Cilantro Sauce

Serves 4; 3 ounces chicken and 2 tablespoons sauce per serving

This dish is so scrumptious that even low-salt skeptics will be clamoring for a sample. You won't have to spend much time in the kitchen, but remember to allow time for marinating.

1 tablespoon olive oil

2 tablespoons lime juice

¼ teaspoon pepper

4 boneless, skinless chicken breast halves (about 4 ounces each), all visible fat discarded

4 ounces fat-free or low-fat plain yogurt

1 tablespoon snipped fresh cilantro

1 tablespoon snipped fresh mint leaves

½ teaspoon ground cumin

Vegetable oil spray (if broiling)

1 medium lime, quartered (optional)

In a large airtight plastic bag, combine the oil, lime juice, and pepper. Add the chicken. Seal the bag and turn to coat. Refrigerate for 30 minutes to 8 hours, turning occasionally. Remove the chicken from the refrigerator 5 to 10 minutes before cooking.

In a small bowl, stir together the yogurt, cilantro, mint, and cumin. Set aside.

Preheat the broiler or preheat the grill on medium high. If using the broiler, lightly spray the broiler rack and pan with vegetable oil spray. Broil the chicken 4 to 5 inches from the heat for 4 to 5 minutes on each side, or until no longer pink in the center, leaving the oven door partially open, basting occasionally with the reserved basting mixture, not the sauce. To prevent transferring harmful bacteria, wash the basting brush after each use.

To serve, transfer the chicken to plates. Spoon the yogurt sauce over the chicken. Garnish with the lime.

PER SERVING

CALORIES 175
TOTAL FAT 5 g
  Saturated 1 g
  Polyunsaturated 0.5 g
  Monounsaturated 3 g
CHOLESTEROL 66 mg
SODIUM 97 mg
CARBOHYDRATES 3 g
  Fiber 0 g
  Sugars 2 g
PROTEIN 28 g
CALCIUM 76 mg
POTASSIUM 377 mg
DIETARY EXCHANGES
  3½ lean meat

Grilled Sesame Chicken

Serves 4; 3 ounces chicken per serving

Sesame seeds give grilled chicken a crunchy difference.

   Vegetable oil spray (optional)

4 boneless, skinless chicken breast halves (about 4 ounces each), all visible fat discarded

   Dash of paprika

   Dash of cayenne

¼ cup fresh lemon juice

¼ cup honey

1 tablespoon dry-roasted sesame seeds

Preheat the grill on medium high or preheat the broiler. If using the broiler, lightly spray the broiler rack and pan with vegetable oil spray.

Lightly season the chicken with the paprika and cayenne.

In a small microwaveable bowl, whisk together the lemon juice and honey. Microwave on 100 percent power (high) for 1 minute, or until the honey is dissolved. Pour 2 tablespoons of the mixture into a small bowl. Stir the sesame seeds into this reserved mixture. Set aside to use as the sauce.

Coat the chicken pieces with about 3 tablespoons of the remaining mixture. Reserve the rest for basting.

Grill the chicken for 5 minutes, or broil 4 to 5 inches from the heat for 5 minutes, leaving the oven door partially open, basting occasionally with the reserved basting mixture, not the sauce. To prevent transferring harmful bacteria, wash the basting brush after each use. Turn the chicken and cook for 5 to 6 minutes, or until no longer pink in the center, basting occasionally.

Spoon the reserved sauce over the chicken just before serving.

PER SERVING

CALORIES 207

TOTAL FAT 2.5 g
  Saturated 0.5 g
  Polyunsaturated 1 g
  Monounsaturated 1 g

CHOLESTEROL 66 mg

SODIUM 76 mg

CARBOHYDRATES 19 g
  Fiber 0 g
  Sugars 18 g

PROTEIN 27 g

CALCIUM 18 mg

POTASSIUM 329 mg

DIETARY EXCHANGES
  1½ other carbohydrate
  3 very lean meat

Chicken with Ginger and Snow Peas

Serve this Asian-inspired dish over brown rice with fruit salad on the side.

½ cup Chicken Broth (page 19) or commercial fat-free, low-sodium chicken broth

1 tablespoon cornstarch

1 tablespoon light soy sauce

1 teaspoon pepper

2 teaspoons canola or corn oil

1¼ pounds boneless, skinless chicken breast tenders, all visible fat discarded

6 ounces snow peas, trimmed (about 2 cups)

2 medium garlic cloves, minced

½ teaspoon minced peeled gingerroot

1 to 2 tablespoons Chicken Broth (page 19), commercial fat-free, low-sodium chicken broth, or water, if needed

In a small bowl, whisk together the ½ cup broth, cornstarch, soy sauce, and pepper.

Heat a wok or large, heavy skillet over high heat. Add the oil and swirl to coat the bottom. Cook the chicken for 4 minutes, stirring frequently.

Stir in the snow peas, garlic, and gingerroot. Cook for 3 minutes, stirring constantly.

Add the broth mixture. Cook for 2 to 3 minutes, or until the sauce thickens and the chicken is no longer pink in the center, stirring constantly. If the mixture begins to burn, remove from the heat momentarily, or add 1 to 2 tablespoons broth or water.

PER SERVING

CALORIES 168
TOTAL FAT 3.5 g
  Saturated 0.5 g
  Polyunsaturated 1 g
  Monounsaturated 1.5 g
CHOLESTEROL 66 mg
SODIUM 157 mg
CARBOHYDRATES 5 g
  Fiber 1 g
  Sugars 1 g
PROTEIN 28 g
CALCIUM 32 mg
POTASSIUM 388 mg
DIETARY EXCHANGES
  1 vegetable
  3 very lean meat

Cumin-Lime Chicken

Serves 4; 3 ounces chicken and 3 tablespoons vegetable mixture per serving

This chicken dish makes its own sauce as it bakes, cutting down on the amount of work for you.

Vegetable oil spray

4 boneless, skinless chicken breast halves (about 4 ounces each), all visible fat discarded

½ medium lime

1 teaspoon ground cumin

½ medium green bell pepper, finely chopped, or ½ cup finely chopped poblano pepper (wear plastic gloves when handling the poblano)

¼ large onion, finely chopped

1 small tomato, chopped

2 tablespoons snipped fresh cilantro

¼ teaspoon salt

½ medium lime

¼ cup fat-free or light sour cream

Preheat the oven to 350°F.

Lightly spray an 11 × 7 × 2-inch baking pan with vegetable oil spray. Place the chicken in a single layer in the pan. Squeeze the juice of ½ lime over the chicken. Sprinkle with the cumin. Top with the bell pepper and onion.

Bake for 28 to 30 minutes, or until no longer pink in the center. Using a slotted spatula, transfer the chicken to plates.

Stir the tomato, cilantro, and salt into the pan residue. Squeeze the juice from the remaining ½ lime into the pan. Stir well.

To serve, spoon the tomato mixture over the chicken. Top with dollops of sour cream.

PER SERVING

CALORIES 159
TOTAL FAT 1.5 g
   Saturated 0.5 g
   Polyunsaturated 0.5 g
   Monounsaturated 0.5 g
CHOLESTEROL 68 mg
SODIUM 235 mg
CARBOHYDRATES 7 g
   Fiber 1 g
   Sugars 3 g
PROTEIN 28 g
CALCIUM 46 mg
POTASSIUM 447 mg
DIETARY EXCHANGES
   1½ vegetable
   3 very lean meat

Arroz con Pollo
(Chicken with Rice)

Serves 6; scant 1¼ cups per serving

Perfect fare for a cold evening, this savory one-dish meal will make you think of Spanish sunshine!

Vegetable oil spray

1½ pounds boneless, skinless chicken breasts, all visible fat discarded

1 tablespoon light stick margarine, melted

1 medium garlic clove, minced

¼ teaspoon pepper

¼ teaspoon paprika

1 teaspoon olive oil

½ to 1 small onion, chopped

¼ medium green bell pepper, chopped

1 cup uncooked rice

2 cups Chicken Broth (page 19) or commercial fat-free, low-sodium chicken broth

2 medium tomatoes, chopped

⅛ teaspoon turmeric

1 cup frozen green peas

Preheat the oven to 350°F. Lightly spray a 13 × 9 × 2-inch casserole dish with vegetable oil spray.

Cut the chicken into bite-size pieces. Put in the casserole dish.

In a small bowl, stir together the margarine, garlic, pepper, and paprika. Brush on the chicken.

Bake for 15 to 20 minutes, or until cooked through.

Meanwhile, heat a large nonstick skillet over medium heat. Add the oil and swirl to coat the bottom. Cook the onion and bell pepper for 3 to 4 minutes, or until soft.

Stir in the rice. Cook for 2 to 3 minutes, or until the rice begins to brown, stirring frequently.

Stir in the broth, tomatoes, and turmeric. Simmer, covered, for 20 minutes.

Stir in the peas and chicken. Simmer, covered, for 10 minutes, or until heated through.

PER SERVING
CALORIES 277
TOTAL FAT 3.5 g
    Saturated 0.5 g
    Polyunsaturated 1 g
    Monounsaturated 1 g
CHOLESTEROL 66 mg
SODIUM 125 mg
CARBOHYDRATES 30 g
    Fiber 2 g
    Sugars 3 g
PROTEIN 31 g
CALCIUM 28 mg
POTASSIUM 504 mg
DIETARY EXCHANGES
    2 starch
    3 very lean meat

Chicken Paprikash

Serves 6; 1 cup per serving

Full-bodied and richly colored with paprika, this traditional Hungarian entrée will satisfy even the most ravenous appetite. This dish goes well with a green salad with Balsamic Vinaigrette (page 57).

2½ cups dried no-yolk noodles

1½ pounds boneless, skinless chicken breasts, all visible fat discarded
    Vegetable oil spray

 1 medium red onion, thinly sliced (about 1 cup)

 2 tablespoons paprika (sweet Hungarian paprika preferred)

 1 medium tomato, peeled if desired and chopped

½ cup Chicken Broth (page 19) or commercial fat-free, low-sodium chicken broth

 2 tablespoons all-purpose flour

½ cup fat-free or low-fat plain yogurt

 2 tablespoons fat-free or light sour cream

Prepare the noodles using the package directions, omitting the salt and oil. Drain well and set aside.

Meanwhile, cut the chicken into bite-size pieces.

Lightly spray a large nonstick skillet with vegetable oil spray. Heat over medium-high heat. Cook the chicken for about 4 minutes, until lightly browned on all sides, stirring occasionally. Transfer to a plate.

Reduce the heat to medium. Put the onion and paprika in the skillet. Cook for 2 to 3 minutes, or until the onion is soft, stirring constantly.

Stir in the tomato and broth. Cook for 2 to 3 minutes, or until hot.

Return the chicken to the skillet. Reduce the heat and simmer, covered, for 30 minutes, or until tender. Using a slotted spoon, transfer the chicken and vegetables to a plate. Set aside.

Sprinkle the flour over the broth mixture. Cook for 2 to 3 minutes, or until the sauce has thickened, whisking constantly.

In a small bowl, whisk together the yogurt and sour cream. Whisk into the sauce.

Stir in the chicken and vegetables.

To serve, spoon the noodles onto plates. Top with the chicken mixture.

PER SERVING
CALORIES 335
TOTAL FAT 2 g
    Saturated 0.5 g
    Polyunsaturated 0.5 g
    Monounsaturated 0.5 g
CHOLESTEROL 67 mg
SODIUM 120 mg
CARBOHYDRATES 42 g
    Fiber 3 g
    Sugars 6 g
PROTEIN 34 g
CALCIUM 81 mg
POTASSIUM 583 mg
DIETARY EXCHANGES
    2½ starch
    1 vegetable
    3 very lean meat

Lettuce Wraps with Chicken and Vegetables

Serves 4; 4 lettuce wraps per serving

Try these crisp lettuce wraps topped with your choice of two sauces. Look for do-ahead tips in the Cook's Tip on page 120.

2   heads iceberg lettuce
1   tablespoon plain rice vinegar
2   teaspoons light soy sauce
½   teaspoon sugar

Sauce 1

¼   cup Chicken Broth (page 19) or commercial fat-free, low-sodium chicken broth
¼   cup plain rice vinegar
2   medium green onions, thinly sliced
1   tablespoon light soy sauce
1   teaspoon sugar
¼   teaspoon toasted sesame oil
⅛   to ¼ teaspoon crushed red pepper flakes

OR

Sauce 2

⅓   cup pineapple juice
2   medium green onions, thinly sliced
2   tablespoons plain rice vinegar
1   tablespoon light soy sauce
¼   teaspoon toasted sesame oil
⅛   to ¼ teaspoon crushed red pepper flakes

Filling

6   shiitake mushrooms (dried preferred)
1   medium carrot
½   medium red bell pepper
2   medium garlic cloves
1   medium zucchini
½   cup canned whole water chestnuts, rinsed and drained
½   cup canned bamboo shoots, rinsed and drained

2 medium green onions
1 pound boneless, skinless chicken breasts, all visible fat discarded,
   or 1 pound lean ground chicken or turkey breast, skin discarded before grinding
⅛ teaspoon white pepper
⅛ teaspoon ground ginger
2 teaspoons canola or corn oil, divided use
2 tablespoons chopped unsalted peanuts

Cut each head of lettuce in half vertically (through the core). Remove the core with a knife. Carefully peel off four outside layers from each half.

In a small bowl, stir together the 1 tablespoon rice vinegar, 2 teaspoons soy sauce, and ½ teaspoon sugar. Set aside.

In another small bowl, stir together all the ingredients for either Sauce 1 or Sauce 2.

If using dried mushrooms, put them in a small bowl and pour in enough boiling water to cover them by 1 inch. Let soak for 15 minutes. Pour off and discard the water, then squeeze the excess water from the mushrooms. Coarsely chop the reconstituted or fresh mushrooms. Set aside.

Meanwhile, dice the carrot and bell pepper and mince the garlic. Set aside together. Dice the zucchini. Set aside. Coarsely chop the water chestnuts and bamboo shoots and thinly slice the green onions. Set aside together.

Cut the chicken into ¼- to ½-inch pieces. Put the chicken pieces or ground chicken in a medium bowl. Sprinkle with the pepper and ginger.

Heat a large nonstick skillet over medium-high heat. Add 1 teaspoon of the oil and swirl to coat the bottom. Cook the chicken pieces for 3 to 4 minutes, or until lightly browned and no longer pink in the center, stirring occasionally (allow 4 to 5 minutes for ground chicken). Transfer to a medium bowl.

Add the remaining 1 teaspoon oil to the skillet and swirl to coat the bottom. Cook the carrot, bell pepper, and garlic for 1 minute, stirring occasionally.

Add the zucchini (and fresh mushrooms if using). Cook for 2 minutes, stirring occasionally.

Add the dried mushrooms, water chestnuts, bamboo shoots, green onions, and rice vinegar mixture. Cook for 1 minute, or until heated through, stirring occasionally.

Stir the chicken into the vegetable mixture.

To serve, spoon the mixture into a decorative bowl. Sprinkle with the peanuts. Place the bowl in the center of a platter. Arrange the lettuce leaves around the bowl. Let each person spoon about ¼ cup poultry mixture into a lettuce wrap, then top with about ½ tablespoon Sauce 1 or Sauce 2. Gently roll the lettuce to enclose the filling. Repeat with the remaining ingredients.

To prepare the ingredients in advance, separate and cover the lettuce leaves with plastic wrap or store in an airtight plastic bag and refrigerate for up to two days. Cover and refrigerate the sauce for up to two days and the chicken mixture for up to four days. At serving time, put the chicken mixture in a microwaveable bowl, cover, and heat on 100 percent power (high) for 1 to 2 minutes.

Use kitchen scissors to trim the edges to make the lettuce wraps manageable, if necessary. Don't worry if the lettuce tears somewhat; you can still use the leaves as wraps if they are large enough to hold the filling.

WITH SAUCE 1
PER SERVING
CALORIES 251
TOTAL FAT 6.5 g
Saturated 1 g
Polyunsaturated 2 g
Monounsaturated 3 g
CHOLESTEROL 66 mg
SODIUM 269 mg
CARBOHYDRATES 18 g
Fiber 5 g
Sugars 7 g
PROTEIN 30 g
CALCIUM 42 mg
POTASSIUM 782 mg
DIETARY EXCHANGES
4 vegetable
3 lean meat

WITH SAUCE 2
PER SERVING
CALORIES 257
TOTAL FAT 6.5 g
Saturated 1 g
Polyunsaturated 2 g
Monounsaturated 3 g
CHOLESTEROL 66 mg
SODIUM 268 mg
CARBOHYDRATES 19 g
Fiber 5 g
Sugars 8 g
PROTEIN 30 g
CALCIUM 42 mg
POTASSIUM 802 mg
DIETARY EXCHANGES
4 vegetable
3 lean meat

Chicken Primavera

Serves 8; 1 cup fettuccine and ¾ cup sauce per serving

Simmer spring vegetables and chunks of chicken in a rich tomato sauce, then serve over warm fettuccine. Round out the meal with a seasonal fruit salad.

1   teaspoon olive oil

1   medium zucchini, chopped

1   medium yellow summer squash, chopped

1   medium red onion, chopped

2   ounces mushrooms (golden Italian preferred), sliced

2   medium garlic cloves, minced

    14.5-ounce can no-salt-added diced tomatoes, undrained

½   cup Chicken Broth (page 19) or commercial fat-free, low-sodium chicken broth

1   teaspoon dried oregano, crumbled

¼   teaspoon pepper

¼   teaspoon crushed red pepper flakes

1   pound dried fettuccine

2   cups cubed cooked skinless chicken breasts, cooked without salt

1   cup frozen green peas

Heat a large saucepan over medium heat. Add the olive oil and swirl to coat the bottom. Cook the zucchini, yellow summer squash, onion, mushrooms, and garlic for 3 to 4 minutes, or until the vegetables are tender-crisp, stirring occasionally.

Stir in the tomatoes with liquid, broth, oregano, pepper, and red pepper flakes. Bring to a simmer over medium-high heat. Reduce the heat to medium-low and cook for 15 to 20 minutes, or until the flavors are blended, stirring occasionally.

Meanwhile, prepare the fettuccine using the package directions, omitting the salt and oil. Drain well. Pour into a large bowl and cover with a dry dish towel to keep warm.

Stir the chicken and peas into the vegetable mixture. Increase the heat to medium and cook for 5 to 10 minutes, or until the chicken and peas are warmed through, stirring occasionally.

To serve, spoon the fettuccine onto plates. Top with the chicken mixture.

PER SERVING
CALORIES 317
TOTAL FAT 3 g
  Saturated 0.5 g
  Polyunsaturated 1 g
  Monounsaturated 1 g
CHOLESTEROL 30 mg
SODIUM 76 mg
CARBOHYDRATES 51 g
  Fiber 4 g
  Sugars 7 g
PROTEIN 21 g
CALCIUM 44 mg
POTASSIUM 399 mg
DIETARY EXCHANGES
  3 starch
  1 vegetable
  1½ very lean meat

Chicken Enchiladas

Serves 4; 2 enchiladas per serving

Cheesy, gooey, and zesty—what more could you ask for in an enchilada? You don't even need salsa or sour cream with these. *¡Olé!*

Vegetable oil spray

Sauce

1 cup fat-free milk

½ cup Chicken Broth (page 19) or commercial fat-free, low-sodium chicken broth

2 tablespoons all-purpose flour

¼ teaspoon pepper

½ cup reduced-fat Monterey Jack cheese

1 teaspoon fresh lime juice

■ ■ ■

8 6-inch corn tortillas

2 cups cubed cooked skinless chicken breasts, cooked without salt (about 10 ounces cooked)

¼ cup thinly sliced green onions

1 medium garlic clove, minced

½ teaspoon ground cumin

¼ teaspoon Chili Powder (page 226) or commercial no-salt-added chili powder

½ cup reduced-fat Monterey Jack cheese

2 to 3 tablespoons canned chopped mild green chiles, rinsed and drained

Preheat the oven to 350°F. Lightly spray a 13 × 9 × 2-inch baking dish with vegetable oil spray. Set aside.

In a medium saucepan, whisk together the milk, broth, flour, and pepper. Bring to a simmer over medium-high heat. Reduce the heat and simmer for 5 to 6 minutes, or until the mixture thickens slightly, whisking occasionally.

Whisk in the ½ cup cheese and lime juice. Remove from the heat. Set aside.

To soften the tortillas, wrap in aluminum foil and warm in the oven for 5 minutes.

Meanwhile, in a medium bowl, stir together the chicken, green onions, garlic, cumin, and Chili Powder.

To assemble, place the tortillas on a flat surface. Spread ¼ cup chicken mixture and 1 tablespoon Monterey Jack in the center of each. Roll up jelly-roll style and place with the seam side down in the baking dish. Pour the sauce over the enchiladas. Sprinkle with the chiles.

Bake for 20 to 25 minutes, or until the filling is warmed through.

PER SERVING
CALORIES 304
TOTAL FAT 8.5 g
    Saturated 4 g
    Polyunsaturated 1.5 g
    Monounsaturated 2 g
CHOLESTEROL 76 mg
SODIUM 344 mg
CARBOHYDRATES 21 g
    Fiber 2 g
    Sugars 4 g
PROTEIN 35 g
CALCIUM 421 mg
POTASSIUM 286 mg
DIETARY EXCHANGES
    1½ starch
    4 lean meat

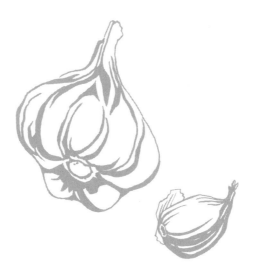

Roasted Lemon-Herb Turkey Breast

Serves 12; 3 ounces per serving

Fresh lemon, fresh parsley, and lots of herbs tucked between the skin and the meat infuse this turkey with sensational flavors.

Vegetable oil spray
2 medium lemons
½ cup snipped fresh parsley
2 tablespoons Lemon-Herb Seasoning (page 224)
1 tablespoon olive oil
1 tablespoon Dijon mustard
5-pound turkey breast with skin
Paprika

Preheat the oven to 325°F. Lightly spray a roasting pan and baking rack with vegetable oil spray.

Cut the lemons in half. Squeeze about ¼ cup juice into a small bowl. Set aside the lemon halves.

Whisk the parsley, seasoning blend, oil, and mustard into the lemon juice.

Using a tablespoon or your fingers, carefully separate the skin from the meat of the turkey. Spread the lemon juice mixture between the skin and meat over as much area as possible, being careful to avoid tearing the skin. Gently pull the skin over the top and sides. Put the turkey on the rack in the pan. Put the lemon halves in the pan, directly under the turkey cavity. Sprinkle the turkey with the paprika.

Roast the turkey, uncovered, for 1 hour 30 minutes to 1 hour 45 minutes, or until a meat thermometer registers 170°F. Let stand for 10 to 15 minutes for easier slicing. Discard the skin before serving the turkey.

PER SERVING
CALORIES 160
TOTAL FAT 2.5 g
  Saturated 0.5 g
  Polyunsaturated 0.5 g
  Monounsaturated 1 g
CHOLESTEROL 89 mg
SODIUM 85 mg
CARBOHYDRATES 1 g
  Fiber 0 g
  Sugars 0 g
PROTEIN 31 g
CALCIUM 30 mg
POTASSIUM 323 mg
DIETARY EXCHANGES
  3 very lean meat

Tarragon Turkey Medallions

Serves 4; 3 ounces turkey per serving

Preparation of this entrée is very fast paced, so have your side dishes ready before you begin cooking it. Mixed salad greens topped with Cider Vinaigrette (page 58) and Rice and Vegetable Pilaf (page 205) make good accompaniments.

Sauce

2 tablespoons fresh lemon juice

2 tablespoons water

1½ teaspoons fresh tarragon leaves or ½ teaspoon dried, crumbled

1 medium garlic clove, minced

¼ teaspoon salt

⅛ teaspoon pepper

■ ■ ■

1-pound turkey tenderloin, all visible fat discarded

Vegetable oil spray

2 teaspoons olive oil

In a small bowl, whisk together the sauce ingredients. Set aside.

Cut the turkey crosswise into ¼-inch slices.

Lightly spray a large nonstick skillet with vegetable oil spray. Heat over high heat. Add the oil and swirl to coat the bottom. Cook the turkey slices in a single layer for 2 minutes. Turn the turkey and cook for 3 minutes, or until no longer pink in the center. Transfer the turkey to a serving plate.

Pour the sauce mixture into the skillet. Cook for 15 to 20 seconds, or until the mixture reduces to 2 tablespoons, stirring constantly with a flat spatula.

To serve, drizzle the sauce over the turkey.

Tarragon Pork Medallions

Substitute a 1-pound pork tenderloin for the turkey; cook as directed above.

TURKEY MEDALLIONS	PORK MEDALLIONS
PER SERVING	**PER SERVING**
CALORIES 149	CALORIES 155
TOTAL FAT 3.5 g	TOTAL FAT 6 g
Saturated 0.5 g	Saturated 1.5 g
Polyunsaturated 0.5 g	Polyunsaturated 0.5 g
Monounsaturated 2 g	Monounsaturated 3 g
CHOLESTEROL 77 mg	CHOLESTEROL 63 mg
SODIUM 196 mg	SODIUM 191 mg
CARBOHYDRATES 1 g	CARBOHYDRATES 1 g
Fiber 0 g	Fiber 0 g
Sugars 0 g	Sugars 0 g
PROTEIN 27 g	PROTEIN 23 g
CALCIUM 17 mg	CALCIUM 9 mg
POTASSIUM 265 mg	POTASSIUM 366 mg
DIETARY EXCHANGES	DIETARY EXCHANGES
3 very lean meat	3 lean meat

Turkey Tenderloin with Rosemary

With this recipe, you season and bake turkey tenderloin, then make a sauce—all in one dish. It's great when you're in a hurry, and even greater when you're the one cleaning up.

Vegetable oil spray

1 tablespoon olive oil

1 tablespoon chopped fresh rosemary leaves or 1 teaspoon dried, crushed

1 teaspoon lemon juice

1 medium garlic clove, minced

¾ teaspoon no-salt-added lemon pepper

1-pound turkey breast tenderloin, all visible fat discarded

¼ cup Chicken Broth (page 19) or commercial fat-free, low-sodium chicken broth

1 tablespoon dry white wine (regular or nonalcoholic), Chicken Broth (page 19), or commercial fat-free, low-sodium chicken broth

Preheat the oven to 350°F.

Spray a 12 × 8 × 2-inch glass baking dish with vegetable oil spray. Put the olive oil, rosemary, lemon juice, garlic, and lemon pepper in the baking dish; stir. Roll the turkey in the mixture, coating well. Tuck the ends under.

Bake for 20 minutes. Turn and bake for 20 to 25 minutes, or until the turkey registers 170°F on a meat thermometer. Transfer the turkey to a cutting board, retaining the liquid in the baking dish and leaving the oven on. Let the turkey stand for 5 minutes. Thinly slice the turkey diagonally across the grain. Arrange on a serving plate.

Meanwhile, pour the broth and wine into the baking dish, scraping to dislodge any browned bits. Stir well. Return the baking dish to the oven for 3 to 4 minutes, or until the broth is heated through. Pour the sauce over the turkey slices.

Pork Tenderloin with Rosemary

Substitute a 1-pound pork tenderloin for the turkey; cook as directed above. Before removing the pork from the oven, make sure it registers 160°F for medium or 170°F for well-done on a meat thermometer.

 Cook's TIP

Fresh Rosemary

Sprigs of rosemary are hardy and will keep for about two weeks in an airtight plastic bag in the refrigerator.

TURKEY TENDERLOIN	PORK TENDERLOIN
PER SERVING	**PER SERVING**
CALORIES 161	**CALORIES** 167
TOTAL FAT 4.5 g	**TOTAL FAT** 7.5 g
Saturated 1 g	Saturated 2 g
Polyunsaturated 0.5 g	Polyunsaturated 0.5 g
Monounsaturated 2.5 g	Monounsaturated 4 g
CHOLESTEROL 77 mg	**CHOLESTEROL** 63 mg
SODIUM 52 mg	**SODIUM** 47 mg
CARBOHYDRATES 1 g	**CARBOHYDRATES** 1 g
Fiber 0 g	Fiber 0 g
Sugars 0 g	Sugars 0 g
PROTEIN 27 g	**PROTEIN** 23 g
CALCIUM 21 mg	**CALCIUM** 12 mg
POTASSIUM 271 mg	**POTASSIUM** 372 mg
DIETARY EXCHANGES	**DIETARY EXCHANGES**
3 lean meat	3 lean meat

Turkey Sausage Patties

Serves 4; 1 patty per serving

These flavorful patties are a leaner version of the breakfast staple. Serve them with Pancakes (page 245) or Blueberry Muffins (pages 250–251).

Vegetable oil spray
12 ounces ground turkey breast, skin discarded before grinding
2 tablespoons water
White of 1 large egg
¼ teaspoon pepper
¼ teaspoon dried basil, crumbled
¼ teaspoon dried sage
¼ teaspoon dried oregano, crumbled
⅛ teaspoon ground allspice
⅛ teaspoon ground nutmeg
⅛ teaspoon dried dillweed, crumbled
⅛ teaspoon garlic powder
⅛ teaspoon Chili Powder (page 226) or commercial no-salt-added variety (optional)
⅛ teaspoon red hot-pepper sauce (optional)

Preheat the broiler. Lightly spray a broiler pan and rack or a roasting pan and baking rack with vegetable oil spray.

In a medium bowl, thoroughly combine the remaining ingredients. Shape into 4 patties. Put the patties on the rack in the pan.

Broil 2 to 4 inches from the heat for 10 minutes. Turn the patties and broil for 5 to 10 minutes, or until no longer pink in the center.

PER SERVING
CALORIES 101
TOTAL FAT 1 g
Saturated 0.5 g
Polyunsaturated 0 g
Monounsaturated 0 g
CHOLESTEROL 58 mg
SODIUM 53 mg
CARBOHYDRATES 1 g
Fiber 0 g
Sugars 0 g
PROTEIN 21 g
CALCIUM 17 mg
POTASSIUM 209 mg
DIETARY EXCHANGES
3 very lean meat

Allspice

Use allspice for a piquant flavor in foods from soups, stews, and meats to cakes and fruit dishes. Allspice is used in the liqueurs Chartreuse and Bénédictine.

Turkey Picadillo

Serve this spicy turkey mixture (pronounced *pee-kah-DEE-yoh*) mixed with rice, or wrap it in a tortilla. Leftovers freeze and reheat beautifully.

2	teaspoons olive oil
1	large red bell pepper, diced
1	medium onion, chopped
4	medium garlic cloves, minced
1½	pounds ground turkey breast, skin discarded before grinding
	28-ounce can no-salt-added crushed tomatoes
⅓	cup dried currants or coarsely chopped raisins
¼	cup coarsely chopped green olives
1	teaspoon ground cumin
½	teaspoon crushed red pepper flakes

Heat a large skillet over medium-high heat. Add the oil and swirl to coat the bottom. Increase the heat to high and cook the bell pepper and onion for 2 minutes, stirring frequently.

Stir in the garlic. Reduce the heat to medium-low and cook for 3 to 4 minutes.

Add the turkey, breaking it up with a fork. Cook until it whitens, about 5 minutes, stirring occasionally.

Stir in the remaining ingredients. Increase the heat to high and bring to a boil. Reduce the heat to medium and cook for 10 minutes, stirring occasionally.

PER SERVING
CALORIES 235
TOTAL FAT 3.5 g
   Saturated 0.5 g
   Polyunsaturated 0.5 g
   Monounsaturated 2 g
CHOLESTEROL 77 mg
SODIUM 248 mg
CARBOHYDRATES 20 g
   Fiber 4 g
   Sugars 12 g
PROTEIN 30 g
CALCIUM 84 mg
POTASSIUM 707 mg
DIETARY EXCHANGES
   ½ fruit
   3 vegetable
   3 lean meat

Turkey Stew

Serves 8; 1½ cups per serving

If you have a household with people eating at different times, this one-pot meal is perfect. You'll probably even have enough for "planned-overs" to serve later in the week.

2   teaspoons corn oil stick margarine

1   medium onion, chopped

4   cups Chicken Broth (page 19) or commercial fat-free, low-sodium chicken broth

1¼ pounds cooked turkey breast, cooked without salt, skin and all visible fat discarded

¼   cup water

2   tablespoons all-purpose flour

6   medium ribs of celery, coarsely chopped

6   medium carrots, coarsely chopped

1   teaspoon poultry seasoning

1   bay leaf

½   teaspoon garlic powder

¼   to ½ teaspoon pepper

6   medium potatoes, coarsely chopped

1½ cups frozen green peas

In a stockpot, melt the margarine over medium-high heat. Cook the onion for 2 to 3 minutes, or until soft, stirring occasionally.

Pour in the broth. Bring to a boil, stirring occasionally.

Meanwhile, cut the turkey into bite-size pieces.

In a small bowl, whisk together the water and flour. Whisk into the broth. Cook for 5 minutes, or until the broth just begins to thicken, whisking constantly.

Stir in the turkey, celery, carrots, poultry seasoning, bay leaf, garlic powder, and pepper. Bring to a boil. Reduce the heat and cook for 15 minutes, or until heated through.

Add the potatoes. Cook, covered, for 30 minutes, or until the vegetables are tender, stirring occasionally.

Stir in the peas. Cook for 5 minutes. Remove the bay leaf before serving the stew.

PER SERVING

CALORIES 251

TOTAL FAT 2 g
  Saturated 0.5 g
  Polyunsaturated 0.5 g
  Monounsaturated 0.5 g

CHOLESTEROL 61 mg

SODIUM 156 mg

CARBOHYDRATES 33 g
  Fiber 6 g
  Sugars 8 g

PROTEIN 28 g

CALCIUM 72 mg

POTASSIUM 1114 mg

DIETARY EXCHANGES
  1½ starch
  2 vegetable
  3 very lean meat

Turkey and Broccoli Stir-Fry

Serves 4; 1½ cups per serving

When you've had enough turkey sandwiches, try this stir-fry to use up Thanksgiving Day leftovers.

1	cup uncooked quick-cooking brown rice
	Vegetable oil spray
½	medium red bell pepper, thinly sliced
½	large onion, thinly sliced
¼	cup water
2	cups small broccoli florets
2	cups diced cooked turkey breast, cooked without salt, skin and all visible fat discarded
3	tablespoons hoisin sauce
2	tablespoons honey
2	to 3 teaspoons fresh lime juice
1	teaspoon toasted sesame oil

In a medium saucepan, prepare the rice using the package directions.

Meanwhile, heat a large nonstick skillet over medium-high heat. Remove from the heat and lightly spray with vegetable oil spray (being careful not to spray near a gas flame). Cook the bell pepper and onion for 5 minutes, or until beginning to lightly brown on the edges, stirring frequently. Transfer to a plate.

Return the skillet to the heat. Pour in the ¼ cup water. Add the broccoli. Cook for 2 minutes, or until the broccoli is just tender-crisp, stirring constantly.

Stir in the bell pepper mixture and the turkey. Remove from the heat. Let stand, covered, for 3 minutes, or until the turkey is heated through.

Meanwhile, in a small microwaveable bowl, stir together the hoisin sauce, honey, lime juice, and sesame oil. Microwave on 100 percent power (high) for 20 seconds, or until hot.

To serve, spoon the rice onto plates. Spoon the turkey mixture over the rice. Top with the sauce.

PER SERVING

CALORIES 265
TOTAL FAT 3 g
  Saturated 0.5 g
  Polyunsaturated 0.5 g
  Monounsaturated 1 g
CHOLESTEROL 66 mg
SODIUM 81 mg
CARBOHYDRATES 30 g
  Fiber 2 g
  Sugars 8 g
PROTEIN 29 g
CALCIUM 30 mg
POTASSIUM 372 mg
DIETARY EXCHANGES
  1½ starch
  ½ fruit
  3 very lean meat

New-Style Turkey Club Sandwich for One

Serves 1; 1 sandwich per serving

Turn a popular sandwich into a heart-healthy, low-sodium lunch by making a few simple substitutions.

   6-inch pita pocket (whole-wheat preferred), cut in half crosswise
2 to 3 ounces sliced roasted turkey, cooked without salt, all visible fat discarded
1 medium Italian plum tomato, sliced
½ medium carrot, shredded
¼ cup finely shredded cabbage
1 teaspoon Hot Mustard (page 221) or commercial honey mustard
½ teaspoon imitation bacon bits

To assemble, stuff each pita half with turkey, tomato, carrot, and cabbage. Spread the mustard on the sandwich stuffing. Sprinkle with the bacon bits.

Low-Sodium Sandwiches

One flavorful way to cut down on the sodium in sandwiches is by using your own home-baked low-sodium breads (pages 234–239). Add leftover meats such as Roasted Lemon-Herb Turkey Breast (page 124) or Easy Roast Beef (pages 134–135) and plenty of vegetables. Our recipes for condiments, such as Hot Mustard, Ketchup, Horseradish, Roasted Tomato Chipotle Salsa, Easy Dill Pickles, Sweet Bread-and-Butter Pickles, or Sweet Pickle Relish (pages 217, 220–222, and 228–231) are designed to add lots of flavor without much sodium.

PER SERVING
CALORIES 302
TOTAL FAT 3 g
   Saturated 0.5 g
   Polyunsaturated 1 g
   Monounsaturated 0.5 g
CHOLESTEROL 61 mg
SODIUM 398 mg
CARBOHYDRATES 42 g
   Fiber 6 g
   Sugars 6 g
PROTEIN 29 g
CALCIUM 45 mg
POTASSIUM 599 mg
DIETARY EXCHANGES
   2½ starch
   1 vegetable
   3 very lean meat

Meats

Easy Roast Beef

You'll be transported back to Grandma's kitchen when you smell this homey dish. The leftovers are excellent for sandwiches and for recipes calling for cooked lean beef, such as Vegetable Beef Soup (page 37).

Vegetable oil spray (olive oil spray preferred)
5-pound beef rump roast, all visible fat discarded
2   tablespoons olive oil
1   tablespoon Chili Powder (page 226) or commercial no-salt-added variety
1   medium onion, thinly sliced
2   medium carrots, thinly sliced
1   large rib of celery, thinly sliced
½   cup dry red wine (regular or nonalcoholic), plus more as needed
1   tablespoon low-sodium Worcestershire sauce
½   teaspoon salt

Preheat the oven to 350°F. Lightly spray a roasting pan with vegetable oil spray.

Rub the meat with the oil. Sprinkle with the Chili Powder. Put the meat in the roasting pan. Arrange the onion, carrots, and celery around the meat.

In a small bowl, stir together the wine and Worcestershire sauce. Pour over the meat.

Bake, uncovered, for 1 hour 30 minutes, or until a meat thermometer inserted in the thickest part of the meat registers the desired doneness. If the meat begins to dry out during cooking, baste with additional wine. Don't use the drippings for basting. Transfer the meat to a cutting board, retaining the pan juices. Lightly cover the meat with aluminum foil. Let sit for 10 to 15 minutes. Thinly slice the meat. Arrange it on a serving platter.

Meanwhile, skim the fat from the pan juices or remove the juices with a bulb baster and discard the fat. Stir the salt into the pan juices. Spoon the pan juices over the meat.

Beef Temperatures

Use a meat thermometer or an instant-read thermometer to determine the internal temperature. To be safe, cook beef to at least 160°F. For well-done, cook to 170°F.

Separating Fat from Pan Juices

A gravy separator, which looks like a measuring cup with a spout coming from the bottom, makes it easy to remove the fat from pan juices. Pour all the pan juices into the separator. After the fat rises to the top, simply pour the fat-free juice out of the bottom until the fat layer falls to the level of the spout. Discard what remains in the separator.

PER SERVING
CALORIES 183
TOTAL FAT 5.5 g
    Saturated 1.5 g
    Polyunsaturated 0.5 g
    Monounsaturated 2.5 g
CHOLESTEROL 71 mg
SODIUM 110 mg
CARBOHYDRATES 2 g
    Fiber 1 g
    Sugars 1 g
PROTEIN 29 g
CALCIUM 12 mg
POTASSIUM 328 mg
DIETARY EXCHANGES
    3 lean meat

Beef Bourguignon

Serves 8; 1 cup per serving

Even though this fancy stew (pronounced *boor-gen-YUN* or *boor-ge-NYON*) takes a while to prepare, it's well worth the time. Packed with beef and vegetables, it's a complete meal in a bowl.

2 tablespoons all-purpose flour
  Pepper to taste
1 pound boneless lean beef chuck roast, all visible fat discarded, cut into 1-inch cubes
  Vegetable oil spray
1 teaspoon canola or corn oil
¼ cup chopped onion
1 medium garlic clove, minced
1 pound small whole button mushrooms
3 medium tomatoes, finely chopped, or 14.5-ounce can no-salt-added diced tomatoes, undrained
1½ cups water, plus more as needed
½ cup dry red wine (regular or nonalcoholic)
1 tablespoon plus 1½ teaspoons Herb Seasoning (page 223) or see Cook's Tip on page 137
4 medium potatoes, peeled and coarsely diced (about 3 cups)
4 medium carrots, coarsely diced

In a large bowl, stir together the flour and pepper.

Add the beef, turning to coat and shaking off the excess.

Lightly spray a Dutch oven with vegetable oil spray. Heat over medium-high heat. Add the oil, swirling to coat the bottom. Cook the beef for 1 to 2 minutes, stirring frequently.

Stir in the onion and garlic. Cook for 2 to 3 minutes, or until the onion is soft, stirring frequently.

Stir in the mushrooms. Cook for 1 to 2 minutes, or until they absorb the liquid.

Stir in the tomatoes, water, wine, and Herb Seasoning. Reduce the heat and simmer, covered, for 2 hours, stirring occasionally and adding water if needed to keep the bottom of the pot covered.

Stir in the potatoes and carrots. Simmer, covered, for 30 minutes, or until the beef and vegetables are tender.

Slow-Cooker Method

Omit the vegetable oil spray and vegetable oil. Put the coated beef cubes in a slow cooker. Add the remaining ingredients and cook on high for 4 to 5 hours or on low for 8 to 9 hours.

 Cook's TIP

If you prefer, replace the Herb Seasoning with a combination of 1 tablespoon snipped fresh parsley; ¼ teaspoon dried thyme, crumbled; ¼ teaspoon dried basil, crumbled; ¼ teaspoon dried oregano, crumbled; ⅛ teaspoon dried rosemary leaves, crushed; and ⅛ teaspoon dried marjoram, crumbled.

PER SERVING
CALORIES 173
TOTAL FAT 3.5 g
  Saturated 1 g
  Polyunsaturated 0.5 g
  Monounsaturated 1.5 g
CHOLESTEROL 33 mg
SODIUM 53 mg
CARBOHYDRATES 23 g
  Fiber 4 g
  Sugars 6 g
PROTEIN 16 g
CALCIUM 40 mg
POTASSIUM 900 mg
DIETARY EXCHANGES
  1 starch
  2 vegetable
  1½ lean meat

Beef Stroganoff

Sour cream sauce is a must in this classic, named for a 19th-century Russian count and diplomat. Stroganoff is usually served with a rice pilaf, such as Rice and Vegetable Pilaf (page 205), or noodles.

1	pound beef tenderloin or boneless sirloin steak, silver skin (for tenderloin) and all visible fat discarded
1/8	teaspoon pepper
1	teaspoon canola or corn oil
8	ounces button mushrooms, sliced
1	medium onion, sliced
2	cups Beef Broth (page 18) or commercial fat-free, no-salt-added beef broth, heated
3	tablespoons all-purpose flour
2	tablespoons no-salt-added tomato paste
2	tablespoons dry sherry
1	teaspoon dry mustard
1/8	teaspoon dried oregano, crumbled
1/8	teaspoon dried dillweed, crumbled
1/4	cup fat-free or light sour cream

Cut the meat into thin strips about 2 inches long. Sprinkle with the pepper.

Heat a large nonstick skillet over medium-high heat. Add the oil and swirl to coat the bottom. Cook the beef for 1 minute.

Stir in the mushrooms and onion. Cook for 2 to 3 minutes, or until the onion is soft, stirring occasionally.

In a medium bowl, whisk together the broth and flour. Pour into the skillet. Bring to a boil. Reduce the heat and simmer for 2 to 3 minutes, or until thickened, stirring constantly.

In a small bowl, whisk together the remaining ingredients except the sour cream. Stir into the beef mixture. Simmer, covered, for 5 to 10 minutes, or until the beef is tender.

Transfer about ¼ cup sauce to a small bowl. Whisk in the sour cream. Stir back into the skillet. Cook for 5 minutes, or until warmed through.

PER SERVING

CALORIES 240
TOTAL FAT 7 g
  Saturated 2 g
  Polyunsaturated 0.5 g
  Monounsaturated 3 g
CHOLESTEROL 55 mg
SODIUM 87 mg
CARBOHYDRATES 15 g
  Fiber 2 g
  Sugars 5 g
PROTEIN 28 g
CALCIUM 60 mg
POTASSIUM 719 mg
DIETARY EXCHANGES
  ½ starch
  1½ vegetable
  3 lean meat

Sirloin with Red Wine and Mushroom Sauce

Serves 4; 3 ounces beef and ¼ cup mushroom sauce per serving

A delicately sweet reduction of red wine, mushrooms, tomato sauce, and herbs crowns tender beef slices.

    1-pound boneless top sirloin (about 1 inch thick), all visible fat discarded
5 ounces button mushrooms, sliced
⅓ cup merlot or other dry red wine (regular or nonalcoholic)
4 ounces no-salt-added tomato sauce
2 medium green onions, finely chopped
1 teaspoon very low sodium beef bouillon granules
1 teaspoon dried basil, crumbled
¾ teaspoon sugar
½ teaspoon dried oregano, crumbled
⅛ teaspoon garlic powder
⅛ teaspoon salt
    Vegetable oil spray
2 tablespoons snipped fresh parsley

In a large airtight plastic bag, combine the steak, mushrooms, and wine. Seal the bag and turn to coat. Refrigerate for 8 to 12 hours, turning occasionally.

In a small bowl, stir together the tomato sauce, green onions, bouillon granules, basil, sugar, oregano, garlic powder, and salt. Set aside.

Heat a large nonstick skillet over medium-high heat. Remove from the heat and lightly spray with vegetable oil spray (being careful not to spray near a gas flame). Remove the steak from the marinade; reserve the marinade. Shake the excess liquid from the steak. Cook the steak for 4 minutes. Turn the steak. Cook for 2 minutes, or until the desired doneness. Transfer to a cutting board.

Pour the reserved marinade with the mushrooms and the tomato sauce mixture into the pan residue in the skillet, scraping the bottom and side to dislodge any browned bits. Cook over medium-high heat for 3 minutes, or until the liquid is reduced to 1 cup.

To serve, slice the steak and transfer to plates. Spoon the mushroom sauce over the steak. Sprinkle with the parsley.

PER SERVING
CALORIES 191
TOTAL FAT 5 g
  Saturated 2 g
  Polyunsaturated 0.5 g
  Monounsaturated 2 g
CHOLESTEROL 46 mg
SODIUM 134 mg
CARBOHYDRATES 6 g
  Fiber 2 g
  Sugars 4 g
PROTEIN 26 g
CALCIUM 35 mg
POTASSIUM 750 mg
DIETARY EXCHANGES
  1 vegetable
  3 lean meat

Cowboy Steak with Portobello Mushrooms

Serves 4; 3 ounces meat and 1/2 cup mushroom mixture per serving

Season the sirloin with a dry rub, sear it to lock in the moisture, then smother it with a portobello and onion mixture.

1   teaspoon dried thyme, crumbled

1   teaspoon ground cumin

1   teaspoon Chili Powder (page 226) or commercial no-salt-added variety

1/4 teaspoon pepper

1   pound boneless top sirloin steak, all visible fat discarded
    Vegetable oil spray

1   medium onion, thinly sliced

8   ounces portobello mushrooms, cut into 1/2-inch slices (about 4 cups)

2   tablespoons Beef Broth (page 18) or commercial fat-free, no-salt-added
    beef broth

1   tablespoon low-sodium Worcestershire sauce

1   medium lime, quartered (optional)

Preheat the oven to 400°F.

In a small bowl, stir together the thyme, cumin, Chili Powder, and pepper.

Cut the steak into 4 pieces. Sprinkle the thyme mixture on both sides. Using your fingertips, gently rub the mixture into the steak.

Heat a large cast-iron or nonstick skillet over medium-high heat. Remove from the heat and lightly spray with vegetable oil spray (being careful not to spray near a gas flame). Cook the steaks for 2 minutes on each side, or until browned. Place the steaks on a baking sheet.

Bake for 3 to 5 minutes, or until the desired doneness. Transfer the steaks to a platter. Cover with aluminum foil to keep warm.

In the same skillet, cook the onion over medium heat for 2 to 3 minutes, or until tender-crisp, stirring occasionally. Stir in the mushrooms, broth, and Worcestershire sauce. Cook for 4 to 5 minutes, or until the mushrooms are tender, stirring occasionally.

To serve, spread the mushroom mixture over the steaks. Arrange the lime wedges around the steaks. Let the diners squeeze the lime wedges over the steak.

 Cook's TIP

Portobello Mushrooms

The gills of portobello mushrooms tend to turn foods dark. You may want to use a spoon to scrape out the gills before slicing the mushrooms. This step is also useful when making stuffed mushrooms, as it allows more room for the stuffing.

PER SERVING

CALORIES 181
TOTAL FAT 5 g
   Saturated 2 g
   Polyunsaturated 0.5 g
   Monounsaturated 2 g
CHOLESTEROL 46 mg
SODIUM 62 mg
CARBOHYDRATES 7 g
   Fiber 2 g
   Sugars 3 g
PROTEIN 26 g
CALCIUM 41 mg
POTASSIUM 615 mg
DIETARY EXCHANGES
   1½ vegetable
   3 lean meat

Sirloin with Tomato, Olive, and Feta Topping

Serves 4; 3 ounces meat and ½ cup topping per serving

Experience the essence of the Mediterranean right in your own home with this excellent entrée.

2 medium garlic cloves, minced

1 teaspoon dried oregano, crumbled

1 teaspoon grated lemon zest

2 tablespoons fresh lemon juice

¼ teaspoon pepper

1 pound boneless top sirloin steak, all visible fat discarded, cut into 4 pieces

Topping

2 cups grape tomatoes or cherry tomatoes, halved

2 tablespoons chopped kalamata olives, rinsed and drained

2 tablespoons crumbled reduced-fat feta cheese, rinsed and drained

1 tablespoon red wine vinegar

■ ■ ■

Vegetable oil spray

In a large airtight plastic bag, combine the garlic, oregano, lemon zest, lemon juice, and pepper. Add the steaks and turn to coat. Seal the bag and refrigerate for 30 minutes to 8 hours, turning occasionally.

Meanwhile, in a medium bowl, stir together the topping ingredients. Cover and refrigerate until ready to serve.

Drain the steaks. Discard the marinade.

Heat a large nonstick skillet over medium-high heat. Remove from the heat and lightly spray with vegetable oil spray (being careful not to spray near a gas flame). Cook the steaks for 4 to 5 minutes on each side, or until the desired doneness. (Or grill or broil 5 to 6 inches from the heat as directed.)

To serve, place each steak on a plate. Spoon the topping over each serving.

PER SERVING	
CALORIES	187
TOTAL FAT	6.5 g
Saturated	2 g
Polyunsaturated	0.5 g
Monounsaturated	2.5 g
CHOLESTEROL	48 mg
SODIUM	145 mg
CARBOHYDRATES	6 g
Fiber	1 g
Sugars	3 g
PROTEIN	26 g
CALCIUM	23 mg
POTASSIUM	565 mg
DIETARY EXCHANGES	
1 vegetable	
3 lean meat	

Filets Mignons with Brandy au Jus

Serves 4; 3 ounces beef and 1 tablespoon sauce per serving

Reducing the liquid for this dish yields an intensely flavored sauce, so a little is all you need. The tip of brandy at the end brings out the deep flavors of the sauce.

¾ cup water
2 tablespoons brandy
1 teaspoon very low sodium beef bouillon granules
1 teaspoon low-sodium Worcestershire sauce
Vegetable oil spray
⅛ teaspoon salt
4 filets mignons without bacon (about 4 ounces each), all visible fat discarded
1 teaspoon light tub margarine
½ teaspoon brandy (optional)
2 tablespoons snipped fresh parsley
¼ teaspoon pepper

Preheat the oven to 200°F.

In a small bowl, stir together the water, 2 tablespoons brandy, bouillon granules, and Worcestershire sauce. Set aside.

Heat a large skillet over high heat. Remove from the heat and lightly spray with vegetable oil spray (being careful not to spray near a gas flame). Sprinkle the salt over the filets. Cook the filets for 2 minutes on each side. Reduce the heat to medium. Cook for 2 to 6 minutes, or until the desired doneness. Transfer the filets to an ovenproof plate. Put in the oven to keep warm.

PER SERVING
CALORIES 186
TOTAL FAT 7 g
Saturated 2.5 g
Polyunsaturated 0.5 g
Monounsaturated 3 g
CHOLESTEROL 67 mg
SODIUM 135 mg
CARBOHYDRATES 1 g
Fiber 0 g
Sugars 0 g
PROTEIN 24 g
CALCIUM 20 mg
POTASSIUM 457 mg
DIETARY EXCHANGES
3 lean meat

Return the skillet with the pan residue to the heat. Increase the heat to high. Pour the brandy mixture into the skillet, scraping the bottom and side to dislodge any browned bits. Bring to a boil. Boil for 4 minutes, or until the liquid is reduced to ¼ cup, stirring constantly. Remove from the heat.

Add the margarine and ½ teaspoon brandy, stirring until the margarine has melted.

To serve, spoon the sauce over the filets. Sprinkle with the parsley and pepper.

Meat Loaf

Serves 8; 2 slices per serving

Capers contribute Mediterranean flavor to this tried-and-true classic. Serve with garlic mashed potatoes and steamed green beans. Don't forget to save some of the meat loaf for sandwiches.

Vegetable oil spray

1/2 cup uncooked quick-cooking oatmeal

1/4 cup fat-free or low-fat plain yogurt

1 pound lean ground beef

1/2 cup chopped onion

1 medium rib of celery, chopped

1 small parsnip or carrot, peeled and shredded

Egg substitute equivalent to 1 egg, or 1 large egg

1 tablespoon capers packed in balsamic vinegar, rinsed and drained

1 tablespoon fresh lemon juice

1/2 teaspoon dried thyme, crumbled

1/4 teaspoon pepper

1/4 teaspoon garlic powder

Preheat the oven to 375°F. Lightly spray a 9-inch square baking pan with vegetable oil spray.

In a large bowl, stir together the oatmeal and yogurt. Let stand for 5 minutes.

Add the remaining ingredients. Combine using your hands or a spoon. Form into a loaf about 8 × 5 inches. Place in the baking pan.

Bake for about 1 hour 15 minutes, or until the internal temperature in the center registers 165°F on a meat or instant-read thermometer. Remove from the oven and let stand for 5 to 10 minutes. Cut into 16 slices.

Cook's TIP

For leftovers with style, make meat loaf sandwiches in low-sodium buns or on low-sodium bread. Top the meat loaf with a mixture of 1 tablespoon Ketchup (page 217) or commercial no-salt-added ketchup and ½ teaspoon Horseradish (page 222) or dried horseradish. Add some crunchy romaine or curly green leaf lettuce, sliced onion, and Easy Dill Pickles (page 228). For a different flavor, spread the meat loaf with Roasted Tomato Chipotle Salsa (page 220) or bottled fat-free salsa with the lowest sodium available.

Cook's TIP

Capers

Small in size but with lots of lively flavor, capers are the flower buds of a bush that grows in Mediterranean countries and parts of Asia. Capers bottled in white balsamic vinegar can be hard to find but are lower in sodium than those bottled in brine. Although either kind should be rinsed well before using, the capers will still provide a salty kick. They are widely available in three sizes: the petite nonpareil, about the size of peppercorns, from France; the slightly larger ones, which come from Italy; and those about the size of cocktail olives, from Spain. They all taste the same, so price, availability, and your preferences can guide you. To retain their tangy flavor and crunchy texture, add capers near the end of the cooking time when possible.

PER SERVING

CALORIES 140
TOTAL FAT 5.5 g
  Saturated 2 g
  Polyunsaturated 0.5 g
  Monounsaturated 2.5 g
CHOLESTEROL 37 mg
SODIUM 88 mg
CARBOHYDRATES 8 g
  Fiber 2 g
  Sugars 2 g
PROTEIN 14 g
CALCIUM 36 mg
POTASSIUM 311 mg
DIETARY EXCHANGES
  ½ starch
  2 lean meat

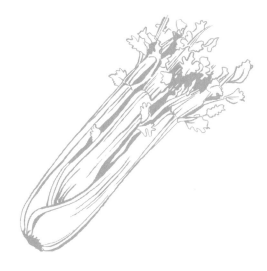

Beef and Pasta Portobello

Serves 4; 1 cup per serving

Portobello mushrooms have a meaty texture that's perfect for this classic meat-lovers' dish.

1   cup dried small shell macaroni

1   pound lean ground beef

1   medium portobello mushroom, stem trimmed, cut into ¾-inch cubes (about 1 cup)

1   cup chopped onion

1   medium garlic clove, minced

    14.5-ounce can no-salt-added diced tomatoes, undrained

    8-ounce can no-salt-added tomato sauce

½   cup water

1   bay leaf

1   teaspoon sugar

1   teaspoon salt-free Italian seasoning

½   teaspoon pepper

½   teaspoon crushed red pepper flakes (optional)

Prepare the macaroni using the package directions, omitting the salt and oil. Drain well and set aside.

Meanwhile, heat a large nonstick saucepan over medium-high heat. Cook the beef, mushroom, onion, and garlic for 8 to 10 minutes, or until the meat is no longer pink and vegetables are soft, stirring occasionally. Put in a colander and drain well. Blot with paper towels to remove excess fat. Wipe the skillet with paper towels. Return the drained mixture to the skillet.

Stir in the remaining ingredients. Bring to a simmer over medium-high heat. Reduce the heat to medium-low and cook for 15 minutes, stirring occasionally.

Stir in the macaroni. Cook for 2 to 3 minutes, or until the macaroni is warmed through. Remove the bay leaf before serving the mixture.

PER SERVING

CALORIES 356

TOTAL FAT 11 g
  Saturated 4 g
  Polyunsaturated 0.5 g
  Monounsaturated 4.5 g

CHOLESTEROL 75 mg

SODIUM 83 mg

CARBOHYDRATES 35 g
  Fiber 3 g
  Sugars 8 g

PROTEIN 29 g

CALCIUM 65 mg

POTASSIUM 957 mg

DIETARY EXCHANGES
  1½ starch
  3 vegetable
  3 lean meat

Spaghetti with Meat Sauce

Serves 12; 1 cup spaghetti and ⅔ cup sauce per serving

When you want to serve a crowd an entrée that you can start cooking, then forget about, this great recipe is the answer.

1	pound lean ground beef
	28-ounce can no-salt-added diced tomatoes, undrained
2	small zucchini, diced
	6-ounce can no-salt-added tomato paste
1	medium onion, chopped
½	cup dry red wine (regular or nonalcoholic)
1½	teaspoons chopped fresh oregano or ½ teaspoon dried, crumbled
1½	teaspoons chopped fresh basil leaves or ½ teaspoon dried, crumbled
1	medium garlic clove, minced
½	teaspoon fennel seeds
⅛	teaspoon pepper
24	ounces dried spaghetti

Heat a large saucepan over medium-high heat. Cook the beef until brown, 3 to 4 minutes, stirring occasionally. Put the beef in a colander and drain to remove the excess fat. Wipe the saucepan with paper towels; return the beef to the saucepan.

Stir in the remaining ingredients except the spaghetti. Cover and simmer for 1 hour 30 minutes, stirring occasionally. If the sauce seems too thick, gradually add water until the desired consistency.

Meanwhile, prepare the spaghetti using the package directions, omitting the salt and oil. Drain well. Spoon the spaghetti onto each plate and top with the sauce.

PER SERVING
CALORIES 315
TOTAL FAT 4.5 g
    Saturated 1.5 g
    Polyunsaturated 0.5 g
    Monounsaturated 1.5 g
CHOLESTEROL 25 mg
SODIUM 48 mg
CARBOHYDRATES 50 g
    Fiber 3 g
    Sugars 6 g
PROTEIN 17 g
CALCIUM 48 mg
POTASSIUM 590 mg
DIETARY EXCHANGES
    3 starch
    1 vegetable
    1 lean meat

Slow-Cooker Beef
and Red Beans

Serves 6; 1 cup beef mixture and ½ cup rice per serving

A smattering of imitation bacon bits adds a smoky flavor to this family-pleasing dish.

1	pound lean ground beef
2	cups Chicken Broth (page 19) or commercial fat-free, low-sodium chicken broth
	15-ounce can no-salt-added red beans, rinsed and drained
	14.5-ounce can no-salt-added diced tomatoes, undrained
1	cup water
2	medium ribs of celery, chopped
½	medium onion, chopped
½	medium green bell pepper, chopped
2	tablespoons imitation bacon bits
1	teaspoon dried thyme, crumbled
2	medium garlic cloves, minced
¼	teaspoon pepper
⅛	to ¼ teaspoon cayenne
1½	cups uncooked instant brown rice
1⅔	cups water
1	teaspoon salt-free all-purpose seasoning blend, such as Herb Seasoning (page 223) or Savory Herb Blend (page 225)

In a large skillet, cook the beef over medium-high heat for 7 to 8 minutes, or until browned on the outside, stirring occasionally to turn and break up the beef. Using a slotted spoon, transfer the beef to a slow cooker. If any liquid remains in the skillet, wipe clean using paper towels.

Stir in the broth, beans, undrained tomatoes, 1 cup water, celery, onion, bell pepper, bacon bits, thyme, garlic, pepper, and cayenne. Cook on high for 3 to 4 hours or on low for 7 to 8 hours.

Prepare the rice using 1⅔ cups water (this may differ from the package directions) and the seasoning blend, omitting the salt and margarine.

To serve, spoon the rice into each bowl. Ladle the beef mixture over each serving.

If you prefer to cook the rice in the slow cooker, stir it in 30 minutes before the end of the cooking time (on low or high setting). If using this method, be sure to add the 1⅔ cups water and the seasoning blend to the slow cooker when you add the beef, beans, and vegetables. You'll save on washing an extra pan, but the presentation won't be quite so attractive.

PER SERVING

CALORIES 304

TOTAL FAT 8.5 g
    Saturated 2.5 g
    Polyunsaturated 0.5 g
    Monounsaturated 3.5 g

CHOLESTEROL 50 mg

SODIUM 145 mg

CARBOHYDRATES 33 g
    Fiber 5 g
    Sugars 3 g

PROTEIN 23 g

CALCIUM 71 mg

POTASSIUM 707 mg

DIETARY EXCHANGES
    2 starch
    1 vegetable
    2½ lean meat

Chili

Serves 4; 1 cup per serving

What could be easier or more welcome during the first cold weekend of the season than a bowl of big red? Before or after the football game, it's a sure winner.

1 pound lean ground beef

½ cup chopped onion

1 to 2 tablespoons chopped fresh jalapeño (wear plastic gloves when handling)

14.5-ounce can no-salt-added stewed tomatoes, undrained

15-ounce can no-salt-added pinto beans, undrained

½ cup water (plus more as needed)

¼ cup stout or beer (regular, light, or nonalcoholic)

1 tablespoon Chili Powder (page 226) or commercial no-salt-added variety

2 teaspoons ground cumin

½ teaspoon dried oregano, crumbled

¼ teaspoon garlic powder

¼ teaspoon salt

⅛ teaspoon pepper

⅛ teaspoon cayenne (optional)

Heat a Dutch oven over high heat. Cook the beef for 3 to 4 minutes, or until brown, stirring frequently. Using a slotted spoon, transfer the beef to a plate. Drain the fat from the Dutch oven. Wipe with paper towels. Return the beef to the Dutch oven.

Reduce the heat to medium-high. Stir in the onion and jalapeño. Cook for 2 to 3 minutes, or until the onion is soft, stirring occasionally.

Stir in the remaining ingredients. Reduce the heat and simmer, covered, for 1 hour 30 minutes, stirring occasionally. Add water as needed for the desired consistency.

PER SERVING

CALORIES 340

TOTAL FAT 10.5 g
  Saturated 4 g
  Polyunsaturated 0.5 g
  Monounsaturated 4.5 g

CHOLESTEROL 75 mg

SODIUM 225 mg

CARBOHYDRATES 27 g
  Fiber 7 g
  Sugars 9 g

PROTEIN 31 g

CALCIUM 99 mg

POTASSIUM 824 mg

DIETARY EXCHANGES
  1 starch
  2 vegetable
  3½ lean meat

Chili Powder

Check the labels on commercial chili powders. Most of them contain salt. Our homemade no-salt-added variety (page 226) provides the flavor without the sodium. Or, in a pinch, substitute a mixture of 2 parts paprika to 1 part ground cumin.

One-Dish Skillet Supper

Serves 4; 1½ cups per serving

Give leftover beef or pork a well-balanced makeover by adding bell pepper, broccoli, and whole-wheat pasta. The result is an easy one-dish meal.

1	teaspoon olive oil
1	medium bell pepper (any color), thinly sliced
1	medium onion, thinly sliced
2	cups Beef Broth (page 18) or commercial fat-free, no-salt-added beef broth
12	ounces cubed cooked lean beef or pork roast, cooked without salt, all visible fat discarded
2	teaspoons low-sodium Worcestershire sauce
1	teaspoon dried savory or dried oregano, crumbled
¼	teaspoon pepper
4	ounces dried whole-wheat pasta, such as rotelle or macaroni
3	ounces broccoli florets (about 1 cup)

Heat a large skillet over medium heat. Add the oil and swirl to coat the bottom. Cook the bell pepper and onion for 3 to 4 minutes, or until tender, stirring occasionally.

Stir in the broth, beef, Worcestershire sauce, savory, and pepper.

Increase the heat to medium-high and bring to a simmer. Stir in the pasta. Reduce the heat and simmer, covered, for 5 minutes.

Stir in the broccoli. Simmer, covered, for 5 minutes, or until the pasta and broccoli are tender.

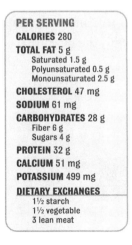

PER SERVING
CALORIES 280
TOTAL FAT 5 g
  Saturated 1.5 g
  Polyunsaturated 0.5 g
  Monounsaturated 2.5 g
CHOLESTEROL 47 mg
SODIUM 61 mg
CARBOHYDRATES 28 g
  Fiber 6 g
  Sugars 4 g
PROTEIN 32 g
CALCIUM 51 mg
POTASSIUM 499 mg
DIETARY EXCHANGES
  1½ starch
  1½ vegetable
  3 lean meat

Cook's TIP

Savory

This interesting herb is worth experimenting with. A member of the mint family, it is slightly peppery. The two most popular varieties are summer savory, which is more delicate, and winter savory, which is spicier and sharper; they are interchangeable. Try savory in bean, pea, and lentil dishes (it is called the bean herb in continental Europe), as well as in stews, marinades, soups, salads, and more.

Chunky Joes

Serves 6; ²/₃ cup pork mixture and 1 bun per serving

Chunks of lean pork replace ground beef in this delightfully messy sandwich. Add some corn for crunch if you wish.

1 pound pork tenderloin or other lean boneless pork, all visible fat discarded
   Vegetable oil spray
1 cup finely chopped onion
1 medium green bell pepper, finely chopped
   14.5-ounce can no-salt-added diced tomatoes, undrained
½ cup frozen whole-kernel corn, thawed (optional)
1 tablespoon plus 1½ teaspoons cider vinegar
1 tablespoon sugar
1 tablespoon plus 1½ teaspoons Chili Powder (page 226) or commercial no-salt-added variety
⅛ teaspoon salt
6 hamburger buns (whole-wheat preferred)

Cut the pork into ¼-inch cubes.

Lightly spray a large nonstick skillet with vegetable oil spray. Heat over high heat. Cook the pork for 3 minutes, or until it just begins to brown and the liquid evaporates, stirring constantly. Transfer to a plate. Set aside.

Lightly spray the skillet with vegetable oil spray (being careful not to spray near a gas flame). Reduce the heat to medium-high. Cook the onion and bell pepper for 2 to 3 minutes, or until the onion is soft, stirring frequently.

Stir in the reserved pork, with any accumulated juices, undrained tomatoes, corn, vinegar, sugar, and Chili Powder. Cook for 10 minutes, or until the mixture has thickened, stirring occasionally. Stir in the salt.

Meanwhile, split and toast the buns.

To serve, spoon the pork mixture over the buns.

Chunky Joe Burritos

Replace hamburger buns with six 6-inch reduced-fat flour tortillas, warmed. Before rolling the mixture in the tortillas, top each serving with 1 tablespoon fat-free or light sour cream. Just be sure to look for the tortillas with the lowest amount of sodium.

For a moister consistency, add 2 to 3 tablespoons of water when you add the salt to the pork mixture.

CHUNKY JOES

PER SERVING

CALORIES 257

TOTAL FAT 5 g
  Saturated 1.5 g
  Polyunsaturated 1.5 g
  Monounsaturated 1.5 g

CHOLESTEROL 42 mg

SODIUM 293 mg

CARBOHYDRATES 35 g
  Fiber 5 g
  Sugars 10 g

PROTEIN 21 g

CALCIUM 85 mg

POTASSIUM 653 mg

DIETARY EXCHANGES
  2 starch
  1 vegetable
  2 lean meat

BURRITOS

PER SERVING

CALORIES 228

TOTAL FAT 3.5 g
  Saturated 1 g
  Polyunsaturated 0.5 g
  Monounsaturated 1 g

CHOLESTEROL 45 mg

SODIUM 293 mg

CARBOHYDRATES 30 g
  Fiber 3 g
  Sugars 7 g

PROTEIN 20 g

CALCIUM 60 mg

POTASSIUM 571 mg

DIETARY EXCHANGES
  1½ starch
  1 vegetable
  2 lean meat

Savory Pork Tenderloin

Serves 4; 3 ounces pork and ½ cup rice per serving

While the pork bakes with its herb-enhanced Dijon glaze, you can prepare brown rice flavored with orange marmalade and steam some broccoli to serve on the side.

2   tablespoons Dijon mustard
1   tablespoon chopped fresh rosemary leaves or 1 teaspoon dried, crushed
1   tablespoon chopped fresh oregano or 1 teaspoon dried, crumbled
2   teaspoons cider vinegar
¼   teaspoon pepper
    1-pound pork tenderloin, all visible fat discarded
1¼ cups Chicken Broth (page 19) or commercial fat-free, low-sodium chicken broth
2   tablespoons all-fruit orange marmalade
1   cup uncooked instant brown rice

Preheat the oven to 350°F.

In a small bowl, stir together the mustard, rosemary, oregano, vinegar, and pepper. Using a pastry brush or spoon, brush over the pork. Place the pork in an 8-inch square nonstick baking dish.

Bake for 40 to 45 minutes, or until the internal temperature reaches 160°F when tested with an instant-read thermometer. Let the pork rest in the baking pan for 5 to 10 minutes, then slice crosswise.

Meanwhile, in a medium saucepan, bring the broth and marmalade to a boil over high heat. Stir in the rice. Reduce the heat and simmer, covered, for 10 minutes, or until the liquid is absorbed and the rice is tender. Set aside, covered.

To serve, spoon the rice mixture onto plates. Arrange the pork slices over the rice.

PER SERVING
CALORIES 252
TOTAL FAT 5 g
    Saturated 1.5 g
    Polyunsaturated 0.5 g
    Monounsaturated 2 g
CHOLESTEROL 63 mg
SODIUM 211 mg
CARBOHYDRATES 24 g
    Fiber 1 g
    Sugars 5 g
PROTEIN 26 g
CALCIUM 19 mg
POTASSIUM 427 mg
DIETARY EXCHANGES
    3 lean meat
    1 starch
    ½ fruit

Hungarian Pork Chops

Serves 4; 3 ounces pork and 3 tablespoons sauce per serving

An Old World comfort dish without the work.

Rub

1 teaspoon paprika

¾ teaspoon dried dillweed, crumbled

½ teaspoon caraway seeds

½ teaspoon onion powder

½ teaspoon garlic powder

■ ■ ■

4 boneless pork loin chops (about 4 ounces each), cut ½ inch thick, all visible fat discarded

Vegetable oil spray

½ cup water

½ cup fat-free or light sour cream

¼ teaspoon salt

2 tablespoons finely chopped green onions

In a small bowl, stir together the rub ingredients. Rub half the mixture on one side of the pork.

Lightly spray a large, heavy nonstick skillet with vegetable oil spray. Heat over medium-high heat. Reduce the heat to medium. Cook the pork with the seasoned side down for 4 minutes. Rub the top side with the remaining mixture. Turn the pork over and cook for 4 to 5 minutes, or until barely pink in the center. Transfer to a plate. Cover with aluminum foil to keep warm.

Increase the heat to high. Pour in the water, scraping the skillet to dislodge any browned bits. Boil for 1 to 2 minutes, or until the liquid is reduced to ¼ cup. Reduce the heat to low.

When the boiling stops, whisk in the sour cream and salt. Cook for 2 to 3 minutes, or until heated through, whisking constantly. Don't let the mixture boil.

To serve, place the pork on plates. Spoon the sauce over the pork. Sprinkle with the green onions.

PER SERVING

CALORIES 199
TOTAL FAT 6.5 g
    Saturated 2.5 g
    Polyunsaturated 0.5 g
    Monounsaturated 3 g
CHOLESTEROL 72 mg
SODIUM 221 mg
CARBOHYDRATES 7 g
    Fiber 1 g
    Sugars 2 g
PROTEIN 26 g
CALCIUM 66 mg
POTASSIUM 395 mg
DIETARY EXCHANGES
    ½ other carbohydrate
    3 lean meat

Caribbean Jerk Pork

Serves 4; 3 ounces pork per serving

Make your own fragrant jerk seasoning to flavor grilled or broiled pork chops.

Vegetable oil spray

Jerk Seasoning Blend

1   to 2 fresh jalapeños
2   tablespoons chopped onion
1   tablespoon ground allspice
1   tablespoon chopped fresh thyme or 1 teaspoon dried, crumbled
1   teaspoon grated orange zest
2   tablespoons fresh orange juice
1   tablespoon honey
2   teaspoons steak sauce
½   teaspoon ground cinnamon

■ ■ ■

4   boneless center-cut pork chops (about 4 ounces each), all visible fat discarded
¼   teaspoon salt
1   medium lime, cut into 8 wedges (optional)

Lightly spray the grill rack with vegetable oil spray. Preheat the grill on high. Or preheat the broiler and lightly spray the broiler rack and pan with vegetable oil spray.

Wearing plastic gloves, cut the jalapeños in half vertically. Discard the stems, ribs, and seeds.

In a food processor or blender, process all the seasoning blend ingredients, including jalapeños, until smooth. Transfer to a large airtight plastic bag.

Put the pork in the bag. Seal the bag and turn to coat. Refrigerate for 15 to 20 minutes, turning the bag occasionally.

Grill the pork for 5 minutes on each side, or until no longer pink in the center. If using a broiler, put the pork on the rack. Broil about 4 inches from the heat for 5 minutes on each side, or until no longer pink in the center.

To serve, put the pork on plates. Sprinkle with the salt. Serve with the lime wedges.

Jerking and Jerk Seasoning

Jerking, a method of cooking in Jamaica, involves rubbing meat with, or marinating it in, a fiery-hot, intensely flavored mixture, then grilling it. Although chicken and pork are the most commonly jerked foods, beef, goat, and fish can also be prepared this way. Jerk seasoning almost always includes some Scotch bonnet or habanero chile, but we lowered the heat a notch here by using jalapeño. Other very typical jerk seasonings are allspice, cinnamon, ginger, nutmeg, cloves, thyme, garlic, and onions.

PER SERVING

CALORIES 191

TOTAL FAT 6.5 g
   Saturated 2.5 g
   Polyunsaturated 0.5 g
   Monounsaturated 3 g

CHOLESTEROL 65 mg

SODIUM 233 mg

CARBOHYDRATES 8 g
   Fiber 1 g
   Sugars 5 g

PROTEIN 24 g

CALCIUM 48 mg

POTASSIUM 364 mg

DIETARY EXCHANGES
   ½ other carbohydrate
   3 lean meat

Pork Chops with Herb Rub

Serves 4; 3 ounces pork per serving

Marjoram, an aromatic herb that tastes like a mild version of oregano, is the key ingredient in the rub that makes these grilled pork chops so tasty.

½ teaspoon dried marjoram, crumbled

⅛ teaspoon garlic powder

⅛ teaspoon onion powder

⅛ teaspoon pepper

4 pork loin chops (about 4 ounces each if boneless, 6 ounces with bone), cut ½ inch thick, all visible fat discarded

Preheat the grill on medium-high or preheat the broiler.

In a small bowl, stir together all the ingredients except the pork. Rub on both sides of the pork.

Grill for 6 minutes on each side, or until browned on the outside and barely pink in the center. If using a broiler, broil about 4 inches from the heat for 5 minutes on each side, or until browned on the outside and barely pink in the center.

PER SERVING

CALORIES 168

TOTAL FAT 10 g
    Saturated 3.5 g
    Polyunsaturated 1 g
    Monounsaturated 4.5 g

CHOLESTEROL 60 mg

SODIUM 57 mg

CARBOHYDRATES 0 g
    Fiber 0 g
    Sugars 0 g

PROTEIN 18 g

CALCIUM 18 mg

POTASSIUM 271 mg

DIETARY EXCHANGES
    3 lean meat

Baked Pork Chops
with Apple Dressing

Serves 4; 3 ounces meat and ½ cup dressing per serving

No more dry pork chops! Just "sandwich" the chops between layers of dressing and bake, leaving them tender and moist. Serve with green beans tossed with lemon zest.

Apple Dressing

2 slices light whole-wheat bread, torn into bite-size pieces

1 medium apple, such as Granny Smith, Gala, Fuji, or Golden Delicious, peeled and finely chopped

1 medium rib of celery, finely chopped

4 medium green onions (green and white parts), thinly sliced

¼ cup Chicken Broth (page 19) or commercial fat-free, low-sodium chicken broth

   Egg substitute equivalent to 1 egg, or 1 large egg

1 teaspoon dried sage

¼ teaspoon pepper

   ■ ■ ■

4 boneless pork loin chops (about 4 ounces each), all visible fat discarded

Preheat the oven to 375°F.

In a medium bowl, stir together the dressing ingredients until the bread is moistened. Spoon half the dressing into an 8-inch square baking pan, smoothing the surface. Place the chops in a single layer on the dressing. Spread the remaining dressing over the chops.

PER SERVING
CALORIES 223
TOTAL FAT 10 g
Saturated 3.5 g
Polyunsaturated 1 g
Monounsaturated 4.5 g
CHOLESTEROL 60 mg
SODIUM 161 mg
CARBOHYDRATES 11 g
Fiber 3 g
Sugars 5 g
PROTEIN 21 g
CALCIUM 32 mg
POTASSIUM 421 mg
DIETARY EXCHANGES
1 fruit
3 lean meat

Bake, covered, for 30 minutes (the pork will be slightly pink in the center). Bake, uncovered, for 10 to 15 minutes, or until the pork is no longer pink in the center and the dressing is golden brown.

To serve, use a wide spatula to transfer the dressing-covered pork to plates. Spoon any remaining dressing over the pork.

Buffalo Baked in Pumpkin

Serves 10; 1 cup pumpkin plus 1 cup stuffing per serving

An ideal one-dish meal for the fall and winter months, this stuffed pumpkin makes a dramatic presentation. Widely available in specialty meat stores and health food stores, buffalo is lower in total fat and saturated fat than beef or pork. If buffalo isn't available, use extra-lean ground beef or turkey breast ground without skin.

1	cup uncooked wild rice, rinsed and drained
2	to 3 fresh jalapeños
	6-pound pumpkin or winter squash (you may need several squash)
¼	cup honey mustard
1	tablespoon canola or corn oil
2	to 3 large onions, chopped
3	large garlic cloves, minced
1½	pounds ground buffalo
¾	cup snipped fresh parsley
2	medium tomatoes, diced (optional)
2	roasted medium yellow or red bell peppers, chopped
¼	cup unsalted shelled pumpkin seeds or dry-roasted pine nuts
1	tablespoon dried thyme, crumbled
1	tablespoon dried cilantro, crumbled
⅛	to ¼ teaspoon cayenne
3	medium green onions, finely chopped (optional)

Prepare the rice using the package directions, omitting the salt, but don't cook the rice until puffy. Keep it al dente (slightly firm); it will cook more during baking.

Meanwhile, wearing plastic gloves, cut the jalapeños in half vertically. Discard the stems, ribs, and seeds. Set aside.

Cut the top off the pumpkin as you would for a jack-o'-lantern. Discard the seeds and stringy fibers. Rinse the pumpkin well and pat dry with paper towels. Using a pastry brush, paint the inside of the pumpkin and lid with the honey mustard. Set aside.

Place an oven rack in the lowest position. Preheat the oven to 325°F.

Heat a large nonstick skillet over medium-high heat. Add the oil and swirl to coat the bottom. Cook the onions for 2 to 3 minutes, or until soft, stirring occasionally.

Stir in the jalapeños and garlic. Cook for 2 minutes, stirring occasionally.

Break the buffalo into pieces and stir into the onion mixture. Cook for 5 minutes, or until the meat is lightly browned, stirring occasionally. Transfer to a large bowl.

Stir in the rice and the remaining ingredients except the green onions.

Gently spoon the mixture into the pumpkin; top with the lid. Place in a roaster or large baking pan. Gently pour in water to a depth of 1½ inches.

Bake for 2 hours to 2 hours and 30 minutes, or until the pumpkin shell is soft to the touch. If the top of the pumpkin begins to brown too quickly, cover with aluminum foil. Check the water level, adding water, if necessary, to keep it at a depth of 1½ inches.

Bring the whole stuffed pumpkin to the table. Slice into 10 wedges. Spoon the stuffing onto the pumpkin. Sprinkle some green onions over each portion.

Cook's TIP

Pumpkin Seeds

If you can't find unsalted pumpkin seeds, simply rinse the salted seeds and let them dry on paper towels.

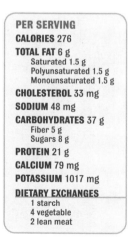

PER SERVING
CALORIES 276
TOTAL FAT 6 g
  Saturated 1.5 g
  Polyunsaturated 1.5 g
  Monounsaturated 1.5 g
CHOLESTEROL 33 mg
SODIUM 48 mg
CARBOHYDRATES 37 g
  Fiber 5 g
  Sugars 8 g
PROTEIN 21 g
CALCIUM 79 mg
POTASSIUM 1017 mg
DIETARY EXCHANGES
  1 starch
  4 vegetable
  2 lean meat

Lamb Curry

Serve this spicy lamb over rice with small bowls of raisins and sliced green onions to sprinkle on top.

3 tablespoons all-purpose flour

⅛ teaspoon pepper

2 pounds boneless lamb chuck roast, all visible fat discarded, cut into cubes

2 teaspoons canola or corn oil

3 cups water

½ cup finely chopped onion

½ cup unsweetened applesauce

2 to 3 teaspoons curry powder

2 teaspoons fresh lemon juice

In a medium plastic or paper bag, combine the flour and pepper.

Add the lamb, a few pieces at a time, and shake to coat. Shake off any excess flour.

In a large nonstick skillet, heat the oil over medium-high heat. Swirl to coat the bottom. Cook the lamb for about 5 minutes, or until brown on all sides, stirring occasionally. Using a slotted spoon, transfer the lamb to a plate. Pour off the excess fat. Wipe the skillet clean with paper towels. Return the lamb to the skillet.

Stir in the remaining ingredients except the lemon juice. Simmer, covered, for 1 hour, or until the lamb is tender, stirring occasionally.

To serve, stir in the lemon juice.

PER SERVING

CALORIES 179

TOTAL FAT 8 g
  Saturated 2.5 g
  Polyunsaturated 1 g
  Monounsaturated 3.5 g

CHOLESTEROL 65 mg

SODIUM 56 mg

CARBOHYDRATES 5 g
  Fiber 1 g
  Sugars 2 g

PROTEIN 20 g

CALCIUM 18 mg

POTASSIUM 283 mg

DIETARY EXCHANGES
  1 vegetable

Eggplant Lasagna

Alfredo Lasagna with Broccoli and Cauliflower

Fettuccine Alfredo

Spaghetti with Exotic Mushroom Sauce

Braised Lentil and Vegetable Medley

Vegetarian Chili

Zucchini Frittata

Vegetarian Entrées

Mexican Omelet for Two

Asian Vegetable and Tofu Stir-Fry

Polenta and Cheese with Fresh Mushrooms
SPICY POLENTA

Gorgonzola Portobello Rounds
PIZZA PORTOBELLOS

Cheese-Topped Stuffed Eggplant

Crustless Garden Quiche

Eggplant Lasagna

Serves 6; 4 × 4-inch piece per serving

If you can, assemble this hearty lasagna a day ahead. Its flavors will be enhanced, plus all you'll need to do for dinner is toss a salad and make a quick fruit dessert while the casserole bakes.

Vegetable oil spray
- 6 dried lasagna noodles
- 3 cups chopped peeled eggplant
- 1 medium green bell pepper, diced
- 1 large onion, chopped
- ¼ cup chopped fresh basil leaves or 1 tablespoon plus 1 teaspoon dried, crumbled
- 3 medium garlic cloves, minced
- 2 8-ounce cans no-salt-added tomato sauce
- 2 teaspoons low-sodium Worcestershire sauce
- ⅛ teaspoon salt
- ¼ teaspoon fennel seeds (optional)
- 1 cup fat-free or low-fat cottage cheese
- 1 cup shredded part-skim mozzarella cheese
- 2 tablespoons shredded or grated Parmesan cheese

Preheat the oven to 350°F. Spray a 12 × 8 × 2-inch glass baking dish with vegetable oil spray. Set aside.

In a large stockpot, prepare the noodles using the package directions, omitting the salt and oil. Drain well.

Meanwhile, lightly spray a large nonstick skillet with vegetable oil spray. Heat over medium-high heat. Cook the eggplant, bell pepper, onion, dried basil (if using fresh basil, add with the tomato sauce), and garlic for 10 minutes, or until the eggplant is soft, stirring occasionally. Reduce the heat to medium if the mixture starts sticking to the skillet.

Add the tomato sauce, fresh basil if using, Worcestershire sauce, salt, and fennel seeds. Bring to a boil. Reduce the heat and simmer for 15 minutes, or until the sauce has slightly thickened and the bell pepper is soft. Remove from the heat.

To assemble, lay 2 noodles lengthwise in the baking dish. Spread a scant 1 cup eggplant mixture over the noodles. Spread ⅓ cup cottage cheese over the eggplant. Sprinkle with ¼ cup mozzarella. Repeat the layers twice, ending with remaining ½ cup mozzarella. Tuck in the ends of the noodles if overhanging. Cover the dish with aluminum foil.

Bake for 30 minutes.

Sprinkle with the Parmesan. Let stand for 5 to 10 minutes to let the cheese melt and make cutting easier.

 ## Cheese

When using fairly small amounts of cheese on top of a casserole, cover the dish with aluminum foil during the baking period to prevent the cheese from over-cooking and drying out. Run the casserole under the broiler for a few seconds if you want to brown the cheese lightly.

PER SERVING
CALORIES 230
TOTAL FAT 4.5 g
  Saturated 2.5 g
  Polyunsaturated 0.5 g
  Monounsaturated 1 g
CHOLESTEROL 15 mg
SODIUM 335 mg
CARBOHYDRATES 33 g
  Fiber 3 g
  Sugars 8 g
PROTEIN 15 g
CALCIUM 231 mg
POTASSIUM 573 mg
DIETARY EXCHANGES
  1½ starch
  2 vegetable
  1 lean meat

Alfredo Lasagna with Broccoli and Cauliflower

Serves 8; ¾ to 1 cup per serving

A creamy Alfredo-type sauce binds layers of noodles, vegetables, and cheeses in this vegetarian lasagna. No tomatoes allowed!

Vegetable oil spray

Sauce

2½ cups fat-free milk

3 tablespoons all-purpose flour

¼ teaspoon pepper

⅛ teaspoon cayenne (optional)

¼ cup shredded or grated Parmesan cheese

■ ■ ■

1 cup fat-free or low-fat ricotta cheese

Egg substitute equivalent to 1 egg, or 1 large egg

1 teaspoon dried oregano, crumbled

¼ teaspoon onion powder

¼ teaspoon garlic powder

4 cups water for fresh vegetables

2 cups chopped fresh (½-inch pieces) or frozen cauliflower, thawed

2 cups chopped fresh (½-inch pieces) or frozen broccoli, thawed

4 oven-ready lasagna noodles, broken in half crosswise

¼ cup roasted red bell pepper, rinsed and drained if bottled, chopped

1 cup shredded part-skim mozzarella cheese, divided use

Crumb Topping

¼ cup plain dry bread crumbs

2 teaspoons olive oil

½ teaspoon salt-free Italian seasoning

Preheat the oven to 375°F. Lightly spray a 2-quart casserole dish with vegetable oil spray. Set aside.

In a medium saucepan, whisk together the sauce ingredients except the Parmesan. Cook over medium-high heat for 4 to 5 minutes, or until the mixture thickens slightly (it will still be somewhat thin), stirring occasionally.

Stir in the Parmesan. Remove from the heat. Set aside.

In a medium bowl, stir together the ricotta, egg substitute, oregano, onion powder, and garlic powder. Set aside.

If using fresh cauliflower and broccoli, bring the water to a boil in a medium saucepan over high heat. Reduce the heat to medium-high and cook the cauliflower for 2 minutes. Add the broccoli. Cook the mixture for 1 minute. Pour into a colander and drain well.

To assemble, pour half the sauce into the casserole dish. Make a layer of 4 lasagna noodle halves. Spread the ricotta mixture over the noodles. Arrange the cauliflower and broccoli over the ricotta mixture. Sprinkle with the bell pepper and ½ cup mozzarella. Top with the remaining noodles, sauce, and mozzarella. Cover the dish with aluminum foil and set on a baking sheet in case the lasagna bubbles over.

Bake for 30 minutes.

Meanwhile, in a small bowl, combine the crumb topping ingredients. After 30 minutes, sprinkle it over the lasagna.

Bake, uncovered, for 8 to 10 minutes, or until the topping is toasted and the noodles are tender. Let stand for 5 to 10 minutes to make cutting easier.

PER SERVING
CALORIES 184
TOTAL FAT 4.5 g
    Saturated 2 g
    Polyunsaturated 0.5 g
    Monounsaturated 1.5 g
CHOLESTEROL 14 mg
SODIUM 291 mg
CARBOHYDRATES 20 g
    Fiber 2 g
    Sugars 6 g
PROTEIN 15 g
CALCIUM 372 mg
POTASSIUM 229 mg
DIETARY EXCHANGES
    1 starch
    ½ skim milk
    1 lean meat

Fettuccine Alfredo

Serves 8; 1 cup per serving

Now you can have all the richness of Alfredo sauce with only a fraction of the calories and sodium. The addition of lemon gives this dish a fresh twist.

1   pound dried fettuccine

¼   cup fat-free milk

2   tablespoons all-purpose flour

1¼   cups fat-free milk

¼   cup shredded or grated Parmesan cheese

2   teaspoons fresh lemon juice

⅛   teaspoon white pepper

2   tablespoons finely snipped fresh parsley

1   tablespoon plus 1½ teaspoons shredded or grated Parmesan cheese

¼   teaspoon salt

1   medium lemon, quartered (optional)

Prepare the fettuccine using the package directions, omitting the salt and oil. Drain well. Cover with aluminum foil to keep warm.

Meanwhile, heat a medium saucepan over medium heat. In a small bowl, whisk together ¼ cup milk and the flour until smooth. Pour the mixture into the saucepan.

Whisk in the remaining 1¼ cups milk. Bring to a boil. Cook for 15 minutes, or until thickened, stirring constantly with a flat spatula to keep the sauce from sticking to the bottom of the pan.

Stir in ¼ cup Parmesan, lemon juice, and pepper.

To serve, transfer the warm fettuccine to a platter. Pour the sauce over the fettuccine. Sprinkle with the parsley, remaining Parmesan, and salt. Garnish with the lemon wedges.

PER SERVING

CALORIES 249
TOTAL FAT 2 g
  Saturated 0.5 g
  Polyunsaturated 0.5 g
  Monounsaturated 0.5 g
CHOLESTEROL 3 mg
SODIUM 160 mg
CARBOHYDRATES 47 g
  Fiber 2 g
  Sugars 4 g
PROTEIN 11 g
CALCIUM 102 mg
POTASSIUM 104 mg
DIETARY EXCHANGES
  3 starch
  ½ very lean meat

Spaghetti with Exotic Mushroom Sauce

Serves 4; 1 cup spaghetti and ½ cup sauce per serving

Use your own favorite exotic mushroom, whatever the produce market is featuring this week, or a mixture to jazz up spaghetti with marinara sauce.

1   tablespoon olive oil

1   cup sliced fresh exotic mushrooms, such as shiitake, cremini, or portobello, or a combination

⅓   cup chopped onion

1   medium garlic clove, minced

   14.5-ounce can no-salt-added diced tomatoes, undrained

   6-ounce can no-salt-added tomato paste

½   cup water

1   tablespoon sugar

1   bay leaf

¾   teaspoon chopped fresh basil leaves or ¼ teaspoon dried, crumbled

¾   teaspoon chopped fresh oregano, or ¼ teaspoon dried, crumbled

⅛   teaspoon pepper

⅛   teaspoon cayenne (optional)

8   ounces dried spaghetti

Heat a large nonstick skillet over medium-high heat. Add the oil and swirl to coat the bottom. Cook the mushrooms, onion, and garlic for 3 to 5 minutes, or until the onion is soft, stirring occasionally.

PER SERVING
CALORIES 318
TOTAL FAT 4.5 g
Saturated 0.5 g
Polyunsaturated 1 g
Monounsaturated 2.5 g
CHOLESTEROL 1 mg
SODIUM 58 mg
CARBOHYDRATES 61 g
Fiber 5 g
Sugars 13 g
PROTEIN 11 g
CALCIUM 64 mg
POTASSIUM 846 mg
DIETARY EXCHANGES
3 starch
3 vegetable
½ fat

Stir in the remaining ingredients except the spaghetti. Bring to a simmer. Lower the heat and simmer, covered, for 1 to 2 hours, stirring occasionally. If the sauce becomes too thick, stir in a small amount of water. Remove the bay leaf.

Prepare the spaghetti using the package directions, omitting the salt and oil. Drain well.

To serve, spoon the spaghetti onto plates. Top each serving with sauce.

Braised Lentil and Vegetable Medley

Serves 4; 1½ cups per serving

An earthy blend of lentils, brown rice, winter squash, and aromatic vegetables, this dish is easy to prepare on the stove or in a slow cooker.

	1¼-pound butternut squash
1	teaspoon olive oil
8	ounces cremini (brown) or button mushrooms, quartered
1	medium red bell pepper, thinly sliced
1	medium onion, thinly sliced
2	medium garlic cloves, minced
3½	cups Vegetable Broth (page 20) or commercial low-sodium vegetable broth
½	teaspoon dried oregano, crumbled
¼	teaspoon pepper
½	cup uncooked lentils, sorted for stones and shriveled lentils and rinsed
¾	cup uncooked instant brown rice

Using a vegetable peeler, peel the squash. Cut the squash in half lengthwise with a large, sharp knife. (Be careful; the squash is very hard and can slip.) Using a spoon, remove and discard the stringy fibers and seeds. Cut crosswise into ½-inch slices.

Heat a large saucepan over medium heat. Add the oil and swirl to coat the bottom. Cook the mushrooms, bell pepper, onion, and garlic for 3 to 4 minutes, or until the bell pepper is tender-crisp and the onion is soft, stirring occasionally.

Stir in the squash. Cook for 2 to 3 minutes, or until the squash is slightly golden brown on the edges.

Stir in the broth, oregano, and pepper. Increase the heat to medium-high and bring to a simmer, stirring occasionally.

Stir in the lentils. Reduce the heat and simmer, covered, for 30 to 35 minutes, or until the lentils and vegetables are tender, stirring once or twice.

Stir in the rice. Simmer, covered, for 10 minutes, or until the rice is tender.

Slow-Cooker Method

Put all the ingredients except the rice in a slow cooker. Cook on high for 2½ to 3½ hours or on low for 7½ to 9½ hours. Stir in the rice. Cook on either setting for 30 minutes, or until the lentils, vegetables, and rice are tender.

 You may substitute 4 cups of your favorite winter squash, such as acorn, golden acorn, buttercup, or hubbard, for the butternut squash. If you prefer to use zucchini or yellow summer squash, you'll need about 1 pound.

PER SERVING

CALORIES 263

TOTAL FAT 2 g
    Saturated 0 g
    Polyunsaturated 0.5 g
    Monounsaturated 1 g

CHOLESTEROL 0 mg

SODIUM 54 mg

CARBOHYDRATES 51 g
    Fiber 10 g
    Sugars 9 g

PROTEIN 14 g

CALCIUM 75 mg

POTASSIUM 716 mg

DIETARY EXCHANGES
    3 starch
    1 vegetable
    ½ very lean meat

Vegetarian Chili

Serves 7; 1¹/₂ cups per serving

When it's time to put logs in the fireplace, it's also time to fire up a big pot of this chili, flavored with lots of cumin and brightened with lemon juice.

Vegetable oil spray

2 teaspoons canola or corn oil

2 large onions, chopped

2 medium green bell peppers, chopped

2 medium garlic cloves, minced

2 cups water

1 cup no-salt-added canned diced tomatoes

1 cup uncooked bulgur

2 tablespoons ground cumin

1 tablespoon plus 1¹/₂ teaspoons Chili Powder (page 226) or commercial no-salt-added chili powder, or to taste

1 tablespoon fresh lemon juice

¹/₂ teaspoon pepper

¹/₄ teaspoon cayenne

2 16-ounce cans no-salt-added kidney beans, rinsed and drained

Lightly spray a large saucepan or Dutch oven with vegetable oil spray. Heat over medium-high heat. Add the oil and swirl to coat the bottom. Cook the onions, bell peppers, and garlic for 8 to 10 minutes, or until the bell peppers are soft, stirring frequently. Reduce the heat if necessary to prevent burning.

Stir in the remaining ingredients except the beans. Reduce the heat and simmer, covered, for 45 to 60 minutes, or until the bulgur is done and the flavors have blended.

Stir in the beans. Simmer, uncovered, for 10 minutes.

PER SERVING

CALORIES 238
TOTAL FAT 2.5 g
  Saturated 0 g
  Polyunsaturated 0.5 g
  Monounsaturated 1 g
CHOLESTEROL 0 mg
SODIUM 20 mg
CARBOHYDRATES 47 g
  Fiber 11 g
  Sugars 6 g
PROTEIN 12 g
CALCIUM 117 mg
POTASSIUM 815 mg
DIETARY EXCHANGES
  2¹/₂ starch
  2 vegetable
  ¹/₂ very lean meat

Zucchini Frittata

Serves 4; 1 wedge per serving

Bursting with Italian flavor, this frittata is equally at home at brunch or dinner.

Whites of 6 large eggs, or egg substitute equivalent to 3 eggs

4 drops yellow food coloring (optional)

Vegetable oil spray

1 medium zucchini, diced

3 medium green onions, sliced

14.5-ounce can no-salt-added tomatoes, drained

2 medium garlic cloves, minced

½ teaspoon salt-free Italian seasoning

¼ teaspoon pepper

2 ounces shredded part-skim mozzarella cheese

1 tablespoon shredded or grated Parmesan cheese

Preheat the oven to 350°F.

In a small bowl, whisk together the egg whites and food coloring. Set aside.

Lightly spray a large nonstick skillet with an ovenproof handle with vegetable oil spray. Heat over medium heat. Cook the zucchini for about 6 minutes, or until soft, stirring occasionally.

Stir in the green onions. Cook for 1 minute.

Stir in the tomatoes, garlic, Italian seasoning, and pepper. Cook for 5 minutes, or until the vegetables are tender and the mixture has slightly thickened, stirring frequently.

Stir in the egg whites.

Sprinkle with the mozzarella.

Bake for 12 minutes, or until a toothpick inserted in the center comes out clean. Leaving the pan in the oven, change the setting to broil. Broil for 3 to 4 minutes, or until golden brown. Sprinkle with the Parmesan.

PER SERVING
CALORIES 105
TOTAL FAT 3 g
 Saturated 1.5 g
 Polyunsaturated 0 g
 Monounsaturated 1 g
CHOLESTEROL 10 mg
SODIUM 211 mg
CARBOHYDRATES 9 g
 Fiber 2 g
 Sugars 5 g
PROTEIN 11 g
CALCIUM 171 mg
POTASSIUM 517 mg
DIETARY EXCHANGES
 2 vegetable
 1 lean meat

Mexican Omelet for Two

Serves 2; 1/2 omelet per serving

These veggie-packed omelets start the day right, especially with a splash of lime to wake up the flavor.

   Vegetable oil spray
3/4   medium green bell pepper, chopped
1/2   cup chopped yellow summer squash
 2   ounces button mushrooms, sliced
   Egg substitute equivalent to 3 eggs, or whites of 6 large eggs
 3   tablespoons fat-free milk
 2   medium green onions, finely chopped
1 1/2   teaspoons low-sodium Worcestershire sauce
 2   tablespoons picante sauce
 1   to 2 tablespoons snipped fresh cilantro
 2   tablespoons fat-free or light sour cream
 2   tablespoons shredded fat-free or reduced-fat sharp Cheddar cheese
1/2   medium lime, cut in half (optional)

Heat a 12-inch nonstick skillet over medium-high heat. Remove from the heat and lightly spray with vegetable oil spray (being careful not to spray near a gas flame). Put the bell pepper, squash, and mushrooms in the skillet. Lightly spray the vegetables with vegetable oil spray. Cook for 4 minutes, or until the bell pepper is just tender-crisp, stirring frequently. Transfer to a plate. Cover with aluminum foil to keep warm. Set aside.

In a small bowl, beat the egg substitute and milk together with a fork. Stir in the green onions.

Wipe the skillet with paper towels. Lightly spray the skillet with vegetable oil spray. Heat over medium heat. Pour in the egg substitute mixture. Swirl to cover the bottom of the skillet. Cook for 2 minutes without stirring. Using a rubber scraper, gently spread the uncooked part of the moist omelet to the edge. Cook for 1 to 2 minutes, or until no longer moist.

Spoon the bell pepper mixture over one half of the omelet. Remove from the heat. Pour the Worcestershire sauce over the vegetables. Fold the other half of the omelet over the vegetables. Cut in half crosswise.

To serve, transfer the omelet halves to dinner plates. Spoon the picante sauce over each serving. Sprinkle with the cilantro. Top with the sour cream. Sprinkle the Cheddar around the edge. Squeeze the lime over the omelets.

 To serve 4, double the recipe. Cook in two batches.

PER SERVING
CALORIES 116
TOTAL FAT 0 g
    Saturated 0 g
    Polyunsaturated 0 g
    Monounsaturated 0 g
CHOLESTEROL 4 mg
SODIUM 356 mg
CARBOHYDRATES 13 g
    Fiber 2 g
    Sugars 8 g
PROTEIN 15 g
CALCIUM 152 mg
POTASSIUM 525 mg
DIETARY EXCHANGES
    ½ other carbohydrate
    1 vegetable
    2 very lean meat

Asian Vegetable and Tofu Stir-Fry

Serves 4; 1 cup vegetable and tofu mixture and 1/2 cup rice per serving

Colorful and quick, this stir-fry is tossed in hoisin sauce and toasted sesame oil, then served over brown rice and garnished with chopped nuts.

1/4 cup Vegetable Broth (page 20) or commercial low-sodium vegetable broth

2 tablespoons hoisin sauce

1 tablespoon light soy sauce

2 teaspoons cornstarch

1 teaspoon toasted sesame oil

1 cup uncooked instant brown rice

1 teaspoon canola or corn oil

2 medium garlic cloves, minced

   12.3-ounce package extra-firm light tofu, cut into 1/2-inch cubes

4 ounces sugar snap peas, trimmed (about 1 cup)

4 medium stalks bok choy (green and white parts), cut into 1/2-inch slices

1/2 cup canned baby corn, rinsed and drained

1/4 cup canned sliced water chestnuts, rinsed and drained

2 tablespoons chopped peanuts, other nuts, or sesame seeds

In a small bowl, whisk together the broth, hoisin sauce, soy sauce, cornstarch, and sesame oil until the cornstarch is dissolved. Set aside.

Prepare the rice using the package directions, omitting the salt and margarine.

Meanwhile, heat a wok or large saucepan over medium-high heat. Add the canola oil and swirl to coat the bottom. Cook the garlic for 15 to 20 seconds, or until soft, stirring occasionally and watching carefully so it doesn't burn.

Stir in the tofu. Cook for 3 to 4 minutes, or until light golden brown and warmed through, stirring constantly.

Stir in the sugar snap peas, bok choy, baby corn, and water chestnuts. Cook for 2 to 3 minutes, or until the vegetables are tender-crisp and the mixture is warmed through, stirring constantly.

Make a well in the center. Pour in the reserved sauce mixture. Bring to a simmer over medium-high heat, stirring constantly until thickened, 2 to 3 minutes. Stir the sauce into the vegetable mixture.

To serve, spoon the rice onto each plate. Spoon the vegetable mixture on top. Sprinkle with the peanuts.

PER SERVING
CALORIES 215
TOTAL FAT 6 g
    Saturated 0.5 g
    Polyunsaturated 2 g
    Monounsaturated 2.5 g
CHOLESTEROL 0 mg
SODIUM 320 mg
CARBOHYDRATES 29 g
    Fiber 5 g
    Sugars 4 g
PROTEIN 11 g
CALCIUM 82 mg
POTASSIUM 190 mg
DIETARY EXCHANGES
    2 starch
    1 lean meat

Polenta and Cheese
with Fresh Mushrooms

Serves 8; 4¼ × 3¼-inch piece per serving

Decorate your dinner plate with rosemary sprigs to give a fresh look to this fancy polenta.

Vegetable oil spray (butter flavor preferred)

1¾ cups chopped mixed fresh mushrooms, such as chanterelles and oyster

5 cups Vegetable Broth (page 20) or commercial low-sodium vegetable broth

1½ cups cornmeal (100% stone-ground preferred)

¼ cup plus 1 tablespoon shredded or grated Parmesan cheese

1 tablespoon olive oil (light preferred)

1 to 1½ teaspoons chopped fresh rosemary leaves

3 tablespoons shredded or grated Parmesan cheese

Fresh rosemary sprigs (optional)

Preheat the oven to 375°F. Spray a 13 × 9 × 2-inch baking dish with vegetable oil spray.

Spray a large nonstick skillet with vegetable oil spray. Cook the mushrooms over medium heat for 5 minutes, or until cooked through, stirring occasionally. Set aside.

In a medium saucepan, bring the broth to a boil over medium heat.

Slowly add the cornmeal, stirring constantly with a wooden spoon. Cook for 20 to 25 minutes, or until thickened and beginning to pull away from the side of the pan, stirring constantly. Remove from the heat.

Stir in the mushrooms, ¼ cup plus 1 tablespoon Parmesan cheese, olive oil, and chopped rosemary. Pour into the baking dish, smoothing the top.

Sprinkle with the remaining Parmesan.

Bake for 20 minutes, or until firm to the touch.

Let cool for 5 to 6 minutes. Cut into eight 4¼ × 3¼-inch pieces or use cookie cutters to cut into your favorite shapes. Garnish with rosemary sprigs.

Spicy Polenta

Using plastic gloves, cut two fresh jalapeños in half lengthwise. Discard the stems, ribs, and seeds. Finely chop the peppers and add with the mushrooms. Substitute Chicken Broth (page 19) or commercial fat-free, low-sodium chicken broth for the Vegetable Broth. Add the yolk of 1 large egg, slightly beaten, when stirring in the olive oil.

If you're having trouble cutting the polenta into shapes, it may have cooled too much. Just reheat it briefly in a microwave oven on 100 percent power (high) for about 3 minutes.

Substitute dried mushrooms that have been reconstituted for fresh mushrooms. A 0.35-ounce package of chanterelles and a 1-ounce package of oyster mushrooms make a great combination. Reconstitute the mushrooms by soaking them in hot water for 20 to 30 minutes. Remove the mushrooms. Strain the soaking liquid in a strainer lined with cheesecloth or in a coffee filter. Use the soaking broth as part of the broth used for cooking the cornmeal.

POLENTA AND CHEESE	SPICY POLENTA
PER SERVING	**PER SERVING**
CALORIES 141	**CALORIES** 145
TOTAL FAT 3.5 g	**TOTAL FAT** 4 g
Saturated 1 g	Saturated 1.5 g
Polyunsaturated 0.5 g	Polyunsaturated 0.5 g
Monounsaturated 2 g	Monounsaturated 2 g
CHOLESTEROL 4 mg	**CHOLESTEROL** 29 mg
SODIUM 116 mg	**SODIUM** 103 mg
CARBOHYDRATES 23 g	**CARBOHYDRATES** 23 g
Fiber 2 g	Fiber 2 g
Sugars 1 g	Sugars 1 g
PROTEIN 6 g	**PROTEIN** 6 g
CALCIUM 69 mg	**CALCIUM** 71 mg
POTASSIUM 131 mg	**POTASSIUM** 169 mg
DIETARY EXCHANGES	**DIETARY EXCHANGES**
1½ starch	1½ starch
½ lean meat	½ lean meat

Gorgonzola Portobello Rounds

Serves 4; 1 stuffed mushroom per serving

Pile fresh spinach leaves, Italian-seasoned vegetables, and Gorgonzola cheese on giant mushrooms, then bake the mixture for a creamy, exotic vegetarian entrée.

4   portobello mushroom caps (about 5 inches wide), stems discarded
    Vegetable oil spray
2   teaspoons olive oil
2   medium red bell peppers, chopped
1   medium red onion, chopped
2   medium garlic cloves, minced
½   teaspoon crushed red pepper flakes
½   cup chopped Italian plum tomatoes
1   tablespoon chopped fresh basil leaves or 1 teaspoon dried, crumbled
1   ounce fresh spinach leaves (about ¾ cup), unrinsed, stems discarded
¼   cup plus 1 tablespoon crumbled Gorgonzola or other blue cheese

Preheat the oven to 350°F.

Lightly spray both sides of the mushrooms with vegetable oil spray. Place with the cap side down on a baking sheet. Brush the oil over the mushrooms.

Bake for 10 to 12 minutes, or until tender when pierced with a fork.

Meanwhile, lightly spray a large nonstick skillet with vegetable oil spray. Heat over medium-high heat. Cook the bell peppers, onion, garlic, and red pepper flakes for 5 minutes, or until the bell peppers are soft, stirring frequently. Remove the skillet from the heat.

Stir in the tomatoes and basil.

Meanwhile, rinse the spinach leaves and shake off the excess water. Don't dry the spinach. Place the spinach on the mushrooms.

Spoon the bell pepper mixture over the spinach. Sprinkle with the Gorgonzola.

Bake for 6 to 7 minutes, or until the cheese begins to melt.

Pizza Portobellos

Substitute ½ cup Spaghetti Sauce (page 214) or bottled low-salt pizza sauce for the spinach. Substitute shredded part-skim mozzarella cheese for the Gorgonzola. Sprinkle each serving with 1 teaspoon shredded or grated Parmesan cheese at serving time.

Portobello Mushrooms

Brushing a small amount of oil on portobello mushrooms before baking or broiling them prevents them from getting a leathery texture.

GORGONZOLA PORTOBELLO ROUNDS
PER SERVING
CALORIES 110
TOTAL FAT 6 g
  Saturated 2.5 g
  Polyunsaturated 0.5 g
  Monounsaturated 2.5 g
CHOLESTEROL 8 mg
SODIUM 159 mg
CARBOHYDRATES 12 g
  Fiber 3 g
  Sugars 6 g
PROTEIN 5 g
CALCIUM 86 mg
POTASSIUM 528 mg
DIETARY EXCHANGES
  2½ vegetable
  1 fat

PIZZA PORTOBELLOS
PER SERVING
CALORIES 111
TOTAL FAT 4.5 g
  Saturated 1.5 g
  Polyunsaturated 0.5 g
  Monounsaturated 2 g
CHOLESTEROL 7 mg
SODIUM 187 mg
CARBOHYDRATES 14 g
  Fiber 4 g
  Sugars 8 g
PROTEIN 6 g
CALCIUM 113 mg
POTASSIUM 471 mg
DIETARY EXCHANGES
  3 vegetable
  1 fat

Cheese-Topped Stuffed Eggplant

Serves 4; 1 eggplant half and 1 cup filling per serving

Mild yet rich-tasting, this easy-to-make dish gets a lot of Mediterranean flavor from the Greek seasoning blend and mozzarella and Parmesan cheeses.

       Vegetable oil spray
2   medium eggplants (about 1 pound each)
1   medium green bell pepper, finely chopped
1   large onion, finely chopped
½   cup water
1   tablespoon dried Greek seasoning blend
8   fat-free, low-sodium saltine crackers, crushed
       8-ounce can no-salt-added tomato sauce
¼   cup snipped fresh parsley
⅛   teaspoon crushed red pepper flakes
4   ounces shredded fat-free or part-skim mozzarella cheese
1   tablespoon plus 1 teaspoon shredded or grated Parmesan cheese

Preheat the oven to 350°F. Lightly spray a 13 × 9 × 2-inch baking pan with vegetable oil spray.

Trim the eggplants. Cut in half lengthwise. Scoop out the centers, leaving a ¼-inch rim. Chop the eggplant pulp. Set aside the pulp and the shells.

Heat a Dutch oven over medium-high heat. Remove from the heat and lightly spray with vegetable oil spray (being careful not to spray near a gas flame). Cook the bell pepper and onion for 4 minutes, or until the onion is soft.

Stir in the chopped eggplant, water, and seasoning blend. Reduce the heat to medium. Cook, covered, for 4 to 5 minutes, or until the eggplant is tender.

Stir in the cracker crumbs, tomato sauce, parsley, and red pepper flakes. Spoon the mixture into the eggplant shells. Place the shells in the baking pan. Sprinkle with the mozzarella.

Bake for 20 minutes, or until the mozzarella has melted and the shells are tender when pierced with a fork.

Remove from the oven. Sprinkle with the Parmesan.

Cook's TIP

If you prefer, you can bake the eggplant mixture in 10-ounce baking cups instead of the shells of the eggplant. For convenience in transporting the baking cups, you may want to place them in a baking pan.

PER SERVING
CALORIES 205
TOTAL FAT 5.5 g
   Saturated 3.5 g
   Polyunsaturated 0.5 g
   Monounsaturated 1.5 g
CHOLESTEROL 19 mg
SODIUM 316 mg
CARBOHYDRATES 29 g
   Fiber 10 g
   Sugars 12 g
PROTEIN 12 g
CALCIUM 295 mg
POTASSIUM 923 mg
DIETARY EXCHANGES
   ½ starch
   5 vegetable
   1 very lean meat

Crustless Garden Quiche

Serves 6; 1 wedge per serving

For a rainy-night supper, serve this "sunshine on a plate."

Vegetable oil spray

8 ounces button mushrooms, sliced

1 medium red bell pepper, thinly sliced

Egg substitute equivalent to 6 eggs

¼ cup fat-free evaporated milk

1 tablespoon Dijon mustard

½ teaspoon low-sodium Worcestershire sauce

¼ teaspoon cayenne

¼ cup shredded reduced-fat sharp Cheddar cheese

10 ounces frozen broccoli and cauliflower, thawed and drained on paper towels

¼ cup snipped fresh parsley

¾ cup shredded reduced-fat sharp Cheddar cheese, divided use

Preheat the oven to 350°F. Spray a 9-inch deep-dish glass pie pan with vegetable oil spray.

Lightly spray a large nonstick skillet with vegetable oil spray. Heat over medium-high heat. Cook the mushrooms for 6 minutes, or until they begin to brown slightly, stirring frequently.

Stir in the bell pepper. Cook for 2 minutes, stirring frequently. Set aside.

In a medium bowl, whisk together the egg substitute, milk, mustard, Worcestershire sauce, cayenne, and ¼ cup Cheddar.

Spread the mushroom mixture in the pie pan. Top with the broccoli and cauliflower, parsley, and ¼ cup Cheddar. Pour the egg mixture over all.

Bake for 30 minutes (the quiche won't be quite set). Sprinkle with the remaining Cheddar. Bake for 5 minutes. Let stand for 5 minutes to absorb liquids.

PER SERVING

CALORIES 121

TOTAL FAT 4 g
  Saturated 2.5 g
  Polyunsaturated 0 g
  Monounsaturated 0.5 g

CHOLESTEROL 10 mg

SODIUM 323 mg

CARBOHYDRATES 7 g
  Fiber 2 g
  Sugars 5 g

PROTEIN 15 g

CALCIUM 244 mg

POTASSIUM 370 mg

DIETARY EXCHANGES
  1½ vegetable
  2 lean meat

Tangy Roasted Asparagus

Baked Beans

Carrot Mash

Green Beans and Corn
SUCCOTASH

Balsamic Beets and Walnuts

Broccoli Pancakes
ZUCCHINI PANCAKES

Thyme-Flavored Cauliflower

Eggplant Mexicana

Vegetables and Side Dishes

- Roasted Red Peppers and Portobello Mushrooms
- Scalloped Potatoes
- Potato Pancakes
- Zesty Oven-Fried Potatoes
- Parmesan-Lemon Spinach
- Sweet Potato Casserole
- Asian Fried Rice with Peas
- Rice and Vegetable Pilaf
- Dilled Summer Squash
- Baked Tomatoes
- Baked Italian Vegetable Mélange

Tangy Roasted Asparagus

Serves 4; 5 spears per serving

Just a tip of Worcestershire is all it takes to give zing to this side dish.

Vegetable oil spray

1 pound asparagus spears (about 20), trimmed and patted dry with paper towels

1 tablespoon light tub margarine

1 teaspoon fresh lemon juice

½ teaspoon low-sodium Worcestershire sauce

¼ teaspoon salt

Preheat the oven to 425°F.

Line a baking sheet with aluminum foil. Lightly spray with vegetable oil spray. Place the asparagus in a single layer on the baking sheet. Lightly spray with vegetable oil spray.

Bake for 10 minutes, or until just tender and beginning to brown lightly on the tips.

In a small saucepan, combine the remaining ingredients. Cook over medium heat for 1 minute, or just until the margarine melts. Stir. Drizzle over the asparagus. Gently roll the asparagus back and forth to coat.

 Cook's TIP

Be sure to pat the asparagus spears dry before placing them on the baking sheet. Otherwise they won't roast, and the taste of the dish will be altered.

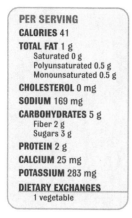

PER SERVING

CALORIES 41
TOTAL FAT 1 g
    Saturated 0 g
    Polyunsaturated 0.5 g
    Monounsaturated 0.5 g
CHOLESTEROL 0 mg
SODIUM 169 mg
CARBOHYDRATES 5 g
    Fiber 2 g
    Sugars 3 g
PROTEIN 2 g
CALCIUM 25 mg
POTASSIUM 283 mg
DIETARY EXCHANGES
    1 vegetable

Baked Beans

Serves 6; ½ cup per serving

No potluck meal or barbecue is complete without baked beans. These cook for a long time but need very little attention. The result is well worth the wait.

½ pound dried navy beans, sorted for stones and shriveled beans and rinsed (about 1 cup)

4 cups water

   Vegetable oil spray

   4-ounce loin-end pork chop, all visible fat discarded

1 cup Chili Sauce (page 218) or 1 cup no-salt-added ketchup plus dash of red hot-pepper sauce

1 cup water

1 medium onion, chopped

2 tablespoons light molasses

1 tablespoon light brown sugar

1½ teaspoons dry mustard

¼ teaspoon garlic powder

In a Dutch oven, bring the beans and water to a boil over high heat. Boil for 2 minutes. Remove from the heat and let stand for 1 hour. Return to the heat and bring to a simmer over high heat. Reduce the heat and simmer, covered, for 1 hour, or until tender. Rinse and drain well.

Preheat the oven to 350°F. Lightly spray a 1½-quart casserole dish with vegetable oil spray. Put the beans in the casserole.

In a small nonstick skillet, brown the pork chop over medium-high heat for 2 to 3 minutes on each side. Cut into small cubes.

Stir the pork and the remaining ingredients into the beans.

Bake, covered, for 4 hours, or until tender. If the beans begin to dry out, add water about ¼ cup at a time.

PER SERVING
CALORIES 244
TOTAL FAT 3 g
   Saturated 0.5 g
   Polyunsaturated 0.5 g
   Monounsaturated 1 g
CHOLESTEROL 10 mg
SODIUM 38 mg
CARBOHYDRATES 44 g
   Fiber 11 g
   Sugars 20 g
PROTEIN 13 g
CALCIUM 105 mg
POTASSIUM 432 mg
DIETARY EXCHANGES
   3 starch
   1 very lean meat

Carrot Mash

Serves 4; ½ cup per serving

Be sure to use regular-size carrots for the proper sweetness and moisture in this delicate, lighter substitute for mashed sweet potatoes.

1   pound carrots, cut crosswise into ½-inch slices

⅓   cup fat-free half-and-half

3   tablespoons firmly packed dark brown sugar

2   tablespoons light tub margarine

½   teaspoon vanilla, butter, and nut flavoring or vanilla extract

1   tablespoon pecan chips, dry roasted (optional)

Steam the carrots for 15 minutes, or until very tender.

In a food processor or blender, process all the ingredients except the pecans until smooth, scraping the bottom and side occasionally.

To serve, spoon the carrot mixture into a shallow bowl. Sprinkle with the pecans.

Pecan Chips

Pecan chips are cut smaller than pecan pieces or chopped pecans, so they help carry the crunch and flavor a longer way.

WITH PECANS

PER SERVING

CALORIES 133

TOTAL FAT 4 g
 Saturated 0 g
 Polyunsaturated 1 g
 Monounsaturated 2 g

CHOLESTEROL 0 mg

SODIUM 147 mg

CARBOHYDRATES 24 g
 Fiber 3 g
 Sugars 17 g

PROTEIN 3 g

CALCIUM 74 mg

POTASSIUM 407 mg

DIETARY EXCHANGES
 1 other carbohydrate
 2 vegetable
 1 fat

Green Beans and Corn

Serves 4; ¹/₂ cup per serving

This pairing of two all-time favorite vegetables is simple but colorful.

¹/₂ cup water

1 cup sliced fresh green beans or frozen French-style green beans

1 cup fresh or frozen whole-kernel corn

1 teaspoon light stick margarine

3 tablespoons chopped onion

¹/₂ teaspoon dried basil, crumbled

¹/₂ teaspoon fresh lemon juice

Dash of pepper

In a medium saucepan, bring the water to a boil over high heat. Stir in the beans and corn. Reduce the heat and simmer, covered, until the beans are just tender, 5 to 8 minutes. Drain well.

In the same saucepan, melt the margarine over medium heat. Cook the onion for 3 to 4 minutes, or until soft.

Return the green beans and corn to the pan. Stir in the remaining ingredients.

Succotash

Substitute fresh or frozen lima beans for the green beans. Simmer for 15 to 20 minutes. Substitute crumbled dried marjoram for the basil.

GREEN BEANS AND CORN	SUCCOTASH
PER SERVING	PER SERVING
CALORIES 49	CALORIES 104
TOTAL FAT 1 g	TOTAL FAT 1 g
Saturated 0 g	Saturated 0 g
Polyunsaturated 0.5 g	Polyunsaturated 0.5 g
Monounsaturated 0.5 g	Monounsaturated 0.5 g
CHOLESTEROL 0 mg	CHOLESTEROL 0 mg
SODIUM 12 mg	SODIUM 69 mg
CARBOHYDRATES 10 g	CARBOHYDRATES 20 g
Fiber 2 g	Fiber 4 g
Sugars 2 g	Sugars 3 g
PROTEIN 2 g	PROTEIN 5 g
CALCIUM 20 mg	CALCIUM 23 mg
POTASSIUM 189 mg	POTASSIUM 358 mg
DIETARY EXCHANGES	DIETARY EXCHANGES
¹/₂ starch	1¹/₂ starch

Balsamic Beets and Walnuts

Serves 6; ½ cup per serving

Dazzle your dinner guests with garnet-colored beets topped with a reduction of balsamic vinegar and brown sugar, then sprinkled with cinnamon-sugar walnuts. This dish is a great complement to dishes such as roasted pork tenderloin and grilled turkey.

2 15-ounce cans no-salt-added sliced beets, drained
2 tablespoons water
½ cup balsamic vinegar
1 tablespoon light brown sugar
   Vegetable oil spray
¼ cup walnut halves
¼ teaspoon ground cinnamon
⅛ teaspoon ground nutmeg
1 teaspoon light brown sugar

In a medium microwaveable bowl, combine the beets and water. Microwave, covered, on 100 percent power (high) for 2 to 3 minutes, or until the beets are warmed through. Keep covered and set aside.

In a small saucepan, stir together the vinegar and 1 tablespoon brown sugar. Bring to a simmer over medium-high heat, stirring constantly until the sugar is dissolved. Simmer for 6 to 8 minutes, or until the mixture is reduced by half (to about ¼ cup), without stirring. Remove from the heat and set aside.

Heat a small nonstick skillet over medium-low heat. Remove from the heat and lightly spray with vegetable oil spray (being careful not to spray near a gas flame). Put the walnuts, cinnamon, and nutmeg in the skillet. Stir together. Dry-roast for 2 to 3 minutes, or until the walnuts are lightly toasted, stirring occasionally. Stir in the remaining brown sugar. Dry-roast for 1 to 2 minutes, or until the mixture is warmed through (the sugar will still be somewhat granulated).

To serve, drain the beets. Transfer to a serving bowl. Drizzle with the balsamic reduction. Sprinkle with the walnuts.

Cook's TIP

If using fresh beets, cut off all but 1 to 2 inches of stems from 2 pounds of beets. Simmer the beets in 2 quarts of boiling water, covered, for 40 to 50 minutes, or until tender. Drain the beets and let cool for about 5 minutes, or until cool enough to handle. Slip the skins off. Slice the beets into ¼-inch slices. Cover to keep warm.

PER SERVING

CALORIES 91
TOTAL FAT 3 g
   Saturated 0.5 g
   Polyunsaturated 2 g
   Monounsaturated 0.5 g
CHOLESTEROL 0 mg
SODIUM 63 mg
CARBOHYDRATES 16 g
   Fiber 2 g
   Sugars 12 g
PROTEIN 2 g
CALCIUM 11 mg
POTASSIUM 44 mg
DIETARY EXCHANGES
   1½ vegetable
   ½ other carbohydrate
   ½ fat

Broccoli Pancakes

Topped with a dollop of fat-free sour cream, these veggie pancakes make either a great side dish with meat, poultry, or seafood or a terrific vegetarian entrée. Or see the Cook's Tip on page 195 for a miniature version to serve as an appetizer.

16 ounces frozen broccoli florets, chopped (about 4 cups)

8 or 9 medium green onions, chopped (green and white parts)

2 medium carrots, shredded

2 tablespoons finely snipped fresh cilantro

1 tablespoon dried dillweed, crumbled

2 teaspoons dried basil, crumbled

½ teaspoon salt

¼ teaspoon white pepper

   Egg substitute equivalent to 2½ eggs, or 1 large egg plus whites of 3 large eggs

½ cup fat-free milk

½ cup all-purpose flour

1¼ cups fat-free or light sour cream

In a large bowl, stir together the broccoli, green onions, carrots, cilantro, dillweed, basil, salt, and pepper.

In a medium bowl, whisk together the egg substitute, milk, and flour until smooth. Stir into the broccoli mixture.

Place a baking sheet in the oven. Preheat the oven to 300°F.

Heat a large nonstick skillet over medium heat. Working in batches, use a ¼-cup measuring cup to drop batter into the skillet. Using the bottom of a measuring cup, slightly flatten the pancakes. Cook for 7 to 10 minutes on each side, or until the pancakes are golden brown and cooked through. If the pancakes begin to burn, reduce the heat to medium low. Transfer the pancakes to the baking sheet in the oven to keep warm. Repeat until all the batter has been used.

To serve, top each pancake with 1 tablespoon sour cream.

Zucchini Pancakes

Substitute 4 cups shredded zucchini for the broccoli. Squeeze the excess liquid from the zucchini before combining the vegetables.

 Serve miniature versions of these pancakes as an appetizer. Simply drop by tablespoonfuls into the skillet, and proceed as directed. Top with a dab of sour cream and a bit of black olive or a dot of caviar.

BROCCOLI PANCAKES

PER SERVING

CALORIES 97

TOTAL FAT 0.5 g
   Saturated 0 g
   Polyunsaturated 0 g
   Monounsaturated 0 g

CHOLESTEROL 5 mg

SODIUM 204 mg

CARBOHYDRATES 17 g
   Fiber 3 g
   Sugars 5 g

PROTEIN 6 g

CALCIUM 104 mg

POTASSIUM 340 mg

DIETARY EXCHANGES
   ½ starch
   2 vegetable
   ½ very lean meat

ZUCCHINI PANCAKES

PER SERVING

CALORIES 93

TOTAL FAT 0 g
   Saturated 0 g
   Polyunsaturated 0 g
   Monounsaturated 0 g

CHOLESTEROL 5 mg

SODIUM 194 mg

CARBOHYDRATES 17 g
   Fiber 2 g
   Sugars 5 g

PROTEIN 5 g

CALCIUM 86 mg

POTASSIUM 373 mg

DIETARY EXCHANGES
   ½ starch
   2 vegetable
   ½ very lean meat

Thyme-Flavored Cauliflower

Serves 4; 1/2 cup per serving

Here's the answer to what to do with cauliflower besides covering it with cheese sauce. Serve with Hungarian Pork Chops (page 157) and cinnamon applesauce.

1 medium head cauliflower (about 1½ pounds) or 10-ounce package frozen cauliflower florets (about 2 cups)

2 tablespoons water

¾ to 1½ teaspoons cider vinegar

½ medium garlic clove, minced

¼ teaspoon dried thyme, crumbled

Dash of pepper

2 teaspoons canola or corn oil

2 teaspoons finely snipped fresh parsley or 1 teaspoon dried, crumbled

If using fresh cauliflower, break into small florets. In a medium saucepan, bring a small amount of water to a boil over high heat. Boil the cauliflower, covered, for 10 to 12 minutes, or until just tender. If using frozen cauliflower, prepare using the package directions, omitting the salt. Drain well.

Meanwhile, in a medium bowl, combine the 2 tablespoons water, vinegar, garlic, thyme, and pepper. Set aside.

Heat a large skillet over medium heat. Add the oil and swirl to coat the bottom. Cook the cauliflower for 2 minutes, stirring occasionally.

Stir in the vinegar mixture. Cook, covered, for 5 to 8 minutes, or until the cauliflower is tender.

To serve, sprinkle with the parsley.

PER SERVING
CALORIES 58
TOTAL FAT 2.5 g
    Saturated 0 g
    Polyunsaturated 1 g
    Monounsaturated 1.5 g
CHOLESTEROL 0 mg
SODIUM 44 mg
CARBOHYDRATES 8 g
    Fiber 4 g
    Sugars 4 g
PROTEIN 3 g
CALCIUM 34 mg
POTASSIUM 443 mg
DIETARY EXCHANGES
    1½ vegetable
    ½ fat

Eggplant Mexicana

Serves 8; 1/2 cup per serving

Want a tasty new way to get vegetables into your diet? Try this eggplant and tomato side dish, which gets a flavor burst from our Chili Powder and fresh cilantro.

1	medium eggplant (about 1 pound), peeled and cubed
4	medium tomatoes, peeled if desired and chopped, or 16-ounce can no-salt-added diced tomatoes
2	tablespoons chopped onion
1	medium garlic clove, minced
1/4	to 1/2 teaspoon Chili Powder (page 226) or commercial no-salt-added chili powder
1/4	teaspoon pepper
2	tablespoons snipped fresh cilantro or parsley

In a large nonstick skillet, stir together all the ingredients except the cilantro. Simmer, covered, for 15 to 20 minutes, or until the eggplant is tender.

Sprinkle with the cilantro.

PER SERVING
CALORIES 29
TOTAL FAT 0.5 g
  Saturated 0 g
  Polyunsaturated 0 g
  Monounsaturated 0 g
CHOLESTEROL 0 mg
SODIUM 5 mg
CARBOHYDRATES 7 g
  Fiber 1 g
  Sugars 2 g
PROTEIN 1 g
CALCIUM 15 mg
POTASSIUM 318 mg
DIETARY EXCHANGES
  1 1/2 vegetable

Roasted Red Peppers and Portobello Mushrooms

Serves 12; ½ cup per serving

Since you serve this unusual side dish at room temperature, it's perfect for a party buffet. It's also a terrific appetizer when served over crostini or low-sodium wheat crackers.

4   medium portobello mushrooms, stems discarded
    Vegetable oil spray (olive oil spray preferred)
1½ cups bottled roasted red bell peppers, rinsed and drained
¼   cup plain rice vinegar
2   teaspoons sugar, or to taste

Spray the mushrooms with vegetable oil spray. Spray a large grill pan (specially designed pan with raised ridges for indoor grilling on stovetop) or grill rack with vegetable oil spray. Heat the pan for several minutes over medium-high heat, or preheat the grill on medium high.

Grill the mushrooms for about 30 minutes, or until meaty and juicy. (Cooking time will vary depending on the size of the mushrooms. If you cook them too long, they will dry out.) Slice the mushrooms to the desired thickness.

Meanwhile, slice the roasted peppers to the desired thickness. Put in a large bowl.

Stir the mushrooms into the roasted peppers.

In a small bowl, whisk together the vinegar and sugar until the sugar is dissolved. Pour over the vegetables. Stir gently. Serve at room temperature.

PER SERVING

CALORIES 10
TOTAL FAT 0 g
    Saturated 0 g
    Polyunsaturated 0 g
    Monounsaturated 0 g
CHOLESTEROL 0 mg
SODIUM 29 mg
CARBOHYDRATES 2 g
    Fiber 0 g
    Sugars 1 g
PROTEIN 0 g
CALCIUM 1 mg
POTASSIUM 71 mg
DIETARY EXCHANGES
    Free

Scalloped Potatoes

Serves 8; ½ cup per serving

You'll attract an audience when you take these yummy potatoes out of the oven. The star of the meal, they go well with almost anything. Try them with Oven-Fried Chicken (page 100) and zucchini or with grilled flank steak and Dilled Summer Squash (page 206).

Vegetable oil spray

1   cup fat-free milk

3   tablespoons all-purpose flour

1   cup Chicken Broth (page 19) or commercial fat-free, low-sodium chicken broth

¼   teaspoon pepper

¼   teaspoon onion powder

¼   teaspoon garlic powder

3   tablespoons shredded or grated Parmesan cheese

4   large potatoes, peeled and thinly sliced (about 4 cups)

½   cup chopped onion

½   cup low-fat shredded Cheddar cheese

⅛   teaspoon paprika

Preheat the oven to 350°F. Lightly spray a 1½-quart casserole dish with vegetable oil spray.

In a medium saucepan, whisk together the milk and flour. Whisk in the broth, pepper, onion powder, and garlic powder. Cook over medium-high heat for 5 to 6 minutes, or until thickened, whisking occasionally.

Whisk in the Parmesan. Remove from the heat.

PER SERVING
CALORIES 105
TOTAL FAT 1 g
Saturated 0.5 g
Polyunsaturated 0 g
Monounsaturated 0.5 g
CHOLESTEROL 3 mg
SODIUM 96 mg
CARBOHYDRATES 18 g
Fiber 2 g
Sugars 3 g
PROTEIN 6 g
CALCIUM 104 mg
POTASSIUM 403 mg
DIETARY EXCHANGES
1 starch
½ very lean meat

To assemble, put the potatoes in the casserole dish. Top with the onion. Gently stir in the sauce.

Bake, covered, for 30 minutes. Gently stir in the Cheddar. Sprinkle with the paprika. Bake, uncovered, for 30 to 40 minutes, or until the potatoes are tender and lightly browned.

Potato Pancakes

Serves 4; 2 pancakes per serving

Try these pancakes for a holiday brunch or a winter supper.

2   cups frozen fat-free shredded potatoes, thawed, or 2 medium potatoes (Idaho or russet preferred)

4   cups water (for fresh potatoes)

1   teaspoon vinegar (for fresh potatoes)

Whites of 2 large eggs

¼   cup all-purpose flour

2   tablespoons finely chopped onion

¾   teaspoon baking powder

¼   teaspoon onion powder

¼   teaspoon garlic powder

⅛   teaspoon pepper

Vegetable oil spray

2   teaspoons olive oil, divided use

For frozen potatoes, drain and put in a medium bowl. For fresh potatoes, stir together the water and vinegar in a medium bowl (to help keep the potatoes from turning brown). Shred the potatoes and put into the water mixture. Let stand for 2 to 3 minutes; drain well. Spread on four layers of paper towels. Cover with two or three layers of paper towels and pat dry. Dry the bowl and return the potatoes to the bowl.

Stir in the egg whites, flour, onion, baking powder, onion powder, garlic powder, and pepper.

Lightly spray a large nonstick skillet with vegetable oil spray. Heat over medium heat. Add 1 teaspoon oil and swirl to coat the bottom. Pour in the batter for 4 pancakes, ¼ cup each, spreading slightly with the back of a spoon. Cook for 3 to 4 minutes, or until golden brown on the bottom. Remove from the heat and lightly spray the tops of the pancakes with vegetable oil spray. Turn the pancakes over. Cook for 3 to 4 minutes, or until golden brown. Transfer to a plate. Cover with aluminum foil to keep warm. Repeat.

PER SERVING
CALORIES 141
TOTAL FAT 2.5 g
    Saturated 0.5 g
    Polyunsaturated 0.5 g
    Monounsaturated 1.5 g
CHOLESTEROL 0 mg
SODIUM 126 mg
CARBOHYDRATES 25 g
    Fiber 2 g
    Sugars 1 g
PROTEIN 5 g
CALCIUM 60 mg
POTASSIUM 346 mg
DIETARY EXCHANGES
    1½ starch
    ½ fat

Zesty Oven-Fried Potatoes

Serves 6; 1/2 cup per serving

This is finger food at its finest! Have everyone over for a meal of these oven-fries, Cajun Snapper (page 80), and Garden Coleslaw (page 41).

Vegetable oil spray
1½ pounds medium red potatoes (4 to 5)
  1 tablespoon olive oil
  ½ to ¾ teaspoon Creole Seasoning (page 227) or commercial salt-free spicy seasoning blend
  ½ teaspoon pepper
  2 tablespoons malt vinegar

Preheat the oven to 400°F. Lightly spray a large baking sheet with vegetable oil spray.

Cut each potato lengthwise into 6 wedges. Place in a single layer on the baking sheet.

In a small bowl, stir together the oil, Creole Seasoning, and pepper. Drizzle over the potatoes. Stir to coat.

Bake for 30 minutes, or until the potatoes are golden and tender.

Sprinkle with the vinegar.

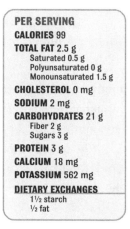

PER SERVING
CALORIES 99
TOTAL FAT 2.5 g
    Saturated 0.5 g
    Polyunsaturated 0 g
    Monounsaturated 1.5 g
CHOLESTEROL 0 mg
SODIUM 2 mg
CARBOHYDRATES 21 g
    Fiber 2 g
    Sugars 3 g
PROTEIN 3 g
CALCIUM 18 mg
POTASSIUM 562 mg
DIETARY EXCHANGES
    1½ starch
    ½ fat

Parmesan-Lemon Spinach

Serves 4; 1/2 cup per serving

A light cream sauce enhanced with Parmesan cheese coats fresh spinach in this side dish. Try it with pork chops, fish fillets, or turkey cutlets.

- 1/2   cup fat-free half-and-half
- 2   tablespoons shredded or grated Parmesan cheese
- 1   tablespoon plus 1 1/2 teaspoons all-purpose flour
- 1   teaspoon olive oil
- 2   medium shallots, finely chopped
- 1/4   cup Chicken Broth (page 19) or commercial fat-free, low-sodium chicken broth
- 1   teaspoon grated lemon zest
- 1/2   teaspoon salt-free all-purpose seasoning blend, such as Herb Seasoning (page 223) or Savory Herb Blend (page 225)
- 1/8   teaspoon cayenne (optional)
- 8   ounces fresh spinach leaves (about 8 cups)

In a medium bowl, whisk together the half-and-half, Parmesan, and flour until smooth. Set aside.

Heat a large nonstick skillet over medium heat. Add the oil and swirl to coat the bottom. Cook the shallots for 2 to 3 minutes, or until tender-crisp, stirring occasionally.

Stir in the broth, lemon zest, seasoning blend, and cayenne. Cook for 1 minute, or until the mixture is warmed through, stirring occasionally.

Add the spinach. Toss with two spoons to lightly coat with the broth mixture. Bring to a simmer, covered, over medium-high heat. Lower the heat and simmer for 2 to 3 minutes, or until the spinach is slightly wilted. Stir. Increase the heat to medium-high. Cook for 1 to 2 minutes, or until the spinach is completely wilted and tender, stirring occasionally.

Stir the reserved half-and-half mixture into the spinach mixture. Simmer for 2 to 3 minutes, or until thickened, stirring occasionally.

PER SERVING

CALORIES 71
TOTAL FAT 2 g
    Saturated 0.5 g
    Polyunsaturated 0 g
    Monounsaturated 1 g
CHOLESTEROL 2 mg
SODIUM 120 mg
CARBOHYDRATES 10 g
    Fiber 2 g
    Sugars 3 g
PROTEIN 5 g
CALCIUM 133 mg
POTASSIUM 356 mg
DIETARY EXCHANGES
    1/2 starch
    1/2 lean meat

Sweet Potato Casserole

Serves 5; ½ cup per serving

You'll soon be replacing the traditional recipe for this southern holiday favorite with our healthful version.

4   medium sweet potatoes or 2 15-ounce cans sweet potatoes, packed with no liquid or in light syrup
    Vegetable oil spray
¼   cup fresh orange juice
2   tablespoons chopped walnuts
¼   teaspoon ground nutmeg
¼   teaspoon brandy flavoring

If using fresh sweet potatoes, boil them whole in a large pot for 25 to 30 minutes, or until tender. Using tongs or a slotted spoon, transfer the potatoes to a large bowl of cold water. Soak until cool enough to handle. Peel. If using canned potatoes, drain thoroughly.

Meanwhile, preheat the oven to 375°F. Lightly spray a 1-quart casserole dish with vegetable oil spray.

In a large bowl, mash the potatoes.

Stir in the remaining ingredients. Spoon into the casserole dish.

Bake for 25 minutes, or until heated through.

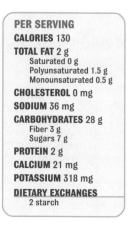

PER SERVING
CALORIES 130
TOTAL FAT 2 g
    Saturated 0 g
    Polyunsaturated 1.5 g
    Monounsaturated 0.5 g
CHOLESTEROL 0 mg
SODIUM 36 mg
CARBOHYDRATES 28 g
    Fiber 3 g
    Sugars 7 g
PROTEIN 2 g
CALCIUM 21 mg
POTASSIUM 318 mg
DIETARY EXCHANGES
    2 starch

Sweet Potatoes and Yams

Although sweet potatoes and yams are similar, they come from different plants. Yams are common in Central and South America, but almost all "yams" sold in the United States are really sweet potatoes.

Asian Fried Rice with Peas

Serves 8; ½ cup per serving

This dish is an excellent accompaniment to almost any Asian entrée. Add some chicken, shrimp, beef, or pork cooked without salt to transform it into a main dish.

1 tablespoon canola or corn oil

4 to 5 medium green onions, thinly sliced

4 cups cooked brown or white rice, chilled or at room temperature

2 tablespoons snipped fresh cilantro

1 tablespoon plus 1½ teaspoons rice vinegar

1 tablespoon light soy sauce

1 teaspoon ground cumin

½ teaspoon sugar

1 cup frozen green peas

2 medium green onions, thinly sliced (optional)

In a large nonstick skillet or wok, heat the oil over medium-high heat and swirl to coat the bottom. Cook the 4 to 5 green onions for 1 minute, or until fragrant, stirring occasionally.

Stir in the rice and cilantro. Cook for 2 minutes, or until heated, stirring constantly to separate the grains.

Stir in the rice vinegar, soy sauce, cumin, and sugar until well combined.

Stir in the peas. Cook for 2 to 3 minutes, or until the mixture is hot and the peas are heated through, stirring occasionally.

To serve, spoon onto plates. Garnish with the remaining green onions.

PER SERVING
CALORIES 146
TOTAL FAT 3 g
Saturated 0.5 g
Polyunsaturated 1 g
Monounsaturated 1.5 g
CHOLESTEROL 0 mg
SODIUM 77 mg
CARBOHYDRATES 27 g
Fiber 3 g
Sugars 2 g
PROTEIN 4 g
CALCIUM 17 mg
POTASSIUM 119 mg
DIETARY EXCHANGES
2 starch

Cook's TIP

For a dramatic presentation, sprinkle some black sesame seeds over the fried rice. Look for them at Asian markets and the international section of some grocery stores.

Rice and Vegetable Pilaf

Serves 6; ½ cup per serving

Full of mushrooms and carrots, this dish tastes great with Herbed Fillet of Sole (page 81).

1 teaspoon olive oil

4 ounces button mushrooms, sliced

2 medium carrots, shredded

1 cup Chicken Broth (page 19) or commercial fat-free, low-sodium chicken broth

¼ teaspoon pepper

½ cup uncooked long-grain rice

½ cup snipped fresh parsley

2 medium green onions, sliced

Heat a medium saucepan over medium-high heat. Add the oil and swirl to coat the bottom. Cook the mushrooms and carrots for 2 to 3 minutes, or until the mushrooms are tender, stirring occasionally.

Add the broth and pepper. Increase the heat to high and bring to a boil.

Stir in the rice. Reduce the heat and simmer, covered, for 20 minutes. Remove from the heat.

Stir in the remaining ingredients. Let stand for 5 minutes. Fluff with a fork before serving.

PER SERVING

CALORIES 78
TOTAL FAT 1 g
 Saturated 0 g
 Polyunsaturated 0 g
 Monounsaturated 0.5 g
CHOLESTEROL 0 mg
SODIUM 26 mg
CARBOHYDRATES 16 g
 Fiber 2 g
 Sugars 2 g
PROTEIN 2 g
CALCIUM 17 mg
POTASSIUM 205 mg
DIETARY EXCHANGES
 1 starch

Dilled Summer Squash

Serves 3; 1/2 cup per serving

This squash is so tender and tasty, you'll double the recipe next time.

1/4 cup water

2 medium yellow summer squash, sliced (about 1 2/3 cups)

1 1/2 teaspoons finely chopped onion

1 1/2 teaspoons snipped fresh dillweed or 1/2 teaspoon dried, crumbled

1/8 teaspoon pepper

Fat-free spray margarine or 1/4 teaspoon light-sodium butter-flavor sprinkles

In a medium saucepan, bring the water to a boil over high heat. Add the remaining ingredients except the spray margarine. Reduce the heat to medium and cook, covered, for 10 minutes, or until the squash is tender. Drain well.

Spray with the spray margarine.

Light-Sodium Butter-Flavor Sprinkles

Look for this no-fat product with the herbs and spices in your supermarket. It is great for flavoring hot vegetables, including baked potatoes. Sprinkle it on the cooked vegetables while they're still hot.

PER SERVING

CALORIES 22

TOTAL FAT 0 g
    Saturated 0 g
    Polyunsaturated 0 g
    Monounsaturated 0 g

CHOLESTEROL 0 mg

SODIUM 3 mg

CARBOHYDRATES 5 g
    Fiber 2 g
    Sugars 3 g

PROTEIN 2 g

CALCIUM 21 mg

POTASSIUM 347 mg

DIETARY EXCHANGES
    1 vegetable

Baked Tomatoes

Serves 4; ½ tomato per serving

Try serving these Italian-flavored tomatoes with Easy Roast Beef (page 134) and fresh corn.

Vegetable oil spray
2   medium tomatoes, halved
1   teaspoon olive oil
1   tablespoon plus 1 teaspoon shredded or grated Parmesan cheese
1   teaspoon snipped fresh parsley or ¼ teaspoon dried parsley, crumbled
¼   teaspoon dried oregano, crumbled
¼   teaspoon dried basil, crumbled

Preheat the oven to 350°F. Lightly spray a 9-inch square baking dish with vegetable oil spray. To assemble, place the tomato halves with the cut side up in the baking dish. Drizzle with the oil. Sprinkle with the remaining ingredients.

Bake for 20 to 25 minutes, or until the tomatoes are heated through.

PER SERVING
CALORIES 31
TOTAL FAT 1.5 g
   Saturated 0.5 g
   Polyunsaturated 0 g
   Monounsaturated 1 g
CHOLESTEROL 1 mg
SODIUM 32 mg
CARBOHYDRATES 3 g
   Fiber 1 g
   Sugars 2 g
PROTEIN 1 g
CALCIUM 32 mg
POTASSIUM 185 mg
DIETARY EXCHANGES
   1 vegetable
   ½ fat

Baked Italian Vegetable Mélange

Serves 4; ½ cup per serving

Roasting veggies over high heat retains those delightful concentrated flavors.

Vegetable oil spray

6 ounces yellow summer squash, sliced (about 1 cup)

½ medium green bell pepper, thinly sliced

½ large onion, thinly sliced

2 medium Italian plum tomatoes, cut crosswise into thin slices (about 1 cup)

⅛ teaspoon crushed red pepper flakes

⅛ teaspoon salt

½ teaspoon dried oregano, crumbled

½ teaspoon dried basil, crumbled

⅛ teaspoon dried fennel seed

2 tablespoons snipped fresh parsley

2 tablespoons shredded or grated Parmesan cheese

Preheat the oven to 400°F.

Lightly spray a 9-inch pie pan with vegetable oil spray.

In the following order, make one layer each of the squash, bell pepper, onion, and tomatoes in the pan. Sprinkle with the red pepper flakes, salt, oregano, basil, and fennel. Lightly spray with vegetable oil spray.

Bake for 25 minutes, or until the vegetables are tender when pierced with a fork. Remove from the oven.

Sprinkle with the parsley and Parmesan. Let stand, covered with aluminum foil, for 5 minutes to absorb flavors and release the juices.

Don't skip the last step. It brings out the flavors while the vegetables "relax" and the juices are released, giving the dish a more intense flavor.

PER SERVING
CALORIES 38
TOTAL FAT 1 g
  Saturated 0.5 g
  Polyunsaturated 0 g
  Monounsaturated 0.5 g
CHOLESTEROL 2 mg
SODIUM 120 mg
CARBOHYDRATES 6 g
  Fiber 2 g
  Sugars 4 g
PROTEIN 2 g
CALCIUM 59 mg
POTASSIUM 275 mg
DIETARY EXCHANGES
  1 vegetable

White Sauce
WHITE SAUCE WITH PARMESAN CHEESE
WHITE SAUCE WITH DIJON MUSTARD
Gourmet Mushroom Sauce
Yogurt Dill Sauce
Creamy Lime and Mustard Sauce
Spaghetti Sauce
Chocolate Sauce
Strawberry Orange Sauce
CINNAMON BLUEBERRY SAUCE
Ketchup
Chili Sauce

Sauces, Condiments, and Seasonings

- Barbecue Sauce
- Roasted Tomato Chipotle Salsa
- Hot Mustard
- Horseradish
- Herb Seasoning
- Lemon-Herb Seasoning
- Savory Herb Blend
- Chili Powder
- Creole Seasoning
- Easy Dill Pickles
- Sweet Bread-and-Butter Pickles
  SWEET PICKLE RELISH
- Rhubarb Mint Chutney

White Sauce

Serves 8; ¼ cup per serving

Whenever you need a basic white sauce, this recipe does the trick. It's also a useful substitute when a casserole recipe calls for a can of condensed creamy soup (usually high in sodium).

2 tablespoons light stick margarine
3 tablespoons all-purpose flour
2 cups fat-free milk
1 teaspoon fresh lemon juice
¼ teaspoon pepper, or to taste

In a medium saucepan, melt the margarine over medium-low heat. Whisk in the flour. Cook for 1 to 2 minutes, whisking occasionally.

Gradually whisk in the milk.

Whisk in the lemon juice and pepper. Increase the heat to medium-high and bring to a simmer, 4 to 5 minutes, whisking constantly. Continue cooking until the sauce has thickened to the desired consistency.

White Sauce with Parmesan Cheese

Add ¼ cup shredded or grated Parmesan cheese with the lemon juice and pepper for a great sauce to serve over pasta.

White Sauce with Dijon Mustard

For a different flavor to go with chicken or fish, add 2 tablespoons Dijon mustard with the lemon juice and pepper.

WHITE SAUCE	WITH PARMESAN CHEESE	WITH DIJON MUSTARD
PER SERVING	PER SERVING	PER SERVING
CALORIES 44	CALORIES 55	CALORIES 49
TOTAL FAT 1.5 g	TOTAL FAT 2 g	TOTAL FAT 1.5 g
Saturated 0.5 g	Saturated 0.5 g	Saturated 0.5 g
Polyunsaturated 0.5 g	Polyunsaturated 0.5 g	Polyunsaturated 0.5 g
Monounsaturated 0.5 g	Monounsaturated 0.5 g	Monounsaturated 0.5 g
CHOLESTEROL 1 mg	CHOLESTEROL 3 mg	CHOLESTEROL 1 mg
SODIUM 45 mg	SODIUM 87 mg	SODIUM 121 mg
CARBOHYDRATES 6 g	CARBOHYDRATES 6 g	CARBOHYDRATES 6 g
Fiber 0 g	Fiber 0 g	Fiber 0 g
Sugars 3 g	Sugars 3 g	Sugars 3 g
PROTEIN 2 g	PROTEIN 3 g	PROTEIN 3 g
CALCIUM 77 mg	CALCIUM 109 mg	CALCIUM 80 mg
POTASSIUM 102 mg	POTASSIUM 104 mg	POTASSIUM 109 mg
DIETARY EXCHANGES	DIETARY EXCHANGES	DIETARY EXCHANGES
½ starch	½ starch	½ starch
	½ fat	

Gourmet Mushroom Sauce

Serves 8; ¼ cup per serving

Simple main dishes, such as broiled or grilled steak, pork chops, or chicken breasts or leftover Meat Loaf (pages 146–147), get all dressed up with the addition of this sauce.

2 tablespoons light stick margarine

8 ounces fresh button or exotic mushrooms, such as shiitake, golden Italian, oyster, or chanterelle, or a combination, sliced (about 2½ cups)

2 medium shallots, finely chopped

3 tablespoons all-purpose flour

2 cups fat-free milk

⅛ teaspoon pepper

⅛ teaspoon garlic powder

1 tablespoon dry white wine (regular or nonalcoholic) or 1 to 2 teaspoons fresh lemon juice

In a large nonstick skillet, melt the margarine over medium heat. Cook the mushrooms and shallots for 4 to 5 minutes, or until the mushrooms are tender, stirring occasionally.

Sprinkle the flour over the mushroom mixture, stirring to combine.

Gradually add the milk, stirring constantly. Stir in the pepper and garlic powder. Increase the heat to medium-high and cook for 4 to 5 minutes, or until the mixture is thickened, stirring occasionally.

Stir in the wine.

PER SERVING
CALORIES 54
TOTAL FAT 1.5 g
    Saturated 0.5 g
    Polyunsaturated 0.5 g
    Monounsaturated 0.5 g
CHOLESTEROL 1 mg
SODIUM 46 mg
CARBOHYDRATES 7 g
    Fiber 1 g
    Sugars 4 g
PROTEIN 3 g
CALCIUM 80 mg
POTASSIUM 204 mg
DIETARY EXCHANGES
    ½ skim milk

Yogurt Dill Sauce

Serves 9; 2 tablespoons per serving

Serve this easy sauce over fish, use it as a dip for raw vegetables, or spoon it over sliced cucumbers.

1 cup fat-free or low-fat plain yogurt

2 tablespoons snipped fresh dillweed or 2 teaspoons dried, crumbled

2 tablespoons fat-free or light sour cream

1 teaspoon Dijon mustard

½ teaspoon sugar

½ teaspoon fresh lemon juice

¼ teaspoon pepper

In a small bowl, whisk together all the ingredients. Cover and refrigerate for at least 1 hour before serving.

PER SERVING

CALORIES 21

TOTAL FAT 0 g
   Saturated 0 g
   Polyunsaturated 0 g
   Monounsaturated 0 g

CHOLESTEROL 1 mg

SODIUM 35 mg

CARBOHYDRATES 3 g
   Fiber 0 g
   Sugars 3 g

PROTEIN 2 g

CALCIUM 60 mg

POTASSIUM 80 mg

DIETARY EXCHANGES
   Free

Creamy Lime and Mustard Sauce

Serves 8; 2 tablespoons per serving

The distinctive combination of capers and Chinese hot mustard makes this sauce a standout. Tasting it over Grilled Salmon Fillet with Fresh Herbs (page 78) will hook you.

¼ cup plus 2 tablespoons fat-free or light mayonnaise

¼ cup plus 2 tablespoons fat-free or low-fat sour cream

1 tablespoon plus 1½ teaspoons to 2 tablespoons fresh lime juice

1 tablespoon finely chopped green onion (green part only)

1 tablespoon finely chopped capers packed in balsamic vinegar, rinsed and drained

1 teaspoon Chinese hot mustard powder, or to taste

⅛ to ¼ teaspoon sugar, or to taste

In a medium glass bowl, whisk together all the ingredients. Cover and refrigerate until ready to serve.

PER SERVING

CALORIES 28
TOTAL FAT 0 g
  Saturated 0 g
  Polyunsaturated 0 g
  Monounsaturated 0 g
CHOLESTEROL 2 mg
SODIUM 133 mg
CARBOHYDRATES 4 g
  Fiber 0 g
  Sugars 2 g
PROTEIN 1 g
CALCIUM 17 mg
POTASSIUM 43 mg
DIETARY EXCHANGES
  Free

Spaghetti Sauce

Serves 6; ½ cup per serving

Make a batch of this wonderful sauce ahead of time for the best blending of flavors. It will keep in the refrigerator for up to a week, or freeze it for longer storage.

- 2   6-ounce cans no-salt-added tomato paste
- 2   cups water
- ¼   cup finely chopped onion
- 2   medium garlic cloves, minced
- 1   teaspoon dried basil, crumbled
- 1   teaspoon dried oregano, crumbled
- ½   teaspoon dried thyme, crumbled
- ½   teaspoon sugar
- ⅛   teaspoon pepper
- ⅛   teaspoon crushed red pepper flakes (optional)

Put the tomato paste in a medium saucepan. Whisk in the water, 1 cup at a time.

Whisk in the remaining ingredients. Bring to a boil over medium-high heat. Reduce the heat and simmer, covered, for 30 minutes, or until the flavors have blended, stirring occasionally.

PER SERVING
CALORIES 54
TOTAL FAT 0.5 g
  Saturated 0 g
  Polyunsaturated 0 g
  Monounsaturated 0 g
CHOLESTEROL 1 mg
SODIUM 58 mg
CARBOHYDRATES 13 g
  Fiber 3 g
  Sugars 7 g
PROTEIN 3 g
CALCIUM 35 mg
POTASSIUM 599 mg
DIETARY EXCHANGES
  2½ vegetable

Chocolate Sauce

Serves 8; 2 tablespoons per serving

Try this chocolate-lover's dream over fresh fruit, such as bananas, raspberries, or strawberries.

1   tablespoon light tub margarine

⅓   cup fat-free milk

½   cup sugar

3   tablespoons unsweetened cocoa powder

1   teaspoon vanilla extract

In a medium skillet, melt the margarine over medium-high heat. Whisk in the milk. Cook for 2 to 3 minutes (no stirring necessary).

Meanwhile, in a small bowl, stir together the sugar and cocoa. Gently whisk into the milk. Bring to a boil, whisking constantly. Remove from the heat.

Whisk in the vanilla. The sauce will thicken as it cools.

PER SERVING

CALORIES 67
TOTAL FAT 1 g
    Saturated 0 g
    Polyunsaturated 0 g
    Monounsaturated 0.5 g
CHOLESTEROL 0 mg
SODIUM 16 mg
CARBOHYDRATES 14 g
    Fiber 0 g
    Sugars 13 g
PROTEIN 1 g
CALCIUM 13 mg
POTASSIUM 119 mg
DIETARY EXCHANGES
    1 other carbohydrate

Strawberry Orange Sauce

Serves 9; ¼ cup per serving

Easy to make, this topping turns angel food cake or fat-free vanilla yogurt or ice cream into a dazzling dessert.

- 1   quart fresh strawberries (about 3½ cups)
- 1   tablespoon orange-flavored liqueur (optional)
- 1   tablespoon orange juice (2 tablespoons if not using liqueur)
- 1   tablespoon sugar

Remove the stems and caps from the strawberries. Slice the strawberries lengthwise.

In a small saucepan, heat the liqueur and orange juice over medium heat.

Stir in half the strawberries. Cook for 2 minutes, stirring frequently.

Stir in the sugar. Cook for 2 to 3 minutes, or until the berries soften. Remove from the heat.

Stir in the remaining strawberries. Serve hot or pour into a small container and refrigerate, covered, until ready to serve.

Cinnamon Blueberry Sauce

Substitute fresh blueberries for the strawberries and ½ teaspoon ground cinnamon for the liqueur. Use 2 tablespoons of orange juice.

STRAWBERRY ORANGE	CINNAMON BLUEBERRY
PER SERVING	PER SERVING
CALORIES 33	CALORIES 44
TOTAL FAT 0 g	TOTAL FAT 0 g
Saturated 0 g	Saturated 0 g
Polyunsaturated 0 g	Polyunsaturated 0 g
Monounsaturated 0 g	Monounsaturated 0 g
CHOLESTEROL 0 mg	CHOLESTEROL 0 mg
SODIUM 1 mg	SODIUM 1 mg
CARBOHYDRATES 7 g	CARBOHYDRATES 11 g
Fiber 1 g	Fiber 2 g
Sugars 5 g	Sugars 8 g
PROTEIN 0 g	PROTEIN 1 g
CALCIUM 11 mg	CALCIUM 6 mg
POTASSIUM 102 mg	POTASSIUM 57 mg
DIETARY EXCHANGES	DIETARY EXCHANGES
½ fruit	1 fruit

Ketchup

Makes 4 cups; 2 tablespoons per serving

It can be difficult to find low-sodium ketchup, so here's a simple recipe to make yourself. The ingredients list is long, but the preparation is almost effortless.

4	cups water
3	6-ounce cans no-salt-added tomato paste
½	cup chopped onion
1	medium rib of celery, chopped
½	cup cider vinegar
½	cup sugar
2	tablespoons light tub or light stick margarine
1	tablespoon light brown sugar
1	teaspoon light molasses
⅛	teaspoon ground cloves
⅛	teaspoon ground cinnamon
⅛	teaspoon dried basil, crumbled
⅛	teaspoon dried tarragon, crumbled
⅛	teaspoon pepper
⅛	teaspoon onion powder
⅛	teaspoon garlic powder

In a food processor or blender, process the water, tomato paste, onion, celery, and vinegar until smooth. Transfer to a medium saucepan.

Stir in the remaining ingredients. Bring to a simmer over medium-high heat. Reduce the heat and simmer, uncovered, for 1 hour 30 minutes, or until the ketchup is reduced to about 1 quart, one-half the original volume, stirring occasionally. Refrigerate in a jar with a tight-fitting lid for up to one month. For longer storage, freeze it in small quantities. (You can use the instructions given in the Cook's Tip on Broth, page 19.)

PER SERVING
CALORIES 32
TOTAL FAT 0.5 g
  Saturated 0 g
  Polyunsaturated 0 g
  Monounsaturated 0 g
CHOLESTEROL 0 mg
SODIUM 24 mg
CARBOHYDRATES 7 g
  Fiber 1 g
  Sugars 6 g
PROTEIN 1 g
CALCIUM 9 mg
POTASSIUM 180 mg
DIETARY EXCHANGES
  1½ vegetable

Chili Sauce

Add some zing to your food, but without the sodium usually found in chili sauce. Drizzle this chili sauce on Spicy Baked Fish (page 68) or shrimp cocktail.

2   16-ounce cans no-salt-added tomato sauce

½   cup sugar

½   cup chopped onion

1   medium rib of celery, chopped

½   medium green bell pepper, chopped

½   cup cider vinegar

2   tablespoons light tub or light stick margarine

1   tablespoon fresh lemon juice

1   teaspoon light brown sugar

1   teaspoon light molasses

¼   teaspoon red hot-pepper sauce

⅛   teaspoon ground cloves

⅛   teaspoon ground cinnamon

⅛   teaspoon pepper

⅛   teaspoon dried basil, crumbled

⅛   teaspoon dried tarragon, crumbled

In a large saucepan, whisk together all the ingredients. Bring to a boil over high heat, whisking frequently. Reduce the heat and simmer, uncovered, for 1 hour 30 minutes, or until reduced to about 3 cups, one-half the original volume, whisking occasionally. Refrigerate in a jar with a tight-fitting lid for up to one month. For longer storage, freeze it in small quantities. (You can use the instructions given in the Cook's Tip on Broth, page 19.)

PER SERVING

CALORIES 36
TOTAL FAT 0.5 g
  Saturated 0 g
  Polyunsaturated 0 g
  Monounsaturated 0 g
CHOLESTEROL 0 mg
SODIUM 15 mg
CARBOHYDRATES 8 g
  Fiber 1 g
  Sugars 7 g
PROTEIN 1 g
CALCIUM 9 mg
POTASSIUM 169 mg
DIETARY EXCHANGES
  1½ vegetable

Barbecue Sauce

Makes 4 cups; 2 tablespoons per serving

After trying our healthful version of barbecue sauce, you'll wonder why you ever bought the bottled kind.

2 cups water

2 6-ounce cans no-salt-added tomato paste

½ cup Ketchup (page 217) or commercial no-salt-added ketchup

¼ cup firmly packed dark brown sugar

¼ cup chopped onion

2 tablespoons Chili Powder (page 226) or commercial no-salt-added chili powder

2 tablespoons fresh lemon juice

2 tablespoons cider vinegar

2 tablespoons canola or corn oil

1 tablespoon snipped fresh parsley

1 teaspoon dry mustard

1 teaspoon paprika

1 medium garlic clove, minced

⅛ teaspoon pepper

Dash of red hot-pepper sauce (optional)

In a large saucepan, whisk together all the ingredients. Bring to a boil over high heat. Reduce the heat and simmer for 20 minutes, or until the flavors have blended, whisking occasionally. Refrigerate in a jar with a tight-fitting lid for up to one month. For longer storage, freeze it in small quantities. (You can use the instructions given in the Cook's Tip on Broth, page 19.)

PER SERVING
CALORIES 30
TOTAL FAT 1 g
   Saturated 0 g
   Polyunsaturated 0.5 g
   Monounsaturated 0.5 g
CHOLESTEROL 0 mg
SODIUM 15 mg
CARBOHYDRATES 5 g
   Fiber 1 g
   Sugars 4 g
PROTEIN 1 g
CALCIUM 10 mg
POTASSIUM 154 mg
DIETARY EXCHANGES
   1 vegetable

Roasted Tomato Chipotle Salsa

Serves 6; 2 tablespoons per serving

Spice up lean grilled hamburgers, chicken breasts, or pork tenderloin with this wonderful salsa, which gets its smoky flavor from the chipotle chile. Regulate the heat from mild to spicy by the amount of chipotle you add.

Vegetable oil spray
1 large tomato
1 large shallot or 1½-inch-thick slice red onion, quartered
2 medium garlic cloves, unpeeled
1 tablespoon whole cilantro leaves
1 to 2 teaspoons fresh lime juice
½ to 2 teaspoons chopped canned chipotle chile in adobo sauce or 1 teaspoon chopped fresh jalapeño (wear plastic gloves when handling)

Preheat the oven to 400°F. Spray a large baking sheet with vegetable oil spray.

Cut the tomato in half crosswise. If desired, squeeze out the tomato seeds. Cut each half in half. Put the tomato quarters on the baking sheet with the shallot and garlic cloves (they will be easier to peel after roasting).

Bake for 20 minutes, or until the garlic is a light golden brown.

Peel the tomato and garlic, discarding the peels. In a food processor or blender, process all the ingredients for 10 to 15 seconds, or until the desired consistency. Cover and refrigerate for up to four days.

PER SERVING

CALORIES 10
TOTAL FAT 0 g
  Saturated 0 g
  Polyunsaturated 0 g
  Monounsaturated 0 g
CHOLESTEROL 0 mg
SODIUM 17 mg
CARBOHYDRATES 2 g
  Fiber 0 g
  Sugars 1 g
PROTEIN 0 g
CALCIUM 6 mg
POTASSIUM 87 mg
DIETARY EXCHANGES
  Free

Hot Mustard

Makes ½ cup; 1 tablespoon per serving

Use this zesty mustard on your favorite sandwich or in our tasty Red-Potato Salad (page 51).

¼ cup all-purpose flour

2 tablespoons sugar

2 tablespoons dry mustard

¼ teaspoon onion powder

¼ teaspoon turmeric

2 tablespoons fresh lemon juice

2 tablespoons water

In a small bowl, whisk together the flour, sugar, dry mustard, onion powder, and turmeric.

Whisk in the lemon juice and water. Put in a jar with a tight-fitting lid and refrigerate.

PER SERVING
CALORIES 40
TOTAL FAT 1 g
    Saturated 0 g
    Polyunsaturated 0 g
    Monounsaturated 0 g
CHOLESTEROL 0 mg
SODIUM 0 mg
CARBOHYDRATES 7 g
    Fiber 0 g
    Sugars 3 g
PROTEIN 1 g
CALCIUM 6 mg
POTASSIUM 27 mg
DIETARY EXCHANGES
    ½ starch

Horseradish

Makes 1½ cups; 1 tablespoon per serving

This great-tasting, low-sodium condiment livens up a wide variety of foods from sour cream sauce on lean roast beef to any spread for sandwiches.

½ medium horseradish root, peeled and cubed (about 12 ounces)
½ cup vinegar

In a food processor or blender, process the horseradish and vinegar to the desired consistency. Put in a jar with a tight-fitting lid and refrigerate for up to one week.

 Cook's TIP

If you don't want to use a food processor or blender, finely grate the horse-radish into a medium bowl. Pour in the vinegar and stir until thoroughly combined.

PER SERVING
CALORIES 9
TOTAL FAT 0 g
  Saturated 0 g
  Polyunsaturated 0 g
  Monounsaturated 0 g
CHOLESTEROL 0 mg
SODIUM 1 mg
CARBOHYDRATES 2 g
  Fiber 0 g
  Sugars 0 g
PROTEIN 0 g
CALCIUM 15 mg
POTASSIUM 79 mg
DIETARY EXCHANGES
  Free

Herb Seasoning

Makes ⅓ cup; ½ teaspoon per serving

An all-purpose replacement for the salt shaker, this flavorful seasoning is perfect for keeping on the table and on the kitchen counter. The mixture is good on vegetables and meats and in casseroles and stews.

1 tablespoon garlic powder

1 teaspoon dried basil, crumbled

1 teaspoon dried marjoram, crumbled

1 teaspoon dried thyme, crumbled

1 teaspoon dried parsley, crumbled

1 teaspoon dried savory, crumbled

1 teaspoon ground mace or nutmeg

1 teaspoon onion powder

1 teaspoon pepper

1 teaspoon sage

½ teaspoon cayenne (optional)

In a small bowl, stir together all the ingredients until well blended. Store in a jar with a tight-fitting lid in a cool, dry, dark place for up to six months.

PER SERVING

CALORIES 2

TOTAL FAT 0 g
  Saturated 0 g
  Polyunsaturated 0 g
  Monounsaturated 0 g

CHOLESTEROL 0 mg

SODIUM 0 mg

CARBOHYDRATES 0 g
  Fiber 0 g
  Sugars 0 g

PROTEIN 0 g

CALCIUM 4 mg

POTASSIUM 7 mg

DIETARY EXCHANGES
  Free

Lemon-Herb Seasoning

Makes ¾ cup; ½ teaspoon per serving

Use a sprinkle of this seasoning to bring out the flavor of seafood, poultry, or green salads.

¼ cup plus 1 tablespoon dried basil, crumbled

¼ cup dried oregano, crumbled

1 tablespoon plus 1½ teaspoons pepper

1 tablespoon plus 1½ teaspoons dried onion flakes, crumbled

1 tablespoon plus 1½ teaspoons whole celery seeds

½ teaspoon garlic powder

½ teaspoon dried grated lemon zest

In a small bowl, stir together all the ingredients until well blended. Store in a jar with a tight-fitting lid in a cool, dry, dark place for up to six months.

PER SERVING

CALORIES 3

TOTAL FAT 0 g
  Saturated 0 g
  Polyunsaturated 0 g
  Monounsaturated 0 g

CHOLESTEROL 0 mg

SODIUM 0 mg

CARBOHYDRATES 1 g
  Fiber 0 g
  Sugars 0 g

PROTEIN 0 g

CALCIUM 13 mg

POTASSIUM 16 mg

DIETARY EXCHANGES
  Free

Savory Herb Blend

Makes 1 cup; ½ teaspoon per serving

The herbs in this blend will make you want to discover salad all over again.

¼   cup dried parsley, crumbled

¼   cup dried marjoram, crumbled

2   tablespoons plus 1½ teaspoons dried basil, crumbled

1   tablespoon plus 1½ teaspoons sesame seeds

1   tablespoon plus 1½ teaspoons crushed red pepper flakes

1   tablespoon plus 1½ teaspoons dried rosemary leaves, crushed

1   tablespoon plus 1¼ teaspoons celery seeds, crushed

2½   teaspoons dried savory, crumbled

2½   teaspoons dried sage

2¼   teaspoons dried thyme, crumbled

2   teaspoons dried onion flakes, crumbled

2   teaspoons dried dillweed, crumbled

1¼   teaspoons pepper

¾   teaspoon garlic powder

In a small bowl, stir together all the ingredients until well blended. Store in a jar with a tight-fitting lid in a cool, dry, dark place for up to six months.

PER SERVING

CALORIES 3

TOTAL FAT 0 g
   Saturated 0 g
   Polyunsaturated 0 g
   Monounsaturated 0 g

CHOLESTEROL 0 mg

SODIUM 1 mg

CARBOHYDRATES 0 g
   Fiber 0 g
   Sugars 0 g

PROTEIN 0 g

CALCIUM 9 mg

POTASSIUM 11 mg

DIETARY EXCHANGES
   Free

Chili Powder

Makes ¼ cup; 1 teaspoon per serving

Try this in your own favorite chili recipe, our Chili (page 152), or Eggplant Mexicana (page 197).

- 3 tablespoons paprika
- 2 teaspoons dried oregano, crumbled
- 1 teaspoon ground cumin
- 1 teaspoon turmeric
- 1 teaspoon garlic powder
- ¼ teaspoon cayenne

In a small bowl, stir together all the ingredients until well blended. Store in a jar with a tight-fitting lid in a cool, dark, dry place for up to six months.

PER SERVING
CALORIES 8
TOTAL FAT 0.5 g
    Saturated 0 g
    Polyunsaturated 0 g
    Monounsaturated 0 g
CHOLESTEROL 0 mg
SODIUM 1 mg
CARBOHYDRATES 1 g
    Fiber 1 g
    Sugars 0 g
PROTEIN 0 g
CALCIUM 8 mg
POTASSIUM 52 mg
DIETARY EXCHANGES
    Free

Creole Seasoning

Makes 2 tablespoons; ½ teaspoon per serving

Use this spicy mix in Zesty Oven-Fried Potatoes (page 201) and any other recipes that call for Creole or Cajun herb mixtures.

- 1 teaspoon Chili Powder (page 226) or commercial no-salt-added chili powder
- 1 teaspoon paprika
- 1 teaspoon ground cumin
- 1 teaspoon dried thyme, crumbled
- ½ teaspoon garlic powder
- ½ teaspoon onion powder
- ½ teaspoon pepper

In a small bowl, stir together all the ingredients. Store in a jar with a tight-fitting lid in a cool, dark, dry place for up to six months.

PER SERVING
CALORIES 3
TOTAL FAT 0 g
   Saturated 0 g
   Polyunsaturated 0 g
   Monounsaturated 0 g
CHOLESTEROL 0 mg
SODIUM 1 mg
CARBOHYDRATES 1 g
   Fiber 0 g
   Sugars 0 g
PROTEIN 0 g
CALCIUM 4 mg
POTASSIUM 16 mg
DIETARY EXCHANGES
   Free

Easy Dill Pickles

Serves 16; ¼ cup per serving

If you've never made pickles before, don't worry. These are so easy! Just let the cucumbers simmer in a flavorful liquid, then cool and refrigerate them. The flavor of these pickles really brightens lean grilled burgers or your favorite potato salad or tuna salad recipe.

- 4 pickling, or Kirby, cucumbers, unpeeled (about 1 pound)
- 1 cup water
- ¾ cup cider vinegar
- 1 tablespoon dill seeds
- 1 tablespoon whole pickling spices
- 1 tablespoon sugar
- 2 medium garlic cloves
- 4 to 5 sprigs fresh dillweed (optional)

With a knife or crinkle cutter, cut the cucumbers crosswise into ¼-inch slices. You should have about 4 cups. Line a colander with two or three paper towels. Put the cucumbers in the colander, cover with a paper towel, and set a plate on top to slightly weigh the cucumbers down (this will help remove any excess moisture). Let stand for 5 to 10 minutes.

In a large saucepan, bring the remaining ingredients to a boil over high heat. Reduce the heat to medium and stir in the cucumbers. Cook for 3 minutes, or until tender-crisp, stirring occasionally. Remove from the heat and let cool for 15 minutes. Transfer to an airtight container large enough to hold the cucumbers and liquid (a clean large pickle jar works well) and refrigerate for at least 4 hours before serving. The pickles will keep in the refrigerator for up to two weeks.

Cook's TIP Pickling, or Kirby, Cucumbers

As its name tells you, this small cucumber variety is primarily used for pickles. It's also used as a garnish in many Asian dishes and can be substituted for the more-common cucumber. Pickling cucumbers have thin skin, are crisp, and have very small seeds. Many groceries carry them regularly, or you can look for them at a local farmers' market or Asian grocery store. A great alternative is the English, or hothouse, cucumber (see Cook's Tip on English Cucumbers, page 42). You can also pickle the common cucumber.

Pickling Spices

You'll find pickling spices in the spice section of the grocery. Commercial brands of this aromatic mix of spices vary but can include allspice, cinnamon, mustard seeds, coriander seeds, ginger, bay leaves, chiles, black pepper, cloves, cardamom, and mace. Use 1 teaspoon to 1 tablespoon of the mixture in marinades, water for cooking shrimp, or soups and stews. Use kitchen twine to tie the spices in a small piece of cheesecloth so you can remove them easily.

PER SERVING
CALORIES 12
TOTAL FAT 0 g
    Saturated 0 g
    Polyunsaturated 0 g
    Monounsaturated 0 g
CHOLESTEROL 0 mg
SODIUM 1 mg
CARBOHYDRATES 3 g
    Fiber 1 g
    Sugars 2 g
PROTEIN 1 g
CALCIUM 18 mg
POTASSIUM 70 mg
DIETARY EXCHANGES
    Free

Sweet Bread-and-Butter Pickles

Serves 16; ¼ cup per serving

Sure to be a hit with your family, these quick-fix pickles have a traditional sweet bread-and-butter pickle taste. Great for a picnic or your next cookout.

4   pickling, or Kirby, cucumbers, unpeeled (about 1 pound)
1   medium onion, sliced
1   cup water
¾   cup cider vinegar
½   cup sugar
1   teaspoon pink peppercorns (optional)
½   teaspoon mustard seeds
¼   teaspoon turmeric

With a knife or crinkle cutter, cut the cucumbers crosswise into ¼-inch slices. You should have about 4 cups. Line a colander with two or three paper towels. Put the cucumbers and onion in the colander, cover with a paper towel, and set a plate on top to slightly weigh the cucumber mixture down (this will help remove any excess moisture). Let stand for 5 to 10 minutes.

In a large saucepan, bring the remaining ingredients to a boil over high heat. Reduce the heat to medium and stir in the cucumbers and onion. Cook for 3 minutes, or until tender-crisp, stirring occasionally. Remove from the heat and let the mixture cool for 15 minutes. Transfer to an airtight container large enough to hold the cucumbers and liquid (a clean large pickle jar works well) and refrigerate for at least 4 hours before serving. The pickles will keep in the refrigerator for up to two weeks.

PER SERVING
CALORIES 34
TOTAL FAT 0 g
   Saturated 0 g
   Polyunsaturated 0 g
   Monounsaturated 0 g
CHOLESTEROL 0 mg
SODIUM 1 mg
CARBOHYDRATES 9 g
   Fiber 1 g
   Sugars 8 g
PROTEIN 0 g
CALCIUM 10 mg
POTASSIUM 77 mg
DIETARY EXCHANGES
   ½ other carbohydrate

Sweet Pickle Relish

Finely chop the cucumbers and onion, and add 1 finely chopped medium green or red bell pepper. Bring all the ingredients to a simmer over medium-high heat, then reduce the heat and simmer for 10 to 15 minutes, or until the relish is thickened, stirring occasionally. Store as directed on page 230.

 Cook's TIP

Pink Peppercorns

These dried berries from the Baies rose plant are not true peppercorns, but are peppery in taste and beautiful in color. Find them in gourmet shops or upscale grocery stores.

PER SERVING

CALORIES 36

TOTAL FAT 0 g
  Saturated 0 g
  Polyunsaturated 0 g
  Monounsaturated 0 g

CHOLESTEROL 0 mg

SODIUM 1 mg

CARBOHYDRATES 9 g
  Fiber 1 g
  Sugars 8 g

PROTEIN 1 g

CALCIUM 11 mg

POTASSIUM 90 mg

DIETARY EXCHANGES
  ½ other carbohydrate

Rhubarb Mint Chutney

Serves 12; 2 tablespoons per serving

This colorful chutney makes a delightful accompaniment for lamb or ham. For an appetizer or snack, use the chutney to top salt-free crackers spread with fat-free or reduced-fat cream cheese.

1   tablespoon light stick margarine

1   small onion, minced

3   cups frozen chopped rhubarb

1   ounce fresh mint leaves, chopped (about 1 cup)

⅓   cup sugar

⅓   cup firmly packed light brown sugar

1   tablespoon grated lemon zest

¼   cup fresh lemon juice

Melt the margarine in a medium saucepan over medium heat. Cook the onion for 3 to 4 minutes, or until soft, stirring occasionally.

Stir in the remaining ingredients. Increase the heat to medium-high and bring to a boil, about 5 minutes. Reduce the heat and simmer for 10 minutes, or until thickened. Serve the chutney warm or at room temperature.

PER SERVING
CALORIES 64
TOTAL FAT 0.5 g
 Saturated 0 g
 Polyunsaturated 0 g
 Monounsaturated 0 g
CHOLESTEROL 0 mg
SODIUM 13 mg
CARBOHYDRATES 15 g
 Fiber 1 g
 Sugars 13 g
PROTEIN 1 g
CALCIUM 88 mg
POTASSIUM 81 mg
DIETARY EXCHANGES
 1 other carbohydrate

Breads and Breakfast Dishes

Basic White Bread

Serves 32; 1 slice per serving

The alluring aroma and superior taste are only two of the rewards of baking your own bread. Another is that you control the sodium content.

¼ cup lukewarm water (105°F to 115°F)
2 ¼-ounce packages active dry yeast
1¾ cups fat-free milk
3 tablespoons sugar
2 tablespoons canola or corn oil
6 cups all-purpose flour (plus more as needed)
  Vegetable oil spray

Pour the water into a large bowl. Add the yeast and stir to dissolve. Let stand for 5 minutes, or until the mixture bubbles.

Stir the milk, sugar, and oil into the yeast mixture.

Gradually stir in 4 cups flour. Beat with a sturdy spoon for about 30 seconds, or until smooth.

Gradually add up to 1½ cups flour, about ¼ cup at a time, stirring after each addition, until the dough starts to pull away from the side of the bowl.

Lightly flour a flat surface. Turn the dough out onto the floured surface. Gradually knead in the remaining flour for 6 to 8 minutes, or until the dough is smooth and elastic. (The dough shouldn't be dry or stick to the surface. You may not need all the flour, or you may need up to ½ cup more if the dough is too sticky.)

Lightly spray a large bowl with vegetable oil spray. Put the dough in the bowl and turn to coat all sides. Cover the bowl with a damp dish towel and let the dough rise in a warm, draft-free place (about 85°F) until doubled in bulk, about 1 hour.

Punch down the dough. Divide in half and shape into loaves. Lightly spray two 10 × 5 × 3-inch loaf pans with vegetable oil spray. Put the dough in the loaf pans. Cover each with a damp dish towel and let the dough rise in a warm, draft-free place (about 85°F) until doubled in bulk, about 30 minutes.

Preheat the oven to 425°F.

Bake the loaves for 25 to 30 minutes, or until the bread registers 190°F on an instant-read thermometer or sounds hollow when rapped with your knuckles. Invert the bread onto cooling racks. Let cool for 15 to 20 minutes before cutting.

(See page 236 for bread machine instructions.)

Practice makes perfect when you're trying to develop a feel for when dough has the proper consistency. You can wind up with a heavy loaf if you knead in too much flour or overknead the dough, making it feel dry and stiff. If you use too little flour or don't knead the dough enough, your loaf may lose its shape during baking.

For basic kneading, fold the dough toward you. Using the heels of one or both hands, push the dough forward and slightly down in almost a rocking motion. Don't knead the dough completely flat against your counter or board. This can cause your dough to become sticky. Rotate the dough a quarter-turn and repeat until the dough is smooth and elastic. Add small amounts of flour to the dough when it starts to stick to the counter or board.

PER SERVING
CALORIES 103
TOTAL FAT 1 g
   Saturated 0 g
   Polyunsaturated 0.5 g
   Monounsaturated 0.5 g
CHOLESTEROL 0 mg
SODIUM 6 mg
CARBOHYDRATES 20 g
   Fiber 1 g
   Sugars 2 g
PROTEIN 3 g
CALCIUM 21 mg
POTASSIUM 55 mg
DIETARY EXCHANGES
   1½ starch

Bread Machine Variation

	1-POUND MACHINE (12 servings)	1½-POUND MACHINE (18 servings)	2-POUND MACHINE (24 servings)
FAT-FREE MILK	²/₃ cup	³/₄ cup plus 2 tablespoons	1¼ cups plus 1 tablespoon
WATER	2 tablespoons	3 tablespoons	¼ cup
CANOLA OR CORN OIL	2¼ teaspoons	1 tablespoon	1 tablespoon plus 1½ teaspoons
ALL-PURPOSE FLOUR	2 cups	3 cups	4 cups
SUGAR	1 tablespoon	1 tablespoon plus 1½ teaspoons	2 tablespoons
ACTIVE DRY YEAST	2 teaspoons	2½ teaspoons	1 tablespoon

Put all the ingredients in the bread machine container in the order given or use the manufacturer's directions. When adding the yeast, use a small spoon to make a well in the dry ingredients. Put the yeast in the well unless your machine has a yeast dispenser. Select the basic/white bread cycle. Proceed as directed. When the bread is done, let it cool on a cooling rack before slicing.

1-POUND
PER SERVING
CALORIES 94
TOTAL FAT 1 g
  Saturated 0 g
  Polyunsaturated 0.5 g
  Monounsaturated 0.5 g
CHOLESTEROL 0 mg
SODIUM 7 mg
CARBOHYDRATES 18 g
  Fiber 1 g
  Sugars 2 g
PROTEIN 3 g
CALCIUM 21 mg
POTASSIUM 57 mg
DIETARY EXCHANGES
  1 starch

1½-POUND
PER SERVING
CALORIES 92
TOTAL FAT 1 g
  Saturated 0 g
  Polyunsaturated 0.5 g
  Monounsaturated 0.5 g
CHOLESTEROL 0 mg
SODIUM 6 mg
CARBOHYDRATES 18 g
  Fiber 1 g
  Sugars 2 g
PROTEIN 3 g
CALCIUM 18 mg
POTASSIUM 52 mg
DIETARY EXCHANGES
  1 starch

2-POUND
PER SERVING
CALORIES 94
TOTAL FAT 1 g
  Saturated 0 g
  Polyunsaturated 0.5 g
  Monounsaturated 0.5 g
CHOLESTEROL 0 mg
SODIUM 6 mg
CARBOHYDRATES 18 g
  Fiber 1 g
  Sugars 2 g
PROTEIN 3 g
CALCIUM 20 mg
POTASSIUM 53 mg
DIETARY EXCHANGES
  1 starch

Whole-Wheat Bread

Serves 32; 1 slice per serving

Get back to basics, and take pleasure in baking your own nourishing bread.

	1-POUND MACHINE (12 servings)	1½-POUND MACHINE (18 servings)	2-POUND MACHINE (24 servings)
FAT-FREE MILK	²/₃ cup	³/₄ cup plus 2 tablespoons	1¼ cups plus 1 tablespoon
WATER	2 tablespoons	3 tablespoons	¼ cup
CANOLA OR CORN OIL	2¼ teaspoons	1 tablespoon	1 tablespoon plus 1½ teaspoons
ALL-PURPOSE FLOUR	1 cup	1½ cups	2 cups
WHOLE-WHEAT FLOUR	1 cup	1½ cups	2 cups
GLUTEN FLOUR	1 tablespoon	1 tablespoon plus 1½ teaspoons	2 tablespoons
MOLASSES	1 tablespoon	1 tablespoon plus 1½ teaspoons	2 tablespoons
ACTIVE DRY YEAST	2 teaspoons	2½ teaspoons	1 tablespoon

Put all the ingredients in the bread machine container in the order given or use the manufacturer's directions. When adding the yeast, use a small spoon to make a well in the dry ingredients. Put the yeast in the well unless your machine has a yeast dispenser. Select the whole-grain cycle or basic/white bread cycle. Proceed as directed. When the bread is done, let cool on a cooling rack before slicing.

1-POUND
PER SERVING
CALORIES 93
TOTAL FAT 1 g
  Saturated 0 g
  Polyunsaturated 0.5 g
  Monounsaturated 0.5 g
CHOLESTEROL 0 mg
SODIUM 8 mg
CARBOHYDRATES 18 g
  Fiber 2 g
  Sugars 2 g
PROTEIN 3 g
CALCIUM 26 mg
POTASSIUM 112 mg
DIETARY EXCHANGES
  1 starch

1½-POUND
PER SERVING
CALORIES 92
TOTAL FAT 1 g
  Saturated 0 g
  Polyunsaturated 0.5 g
  Monounsaturated 0.5 g
CHOLESTEROL 0 mg
SODIUM 7 mg
CARBOHYDRATES 18 g
  Fiber 2 g
  Sugars 2 g
PROTEIN 3 g
CALCIUM 24 mg
POTASSIUM 107 mg
DIETARY EXCHANGES
  1 starch

2-POUND
PER SERVING
CALORIES 93
TOTAL FAT 1 g
  Saturated 0 g
  Polyunsaturated 0.5 g
  Monounsaturated 0.5 g
CHOLESTEROL 0 mg
SODIUM 7 mg
CARBOHYDRATES 18 g
  Fiber 2 g
  Sugars 2 g
PROTEIN 3 g
CALCIUM 26 mg
POTASSIUM 108 mg
DIETARY EXCHANGES
  1 starch

Rosemary Rye Bread

It won't take you long to do the actual preparation for this aromatic bread. During its resting and baking times, you can take a walk, fix dinner, or just relax.

Vegetable oil spray (olive oil spray preferred)

1¼ cups all-purpose flour

¾ cup rye flour

1 tablespoon gluten flour

1 tablespoon fresh rosemary leaves, chopped, or 1 teaspoon dried, crushed

1 tablespoon caraway seeds

1 tablespoon olive oil

2 teaspoons fast-rising yeast

½ teaspoon salt

1¼ cups warm water (120°F to 130°F)

1 cup all-purpose flour (plus more as needed)

Spray a baking sheet with the vegetable oil spray. Set aside.

In a large bowl, stir together the 1¼ cups all-purpose flour, rye flour, gluten flour, rosemary, caraway seeds, olive oil, yeast, and salt.

Add the water, stirring with a sturdy spoon for about 30 seconds.

Gradually add some of the remaining 1 cup all-purpose flour, beating with a sturdy spoon after each addition, until the dough starts to pull away from the side of the bowl. Add more flour if necessary to make the dough smooth enough to handle.

Turn the dough out onto a lightly floured surface. Gradually knead in enough of the remaining flour to make the dough smooth and elastic, 6 to 7 minutes. (The dough shouldn't be dry or stick to the surface. You may not need all the flour, or you may need up to ½ cup more if the dough is too sticky.) Cover the dough with a damp dish towel and let it rest for 10 minutes.

Shape the dough into a 9 × 5-inch oval loaf. Set on the baking sheet and flatten slightly. Cut a few horizontal slashes about 3 inches long and ½ inch deep in the top of the loaf. Cover with a dry dish towel and let rise for 30 to 45 minutes, or until doubled in bulk. Near the end of the rising cycle, preheat the oven to 375°F.

PER SERVING

CALORIES 93

TOTAL FAT 1 g
  Saturated 0 g
  Polyunsaturated 0 g
  Monounsaturated 0.5 g

CHOLESTEROL 0 mg

SODIUM 74 mg

CARBOHYDRATES 18 g
  Fiber 2 g
  Sugars 0 g

PROTEIN 3 g

CALCIUM 8 mg

POTASSIUM 52 mg

DIETARY EXCHANGES
  1 starch

Bake for 35 to 40 minutes, or until the bread registers 190°F on an instant-read thermometer or sounds hollow when rapped with your knuckles. Invert the bread onto a cooling rack. Let cool for 15 minutes before slicing.

Bread Machine Instructions

Follow the manufacturer's instructions for the quick baking cycle. If you prefer, use the quick dough cycle, shape the loaf by hand when the dough is ready, and bake the bread in the oven as directed above.

	1-POUND MACHINE (12 servings)	1½-POUND MACHINE (18 servings)	2-POUND MACHINE (24 servings)
WATER (TAP)	¾ cup	1¼ cups	1½ cups
OLIVE OIL	1 tablespoon	1 tablespoon plus 1½ teaspoons	2 tablespoons
ALL-PURPOSE FLOUR	1½ cups	2¼ cups	3 cups
RYE FLOUR	½ cup	¾ cup	1 cup
GLUTEN FLOUR	2 teaspoons	1 tablespoon	1 tablespoon plus 1 teaspoon
FRESH ROSEMARY LEAVES, CHOPPED	2 teaspoons	1 tablespoon	1 tablespoon plus 1 teaspoon
(or dried rosemary, crushed)	½ teaspoon	1 teaspoon	1½ teaspoons
CARAWAY SEEDS	2 teaspoons	1 tablespoon	1 tablespoon plus 1 teaspoon
SALT	¼ teaspoon	½ teaspoon	½ teaspoon
FAST-RISING YEAST	1 teaspoon	1½ teaspoons	2 teaspoons

1-POUND
PER SERVING
CALORIES 86
TOTAL FAT 1.5 g
  Saturated 0 g
  Polyunsaturated 0 g
  Monounsaturated 1 g
CHOLESTEROL 0 mg
SODIUM 50 mg
CARBOHYDRATES 16 g
  Fiber 1 g
  Sugars 0 g
PROTEIN 2 g
CALCIUM 7 mg
POTASSIUM 44 mg
DIETARY EXCHANGES
  1 starch

1½-POUND
PER SERVING
CALORIES 96
TOTAL FAT 1.5 g
  Saturated 0 g
  Polyunsaturated 0.5 g
  Monounsaturated 1 g
CHOLESTEROL 0 mg
SODIUM 74 mg
CARBOHYDRATES 18 g
  Fiber 1 g
  Sugars 0 g
PROTEIN 3 g
CALCIUM 8 mg
POTASSIUM 49 mg
DIETARY EXCHANGES
  1 starch

2-POUND
PER SERVING
CALORIES 86
TOTAL FAT 1.5 g
  Saturated 0 g
  Polyunsaturated 0 g
  Monounsaturated 1 g
CHOLESTEROL 0 mg
SODIUM 50 mg
CARBOHYDRATES 16 g
  Fiber 1 g
  Sugars 0 g
PROTEIN 2 g
CALCIUM 7 mg
POTASSIUM 44 mg
DIETARY EXCHANGES
  1 starch

Bread Machine Cinnamon Rolls

Serves 32; 1 roll per serving

When these come out of the oven, stand back! All the neighbors may drop by for a sample.

1 recipe Basic White Bread (pages 234–235)
   Vegetable oil spray
   Flavorings (see chart, page 241)
   Glaze (see chart, page 241)

Prepare the white bread dough using the bread machine variation for your size machine (select the dough cycle).

Lightly spray a large baking sheet with vegetable oil spray.

On a lightly floured flat surface, roll the dough into a rectangle (refer to the chart on page 241 for the size of the rectangle and for ingredient measurements). Brush the melted margarine over the dough. Sprinkle the cinnamon, brown sugar, and pecans over the dough. Starting on one long side, roll the dough jelly-roll style into a cylinder and cut in 1-inch slices (refer to the chart for the number of rolls).

Place ½ inch apart on the baking sheet (for the 2 end pieces, place with the cut side up). Cover with a dry dish towel and allow to rise until almost doubled in size, 30 to 35 minutes.

Preheat the oven to 375°F.

Bake for 15 to 20 minutes, or until golden brown. Let the rolls partially cool on a cooling rack.

Meanwhile, for the glaze, whisk together the confectioners' sugar, vanilla, and water in a small bowl. Drizzle over the warm rolls.

	1-POUND MACHINE (12 rolls)	1½-POUND MACHINE (18 rolls)	2-POUND MACHINE (24 rolls)
SIZE OF RECTANGLE	8 × 12 inches	12 × 18 inches	12 × 24 inches
FLAVORINGS			
LIGHT STICK MARGARINE, MELTED	1 tablespoon plus 1½ teaspoons	2 tablespoons	3 tablespoons
CINNAMON	1 teaspoon	1½ teaspoons	2 teaspoons
BROWN SUGAR	⅓ cup, firmly packed	½ cup, firmly packed	⅔ cup, firmly packed
CHOPPED PECANS	3 tablespoons	¼ cup	⅓ cup
GLAZE (MIX SEPARATELY)			
CONFECTIONERS' SUGAR	⅓ cup	½ cup	⅔ cup
VANILLA EXTRACT	¼ teaspoon	½ teaspoon	¾ teaspoon
WATER	1 to 2 teaspoons	1½ teaspoons to 1 tablespoon	1 tablespoon plus 1½ teaspoons

1-POUND
PER SERVING
CALORIES 150
TOTAL FAT 3 g
  Saturated 0.5 g
  Polyunsaturated 1 g
  Monounsaturated 1.5 g
CHOLESTEROL 0 mg
SODIUM 18 mg
CARBOHYDRATES 28 g
  Fiber 1 g
  Sugars 11 g
PROTEIN 3 g
CALCIUM 30 mg
POTASSIUM 87 mg
DIETARY EXCHANGES
  2 starch
  ½ fat

1½-POUND
PER SERVING
CALORIES 146
TOTAL FAT 3 g
  Saturated 0.5 g
  Polyunsaturated 1 g
  Monounsaturated 1.5 g
CHOLESTEROL 0 mg
SODIUM 17 mg
CARBOHYDRATES 28 g
  Fiber 1 g
  Sugars 11 g
PROTEIN 3 g
CALCIUM 27 mg
POTASSIUM 82 mg
DIETARY EXCHANGES
  2 starch
  ½ fat

2-POUND
PER SERVING
CALORIES 148
TOTAL FAT 3 g
  Saturated 0.5 g
  Polyunsaturated 1 g
  Monounsaturated 1.5 g
CHOLESTEROL 0 mg
SODIUM 18 mg
CARBOHYDRATES 28 g
  Fiber 1 g
  Sugars 11 g
PROTEIN 3 g
CALCIUM 29 mg
POTASSIUM 83 mg
DIETARY EXCHANGES
  2 starch
  ½ fat

Oatmeal Banana Breakfast Bread

Serves 16; 1 slice per serving

Banana, cranberries, and orange zest give this bread a lively flavor that will get your day off to just the right start.

Vegetable oil spray

¾ cup fat-free milk

½ cup uncooked quick-cooking oatmeal

½ cup firmly packed light brown sugar

1 medium banana, mashed (about ½ cup)

½ cup dried cranberries, raisins, or dried mixed fruit bits (optional)

Egg substitute equivalent to 1 egg, or 1 large egg

2 tablespoons canola or corn oil

1½ to 2 teaspoons grated orange zest or ½ teaspoon dried orange peel (see Cook's Tip, page 243)

1½ cups all-purpose flour

½ cup oat bran

2 teaspoons baking powder

1 to 1½ teaspoons ground cinnamon

¼ teaspoon baking soda

1 tablespoon uncooked quick-cooking oatmeal (optional)

Preheat the oven to 350°F. Spray an 8½ × 4½ × 2½-inch loaf pan with vegetable oil spray.

In a medium bowl, stir together the milk, ½ cup oatmeal, brown sugar, banana, dried cranberries, egg substitute, oil, and orange zest.

In another medium bowl, stir together the remaining ingredients except 1 tablespoon oatmeal. Add to the milk mixture, stirring just until moistened. Don't overmix; the batter should be lumpy. Pour the batter into the loaf pan. Sprinkle with the remaining oatmeal.

Bake for 45 to 50 minutes, or until a wooden toothpick or cake tester inserted in the center comes out clean. Invert the bread onto a cooling rack. Let cool for at least 10 minutes before slicing.

Bottled Citrus Peel

Stock a bottle of dried grated lemon peel and one of orange peel in your spice rack to add citrus flavor to your favorite salad dressings, marinades, and baked goods.

Bananas and Potassium

Potassium is necessary for the growth and maintenance of your body, including controlling a normal water balance between the cells and body fluids. Potassium also may help lower blood pressure. When medication for certain heart diseases is used to prevent retention of sodium and water, a potassium deficiency may occur. Eating a healthful, balanced diet can help you get enough potassium (about 4,700 milligrams per day for the average adult). One of the best sources is the banana; one medium banana has about 420 milligrams of potassium, as well as a good amount of fiber and vitamin C. (Appendix E, page 311, lists a number of other foods that are good sources of potassium.)

It's easy to keep a supply of bananas on hand. They are available year-round and usually are inexpensive. If you have bananas that are ripening too fast, store them in the refrigerator for up to two weeks or peel and freeze them, whole or in chunks, in an airtight bag for longer periods. The skins of refrigerated bananas will turn dark, but the fruit will be fine. In addition to eating bananas raw, you can bake, grill, or broil them. Add frozen bananas to smoothies, shakes, and other beverages for a thick consistency and smooth, creamy texture, or eat them frozen for a snack. Thaw them for use in puddings, pie fillings, or muffin, quick bread, or cake batter.

PER SERVING
CALORIES 114
TOTAL FAT 2.5 g
  Saturated 0 g
  Polyunsaturated 0.5 g
  Monounsaturated 1 g
CHOLESTEROL 0 mg
SODIUM 86 mg
CARBOHYDRATES 22 g
  Fiber 1 g
  Sugars 8 g
PROTEIN 3 g
CALCIUM 59 mg
POTASSIUM 113 mg
DIETARY EXCHANGES
  1½ starch
  ½ fat

Chocolate Chip Banana Bread

Serves 16; 1 slice per serving

Slices of this moist bread, with its banana flavor, surprise chocolate chips in the center, and crunchy vanilla wafer topping, are particularly inviting for a snack with a cup of hot tea.

Vegetable oil spray

1¾ cups all-purpose flour

⅔ cup sugar

⅓ cup semisweet chocolate chips

2 teaspoons baking powder

¼ teaspoon ground cinnamon

⅛ teaspoon ground nutmeg

1 cup mashed banana

⅓ cup unsweetened applesauce

Egg substitute equivalent to 1 egg, or 1 large egg

1 tablespoon canola or corn oil

6 reduced-fat vanilla wafer cookies, crushed (about ¼ cup)

Preheat the oven to 350°F. Lightly spray an 8½ × 4½ × 2½-inch loaf pan with vegetable oil spray.

In a large bowl, stir together the flour, sugar, chocolate chips, baking powder, cinnamon, and nutmeg. Make a well in the center.

Add the remaining ingredients except the cookie crumbs, stirring until just moistened. Don't overmix; the batter should be lumpy. Pour into the loaf pan. Sprinkle with the cookie crumbs.

Bake for 55 minutes, or until a wooden toothpick or cake tester inserted in the center comes out clean. Invert the bread onto a cooling rack and let cool before slicing.

PER SERVING

CALORIES 129

TOTAL FAT 2 g
    Saturated 0.5 g
    Polyunsaturated 0.5 g
    Monounsaturated 1 g

CHOLESTEROL 0 mg

SODIUM 64 mg

CARBOHYDRATES 26 g
    Fiber 1 g
    Sugars 13 g

PROTEIN 2 g

CALCIUM 37 mg

POTASSIUM 89 mg

DIETARY EXCHANGES
    1 starch
    ½ fruit
    ½ fat

Blueberry Muffins

Serves 12; 1 muffin per serving

Plump blueberries in a lemon-scented muffin really hit the spot for breakfast or an afternoon break.

Vegetable oil spray (optional)

1¾ cups all-purpose flour

⅓ cup sugar

2½ teaspoons baking powder

½ cup fat-free milk

Egg substitute equivalent to 1 egg, or whites of 2 large eggs

¼ cup unsweetened applesauce

1 teaspoon grated lemon zest

1 tablespoon canola or corn oil

1 cup fresh or frozen blueberries

1 teaspoon sugar

Preheat the oven to 400°F. Lightly spray a 12-cup muffin pan with vegetable oil spray or line with aluminum foil or paper muffin cups.

In a large bowl, stir together the flour, ⅓ cup sugar, and baking powder.

In a small bowl, whisk together the milk, egg substitute, applesauce, lemon zest, and oil. Pour into the flour mixture and stir just until moistened. Don't overmix; the batter should be lumpy.

With a rubber scraper, carefully fold in the blueberries. Pour about ¼ cup batter into each muffin cup. Sprinkle with the remaining sugar.

Bake for 20 to 22 minutes, or until a wooden toothpick or cake tester inserted in the center of the muffin comes out clean.

Cook's TIP

Paper Muffin Cups

Let the muffins cool completely before removing the paper muffin cups. This will keep the paper from sticking and pulling off part of the muffin.

PER SERVING
CALORIES 115
TOTAL FAT 1.5 g
  Saturated 0 g
  Polyunsaturated 0.5 g
  Monounsaturated 0.5 g
CHOLESTEROL 0 mg
SODIUM 99 mg
CARBOHYDRATES 23 g
  Fiber 1 g
  Sugars 8 g
PROTEIN 3 g
CALCIUM 68 mg
POTASSIUM 56 mg
DIETARY EXCHANGES
  1½ starch

Oat Bran and Yogurt Muffins

Serves 12; 1 muffin per serving

These muffins boast more nutrition than a high-calorie snack bar. Pack two in your lunchbox, and share your heart-healthy treat with a friend.

Vegetable oil spray (optional)
3/4 cup all-purpose flour
1/2 cup whole-wheat flour
1/2 cup oat bran
1/2 cup raisins
1/3 cup sugar
2 teaspoons baking powder
1/4 teaspoon baking soda
1 cup fat-free or low-fat plain yogurt
Egg substitute equivalent to 1 egg, or 1 large egg
1 tablespoon canola or corn oil

Preheat the oven to 425°F. Lightly spray a 12-cup muffin pan with vegetable oil spray or line with aluminum foil or paper muffin cups.

In a large bowl, stir together the flours, oat bran, raisins, sugar, baking powder, and baking soda.

In a small bowl, whisk together the remaining ingredients. Pour into the flour mixture and stir just until moistened. Don't overmix; the batter should be lumpy. Pour about 1/4 cup batter into each muffin cup.

Bake for 16 to 18 minutes, or until a wooden toothpick or cake tester inserted in the center of the muffin comes out clean.

Make an extra batch of these muffins for future snacks-on-the-go. Put each cooled muffin into a small airtight freezer bag and freeze them for up to one month. On your way out the door, grab a muffin and a piece of fruit or a can of juice to take with you for a quick, heart-healthy snack.

Cook's TIP

Oat Bran

Oat bran, the ground outer casing of the oat kernel, is high in both soluble and insoluble fiber. That is important because soluble fiber has been shown to help lower blood cholesterol when eaten regularly as part of a diet low in saturated and trans fats and cholesterol. Insoluble fiber is an important aid in digestion, helping maintain normal bowel function. A half-cup of cooked oat bran contains only 40 calories and 1 milligram of sodium, less than 1 gram of saturated fat, and no cholesterol. It's not just a breakfast cereal, though; give yogurt a nutritional boost by adding oat bran, or add about a half-cup per pound to lean ground meat mixtures, such as casseroles, meatballs, meat loaf, and chili. You can also substitute oat bran for flour in baking. However, oat bran can impart a slightly bitter taste when used in large amounts and it lacks gluten, which is needed for dough to rise, so replace only about one-quarter to one-third of the flour with oat bran.

PER SERVING

CALORIES 121
TOTAL FAT 1.5 g
    Saturated 0 g
    Polyunsaturated 0.5 g
    Monounsaturated 1 g
CHOLESTEROL 0 mg
SODIUM 120 mg
CARBOHYDRATES 25 g
    Fiber 2 g
    Sugars 11 g
PROTEIN 4 g
CALCIUM 91 mg
POTASSIUM 162 mg
DIETARY EXCHANGES
    1½ starch

Corn Muffins

Homemade corn muffins make mealtime special. Any leftovers are super for a quick snack on the go, or crumble a muffin into a bowl and top it with some beef taco filling. Add chopped bell peppers, onions, tomatoes, and shredded lettuce for a "taco in a bowl."

Vegetable oil spray
1 cup all-purpose flour
¾ cup yellow or white cornmeal
1 tablespoon sugar (optional)
2 teaspoons baking powder
1 cup fat-free milk
Egg substitute equivalent to 1 egg, or 1 large egg
1 tablespoon canola or corn oil
1 tablespoon light stick margarine, melted

Preheat the oven to 425°F. Lightly spray a 12-cup muffin pan with vegetable oil spray.

In a large bowl, stir together the flour, cornmeal, sugar, and baking powder.

In a small bowl, whisk together the remaining ingredients. Pour all at once into the dry ingredients, stirring just until moistened. Don't overmix; the batter should be slightly lumpy. Fill each muffin cup with about ¼ cup batter.

Bake for 15 to 20 minutes, or until a wooden toothpick or cake tester inserted in the center of the muffin comes out clean. Invert the muffins onto a cooling rack. Let cool for at least 2 minutes before serving.

PER SERVING
CALORIES 92
TOTAL FAT 2 g
    Saturated 0 g
    Polyunsaturated 0.5 g
    Monounsaturated 1 g
CHOLESTEROL 0 mg
SODIUM 92 mg
CARBOHYDRATES 16 g
    Fiber 1 g
    Sugars 1 g
PROTEIN 3 g
CALCIUM 69 mg
POTASSIUM 65 mg
DIETARY EXCHANGES
    1 starch

Corn Bread

Lightly spray an 8-inch square baking pan with vegetable oil spray. Pour in the batter. Bake for 20 to 25 minutes, or until a wooden toothpick or cake tester inserted in the center comes out clean. Invert onto a cooling rack. Cut into 12 squares. Serves 12; 1 square per serving.

Mexican Corn Muffins

To the milk mixture, add 1 cup no-salt-added canned or frozen whole-kernel corn, drained if canned or thawed if frozen; ½ cup fat-free shredded Cheddar cheese; 2 tablespoons canned mild green chiles, rinsed and drained; and 1 teaspoon Chili Powder (page 226) or commercial no-salt-added chili powder. Continue with the recipe as directed on page 248. Serves 12; 1 muffin per serving.

CORN BREAD	
PER SERVING	
CALORIES 92	
TOTAL FAT 2 g	
Saturated 0 g	
Polyunsaturated 0.5 g	
Monounsaturated 1 g	
CHOLESTEROL 0 mg	
SODIUM 92 mg	
CARBOHYDRATES 16 g	
Fiber 1 g	
Sugars 1 g	
PROTEIN 3 g	
CALCIUM 69 mg	
POTASSIUM 65 mg	
DIETARY EXCHANGES	
1 starch	

MEXICAN CORN MUFFINS	
PER SERVING	
CALORIES 114	
TOTAL FAT 2 g	
Saturated 0.5 g	
Polyunsaturated 0.5 g	
Monounsaturated 1 g	
CHOLESTEROL 1 mg	
SODIUM 146 mg	
CARBOHYDRATES 20 g	
Fiber 1 g	
Sugars 2 g	
PROTEIN 5 g	
CALCIUM 116 mg	
POTASSIUM 108 mg	
DIETARY EXCHANGES	
1½ starch	

Pancakes

Whether you serve these pancakes for breakfast, brunch, lunch, or dinner, they'll soon be a family favorite.

1   cup all-purpose flour
2   tablespoons sugar
2   teaspoons baking powder
⅛   teaspoon ground cinnamon
¾   cup plus 2 tablespoons fat-free milk
    Egg substitute equivalent to 1 egg, or 1 large egg
2   teaspoons canola or corn oil
¼   teaspoon vanilla extract
    Vegetable oil spray

In a medium bowl, stir together the flour, sugar, baking powder, and cinnamon.

In a small bowl, whisk together the remaining ingredients except the vegetable oil spray. Pour into the flour mixture. Gently whisk until just moistened. Don't over-mix; the batter should be lumpy.

Preheat the oven to 200°F. Heat a nonstick griddle over medium heat. Test the temperature by sprinkling a few drops of water on the griddle. If the water evaporates quickly, the griddle is ready. Remove it from the heat and lightly spray with vegetable oil spray (being careful not to spray near a gas flame). Spoon ¼ cup batter onto the griddle for each pancake, making 4 pancakes. Cook for 2 to 3 minutes, or until bubbles appear all over the surface. Flip the pancakes. Cook for 2 minutes, or until the bottoms are golden brown. Transfer the pancakes to a plate. Put in the oven to keep warm. Repeat with the remaining batter.

PER SERVING
CALORIES 185
TOTAL FAT 2.5 g
  Saturated 0 g
  Polyunsaturated 1 g
  Monounsaturated 1.5 g
CHOLESTEROL 1 mg
SODIUM 254 mg
CARBOHYDRATES 33 g
  Fiber 1 g
  Sugars 9 g
PROTEIN 7 g
CALCIUM 198 mg
POTASSIUM 139 mg
DIETARY EXCHANGES
  2 starch
  ½ skim milk

Blueberry Pancakes

Add ½ cup fresh or frozen blueberries to the batter after combining the ingredients.

Blueberries

When selecting blueberries, an excellent source of fiber, look for plump, firm berries with a powdery coating. That protective shield preserves moisture and keeps them fresh longer than most other berries. Choose dark blue berries for eating raw; the reddish ones are fine for cooking but are quite tart. Blueberries freeze well. Place the unwashed berries in a single layer on a baking sheet so they don't touch, let them freeze solid, then put them in an airtight freezer bag. Just before use, rinse the frozen berries, but don't thaw them or they will bleed on your hands or other food.

PER SERVING
CALORIES 196
TOTAL FAT 2.5 g
    Saturated 0 g
    Polyunsaturated 1 g
    Monounsaturated 1.5 g
CHOLESTEROL 1 mg
SODIUM 255 mg
CARBOHYDRATES 36 g
    Fiber 1 g
    Sugars 11 g
PROTEIN 7 g
CALCIUM 199 mg
POTASSIUM 153 mg
DIETARY EXCHANGES
    2 starch
    ½ skim milk

Oatmeal-Banana Waffles with Strawberry Sauce

Serves 12; 1 waffle and 2 tablespoons sauce per serving

You'll be tempted to start a weekend tradition of serving waffles for a special breakfast treat.

Strawberry Sauce

1 pound strawberries, stemmed and halved (about 2 cups)

1 tablespoon honey

Waffles

1½ cups fat-free or low-fat buttermilk

½ cup uncooked quick-cooking oatmeal

1 large banana, mashed (about ½ cup)

Egg substitute equivalent to 2 eggs, or 2 large eggs

3 tablespoons light brown sugar

1 tablespoon canola or corn oil

1 cup all-purpose flour

½ cup whole-wheat flour

2 teaspoons baking powder

¼ teaspoon baking soda

■ ■ ■

Vegetable oil spray

¼ cup chopped pecans, dry-roasted

In a food processor or blender, process the strawberries and honey until smooth. Pour the mixture into a small bowl. Cover and refrigerate until ready to use (it will keep for up to three days). (If you prepare the sauce ahead of time, you may want to let it come to room temperature before spooning it over the waffles.)

In a medium bowl, stir together the buttermilk, oatmeal, banana, egg substitute, brown sugar, and oil until the oatmeal is moistened. Let the mixture sit for 5 minutes to soften the oatmeal.

Meanwhile, preheat a waffle iron using the manufacturer's directions. Preheat the oven to 200°F. Line a baking sheet with aluminum foil.

In a small bowl, stir together the flours, baking powder, and baking soda. Pour into the buttermilk mixture. Whisk together until the flour mixture is just moistened but still slightly lumpy. Do not overmix, or the waffles will be tough.

Lightly spray the heated waffle iron with vegetable oil spray. Spoon the batter for the first waffle over the waffle iron. Following the manufacturer's directions for timing, cook until the steaming stops and the waffle is golden brown. Watch the first batch closely; adjust the time as necessary. Transfer the waffle to the baking sheet. Put in the oven and keep warm, uncovered, for up to 45 minutes. Repeat with the remaining batter.

To serve, spoon 2 tablespoons strawberry sauce over each waffle. Sprinkle 1 teaspoon pecans over each.

Banana Split Waffles

Serves 12; 1 waffle with toppings per serving

1	recipe Oatmeal-Banana Waffles (above), prepared
1½	cups drained crushed pineapple canned in its own juice
¾	cup fat-free or light nondairy frozen whipped topping, thawed
12	maraschino cherries, drained
¾	cup light chocolate syrup

Put 1 waffle on each plate. Top each with 2 tablespoons pineapple, 1 tablespoon whipped topping, 1 cherry, and 1 tablespoon chocolate syrup.

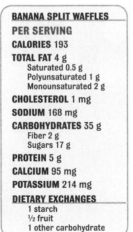

OATMEAL-BANANA WAFFLES	BANANA SPLIT WAFFLES
PER SERVING	**PER SERVING**
CALORIES 153	**CALORIES** 193
TOTAL FAT 4 g	**TOTAL FAT** 4 g
Saturated 0.5 g	Saturated 0.5 g
Polyunsaturated 1 g	Polyunsaturated 1 g
Monounsaturated 2 g	Monounsaturated 2 g
CHOLESTEROL 1 mg	**CHOLESTEROL** 1 mg
SODIUM 148 mg	**SODIUM** 168 mg
CARBOHYDRATES 26 g	**CARBOHYDRATES** 35 g
Fiber 3 g	Fiber 2 g
Sugars 10 g	Sugars 17 g
PROTEIN 5 g	**PROTEIN** 5 g
CALCIUM 95 mg	**CALCIUM** 95 mg
POTASSIUM 225 mg	**POTASSIUM** 214 mg
DIETARY EXCHANGES	**DIETARY EXCHANGES**
1 starch	1 starch
½ fruit	½ fruit
½ fat	1 other carbohydrate

Biscuits

Serves 14; 1 biscuit per serving

Split open one of these steaming, fluffy biscuits and spoon some all-fruit peach preserves on top. Or make your own sausage biscuits with Turkey Sausage Patties (page 128). Good for breakfast any time of day!

  Vegetable oil spray
2 cups all-purpose flour
2 teaspoons baking powder
¼ cup light stick margarine
¾ cup fat-free milk
  Flour for rolling out dough

Preheat the oven to 450°F. Lightly spray a baking sheet with vegetable oil spray.

In a medium bowl, stir together 2 cups flour and baking powder. Using a pastry blender, a fork, or two knives, cut the margarine in until the margarine pieces are about pea-size.

Pour the milk into the mixture. Stir with a fork until the dough clings together.

Lightly flour a flat surface. Turn out the dough and knead lightly 4 or 5 times. Pat the dough until it is about ½ inch thick. Dip the edge of a 2-inch round cutter (or drinking glass) into the flour to keep the dough from sticking. Reflouring the cutter as necessary, cut out the biscuits and place on the baking sheet with the edges of the biscuits touching.

Bake for 12 to 15 minutes, or until golden brown.

PER SERVING
CALORIES 84
TOTAL FAT 2 g
  Saturated 0.5 g
  Polyunsaturated 0.5 g
  Monounsaturated 0.5 g
CHOLESTEROL 0 mg
SODIUM 84 mg
CARBOHYDRATES 14 g
  Fiber 1 g
  Sugars 1 g
PROTEIN 2 g
CALCIUM 53 mg
POTASSIUM 41 mg
DIETARY EXCHANGES
  1 starch

Herb-Seasoned Biscuits

Add one or more of the following to the flour mixture: 1 teaspoon garlic powder; 1 teaspoon onion powder; 2 teaspoons dried parsley, crumbled; 2 teaspoons dried dillweed, crumbled; or ½ teaspoon dried sage.

Drop Biscuits

Increase the milk by 2 tablespoons. Stir the dough until well mixed. Make 14 biscuits, dropping the dough by heaping tablespoonfuls onto the baking sheet.

HERB-SEASONED BISCUITS
PER SERVING
CALORIES 84
TOTAL FAT 2 g
Saturated 0.5 g
Polyunsaturated 0.5 g
Monounsaturated 0.5 g
CHOLESTEROL 0 mg
SODIUM 85 mg
CARBOHYDRATES 15 g
Fiber 1 g
Sugars 1 g
PROTEIN 2 g
CALCIUM 54 mg
POTASSIUM 43 mg
DIETARY EXCHANGES
1 starch

DROP BISCUITS
PER SERVING
CALORIES 85
TOTAL FAT 2 g
Saturated 0.5 g
Polyunsaturated 0.5 g
Monounsaturated 0.5 g
CHOLESTEROL 0 mg
SODIUM 85 mg
CARBOHYDRATES 15 g
Fiber 1 g
Sugars 1 g
PROTEIN 2 g
CALCIUM 56 mg
POTASSIUM 44 mg
DIETARY EXCHANGES
1 starch

Peach and Dried Cherry Coffee Cake

Serves 16; 2¼- × 3¼-inch piece per serving

When it's your turn to bring a breakfast treat, try this adaptation of a quick mix.

Vegetable oil spray

½ cup water

⅓ cup dried sweetened cherries or dried sweetened cranberries

16.9-ounce box quick bread and coffee cake mix with streusel packet

¾ cup water

Whites of 4 large eggs, or egg substitute equivalent to 2 eggs

2 cups chopped fresh or frozen unsweetened peaches, thawed if frozen

Preheat the oven according to the directions on the mix package. Lightly spray a 13 × 9 × 2-inch baking pan with vegetable oil spray.

In a microwaveable bowl, combine the ½ cup water and cherries. Microwave on 100 percent power (high) for about 1½ minutes, or until the water just begins to boil. Drain well. Set aside.

In a medium bowl, stir together the quick bread mix, ¾ cup water, and egg whites until just blended. Spoon into the baking pan, smoothing evenly. Arrange the peaches and cherries on top. Sprinkle with the contents of the streusel packet. Top with the contents of the pecan packet, if included.

Bake for 25 minutes, or until a wooden toothpick or cake tester inserted in the center comes out almost clean. Place on a cooling rack to cool slightly before serving. Serve warm or at room temperature.

Flavors and texture are at their peak if this cake is served the day you bake it.

PER SERVING

CALORIES 153

TOTAL FAT 4.5 g
   Saturated 1 g
   Polyunsaturated 0 g
   Monounsaturated 0 g

CHOLESTEROL 0 mg

SODIUM 133 mg

CARBOHYDRATES 26 g
   Fiber 0 g
   Sugars 17 g

PROTEIN 2 g

CALCIUM 2 mg

POTASSIUM 55 mg

DIETARY EXCHANGES
   1½ starch
   ½ fat

Lemon Chiffon Angel Food Cake

Denver Chocolate Pudding Cake

Chocolate Cake

Carrot Cake

Quick Lemon Frosting

QUICK CHOCOLATE FROSTING

Gingerbread

Apple Pie with Raisins

Deep-Dish Cherry Pie

DEEP-DISH BLUEBERRY PIE

Pumpkin Pie

Nectarine Crumble

Matzo Crumb Piecrust

Piecrust

Desserts

- Brownies
- Peanut Butter Cookies
- Oatmeal Cookies
- Gingerbread Cookie Cutouts
- Praline Cookies
- Fudge
  PEANUT BUTTER FUDGE

- Lemon Cream with Raspberries and Gingersnap Topping
- Flan Caramel
- Spiced Fruit
- Ice Cream with Hot Tropical Fruit
- Strawberry Banana Sorbet
- Frozen Mini Chocolate Mousse Soufflés

Lemon Chiffon Angel Food Cake

Serves 16; 1 slice of cake, ¼ cup raspberries, and 1½ tablespoons whipped topping per serving

Enhance an easy-to-prepare angel food cake mix with lemon zest, nutmeg, and chopped pistachios. Top each slice with fresh, juicy raspberries and lemon-scented whipped topping. Pure bliss!

  16-ounce package angel food cake mix
2 teaspoons grated lemon zest
1 teaspoon lemon extract
½ teaspoon yellow food coloring (optional)
¼ cup chopped unsalted pistachios
1½ cups frozen fat-free or light whipped topping, thawed
1 teaspoon grated lemon zest
4 cups raspberries

In a large mixing bowl, stir together the cake mix, 2 teaspoons lemon zest, lemon extract, and food coloring. Prepare the cake using the package directions. Stir in the pistachios.

Put the whipped topping in a medium bowl. Fold in 1 teaspoon lemon zest.

To serve, place slices of cake on plates. Top each slice with ¼ cup raspberries and 1½ tablespoons whipped topping.

PER SERVING
CALORIES 144
TOTAL FAT 1 g
  Saturated 0 g
  Polyunsaturated 0.5 g
  Monounsaturated 0.5 g
CHOLESTEROL 0 mg
SODIUM 251 mg
CARBOHYDRATES 30 g
  Fiber 2 g
  Sugars 20 g
PROTEIN 3 g
CALCIUM 40 mg
POTASSIUM 68 mg
DIETARY EXCHANGES
  2 other carbohydrate

Denver Chocolate Pudding Cake

Serves 9; 3-inch square per serving

This cake is so easy to prepare. Just bake it and, *voilà*, the topping magically appears.

Vegetable oil spray
1 cup all-purpose flour
¾ cup sugar
3 tablespoons unsweetened cocoa powder (Dutch process preferred)
2 teaspoons baking powder
½ cup fat-free milk
3 tablespoons light stick margarine, melted
½ teaspoon vanilla extract
½ cup firmly packed light brown sugar
½ cup sugar
¼ cup unsweetened cocoa powder (Dutch process preferred)
1½ cups cold water or cold coffee

Preheat the oven to 350°F. Lightly spray a 9-inch square baking pan with vegetable oil spray.

In a large bowl, sift together the flour, ¾ cup sugar, 3 tablespoons cocoa, and baking powder.

Whisk in the milk, margarine, and vanilla.

PER SERVING
CALORIES 243
TOTAL FAT 2.5 g
   Saturated 0.5 g
   Polyunsaturated 0.5 g
   Monounsaturated 0.5 g
CHOLESTEROL 0 mg
SODIUM 126 mg
CARBOHYDRATES 54 g
   Fiber 1 g
   Sugars 40 g
PROTEIN 3 g
CALCIUM 84 mg
POTASSIUM 293 mg
DIETARY EXCHANGES
   3½ other carbohydrate
   ½ fat

Pour the batter into the pan. Sprinkle in order with the brown sugar, ½ cup sugar, and ¼ cup cocoa powder; don't mix. Pour the water evenly over the batter; don't mix.

Bake for 40 minutes, or until the top of the cake looks dry and is firm to the touch.

To serve, cut the cake into 9 pieces. Invert each piece onto a dessert plate so the sauce is on top.

Chocolate Cake

Serves 24; 1 slice per serving

A wonderfully moist cake, this is good with Quick Chocolate Frosting (page 263) or without.

	Vegetable oil spray
2½	cups all-purpose flour
⅓	cup unsweetened cocoa powder (Dutch process preferred)
1	tablespoon plus ½ teaspoon baking powder
¾	cup water
⅔	cup fat-free milk
	4-ounce jar baby-food prunes
¼	cup canola or corn oil
1	teaspoon vanilla extract
	Whites of 4 large eggs
¼	teaspoon cream of tartar
1¾	cups sugar

Preheat the oven to 375°F. Lightly spray a 13 × 9 × 2-inch cake pan or two 8-inch square or 9-inch square cake pans with vegetable oil spray. Line the pan(s) with wax paper or cooking parchment cut to fit the bottom.

In a large bowl, sift together the flour, cocoa powder, and baking powder. Make a well in the center.

In a small bowl, whisk together the water, milk, prunes, oil, and vanilla. Pour into the well in the flour mixture, stirring until well combined. The batter will resemble a thick paste.

In a medium mixing bowl, beat the egg whites with an electric mixer until foamy. Add the cream of tartar. Gradually add the sugar, beating after each addition until the egg whites form soft peaks. Gently fold the egg whites into the batter. Pour into the prepared pan(s).

Bake for 35 to 40 minutes, or until a wooden toothpick or cake tester inserted in the center comes out clean. Set on a cooling rack for 5 minutes. Turn out the cake; peel off the wax paper or cooking parchment. Serve the cake warm or at room temperature.

Cocoa Powder

Made from roasted cocoa beans with most of the fat (cocoa butter) removed, unsweetened cocoa powder can substitute for solid chocolate in baking recipes. Use 3 tablespoons of cocoa powder plus 1 tablespoon of oil, such as canola or corn, for 1 ounce of unsweetened baking chocolate. You'll cut the total fat by 50 to 75 percent. Cocoa powder has many other advantages. It costs less per ounce than baking chocolate and goes almost twice as far. It blends more easily than chocolate, so there's less chance of lumpy batters. If you store cocoa powder in a cool, dry place, it will keep almost indefinitely. Dutch process cocoa has been treated with alkali to remove its natural acidity, making it darker in color, richer in flavor, and usually a little more expensive than all-purpose, or American process, cocoa powder. The two types have about the same calorie and fat counts and are interchangeable in recipes.

PER SERVING
CALORIES 140
TOTAL FAT 2.5 g
   Saturated 0.5 g
   Polyunsaturated 0.5 g
   Monounsaturated 1.5 g
CHOLESTEROL 0 mg
SODIUM 71 mg
CARBOHYDRATES 27 g
   Fiber 1 g
   Sugars 16 g
PROTEIN 3 g
CALCIUM 47 mg
POTASSIUM 114 mg
DIETARY EXCHANGES
   2 other carbohydrate
   ½ fat

Carrot Cake

Serves 16; 2 × 3-inch piece per serving

This snack cake gives you a double dose of carrots—a scrumptious way to eat your vegetables!

Vegetable oil spray

Cake

1 cup honey

2 tablespoons canola or corn oil

4-ounce jar baby-food carrots

Egg substitute equivalent to 1 egg, or whites of 2 large eggs

1 teaspoon vanilla extract

2 cups shredded carrots

1 cup all-purpose flour

1 cup whole-wheat flour

¼ cup fat-free dry milk

2 teaspoons baking powder

1 teaspoon ground cinnamon

⅛ teaspoon ground nutmeg

Topping

2 cups frozen fat-free or light whipped topping, thawed (optional)

½ teaspoon ground nutmeg or cinnamon (optional)

Preheat the oven to 350°F. Lightly spray a 13 × 9 × 2-inch baking pan with vegetable oil spray.

PER SERVING
CALORIES 149
TOTAL FAT 2 g
Saturated 0 g
Polyunsaturated 0.5 g
Monounsaturated 1 g
CHOLESTEROL 0 mg
SODIUM 77 mg
CARBOHYDRATES 31 g
Fiber 2 g
Sugars 19 g
PROTEIN 3 g
CALCIUM 57 mg
POTASSIUM 135 mg
DIETARY EXCHANGES
2 other carbohydrate
½ fat

For the cake, in a medium bowl, stir together the honey and oil until smooth. Stir in the baby-food carrots, egg substitute, and vanilla. Stir in the shredded carrots.

In a large bowl, stir together the remaining cake ingredients. Stir in the carrot mixture. Pour into the baking pan.

Bake for 25 minutes, or until a wooden toothpick or cake tester inserted in the center comes out clean. Let cool on a cooling rack before cutting into 16 slices.

In a small bowl, stir together the whipped topping and nutmeg. Dollop about 2 tablespoons mixture onto each piece of cake.

Quick Lemon Frosting

Frosts 13 × 9 × 2-inch or two-layer cake
Serves 16; 2 tablespoons per serving

Need some frosting in a hurry? This easy-to-do recipe is your answer. Try it on Carrot Cake (page 262).

1 cup confectioners' sugar

2 tablespoons fat-free milk

½ teaspoon lemon zest

1 tablespoon plus 1½ teaspoons fresh lemon juice

1 teaspoon vanilla extract

2 cups frozen fat-free or light whipped topping, thawed

In a medium bowl, using a rubber scraper, stir together all the ingredients except the whipped topping. Gently fold in the whipped topping.

Quick Chocolate Frosting

Frosts 13 × 9 × 2-inch or two-layer cake
Serves 16; 2 tablespoons per serving

1 cup confectioners' sugar

¾ cup unsweetened cocoa powder (Dutch process preferred)

3 tablespoons fat-free milk

1¼ teaspoons vanilla extract

2 cups frozen fat-free or light whipped topping, thawed

In a medium bowl, using a rubber scraper, stir together all the ingredients except the whipped topping. Gently fold in the whipped topping.

QUICK LEMON FROSTING
PER SERVING
CALORIES 46
TOTAL FAT 0 g
   Saturated 0 g
   Polyunsaturated 0 g
   Monounsaturated 0 g
CHOLESTEROL 0 mg
SODIUM 6 mg
CARBOHYDRATES 11 g
   Fiber 0 g
   Sugars 9 g
PROTEIN 0 g
CALCIUM 3 mg
POTASSIUM 5 mg
DIETARY EXCHANGES
   ½ other carbohydrate

QUICK CHOCOLATE FROSTING
PER SERVING
CALORIES 52
TOTAL FAT 0 g
   Saturated 0 g
   Polyunsaturated 0 g
   Monounsaturated 0 g
CHOLESTEROL 0 mg
SODIUM 6 mg
CARBOHYDRATES 12 g
   Fiber 0 g
   Sugars 9 g
PROTEIN 0 g
CALCIUM 4 mg
POTASSIUM 73 mg
DIETARY EXCHANGES
   1 other carbohydrate

Gingerbread

Serves 8; 3-inch square per serving

Adding fruit gives this gingerbread a deep sweetness.

  5-ounce can fat-free evaporated milk
2 teaspoons cider vinegar
  Vegetable oil spray
1 cup all-purpose flour
1 cup whole-wheat flour
1 teaspoon ground ginger
½ teaspoon baking soda
½ teaspoon ground cinnamon
¾ cup honey
  6-ounce jar baby-food sweet potatoes
2 tablespoons egg substitute, or white of 1 large egg
1 tablespoon plus 2 teaspoons canola or corn oil
½ cup raisins, dried cherries, dried cranberries, or chopped peeled apple

In a medium bowl, stir together the milk and vinegar. Let stand for 10 minutes.

Preheat the oven to 350°F. Lightly spray a 9-inch square baking pan with vegetable oil spray.

In another medium bowl, stir together the flours, ginger, baking soda, and cinnamon.

PER SERVING
CALORIES 292
TOTAL FAT 3.5 g
  Saturated 0.5 g
  Polyunsaturated 1 g
  Monounsaturated 2 g
CHOLESTEROL 1 mg
SODIUM 113 mg
CARBOHYDRATES 63 g
  Fiber 3 g
  Sugars 36 g
PROTEIN 6 g
CALCIUM 72 mg
POTASSIUM 295 mg
DIETARY EXCHANGES
  3 starch
  1 other carbohydrate

Add the remaining ingredients except the raisins to the milk mixture. Beat with an electric mixer on medium until blended.

Gradually add the flour mixture, stirring well after each addition. Fold in the raisins. Pour into the pan.

Bake for 30 minutes, or until a wooden toothpick or cake tester inserted in the center comes out clean. Let cool on a cooling rack for at least 10 minutes before slicing.

Apple Pie with Raisins

Serves 8; 1 slice per serving

This recipe combines the ingredients of apple strudel to give you the same taste without as much work.

Vegetable oil spray

²⁄₃ cup sugar

1 teaspoon ground cinnamon

2½ pounds tart, firm apples, peeled and sliced (about 8 medium)

½ cup raisins

1 recipe Piecrust (page 270), unbaked

Preheat the oven to 425°F. Lightly spray a 9-inch pie pan with vegetable oil spray.

In a large bowl, stir together the sugar and cinnamon.

Stir in the apples and raisins. Pour into the pie pan.

Top the apple mixture with the crust. Cut off the excess crust. Crimp the crust around the edge to create a ruffle. Make four to six slits in the crust about ½ inch deep. Cover the rim of the pie with aluminum foil to prevent overbrowning.

Bake for 25 minutes. Remove the foil and bake for 15 to 20 minutes, or until the crust is lightly browned.

PER SERVING
CALORIES 237
TOTAL FAT 3 g
   Saturated 0.5 g
   Polyunsaturated 1 g
   Monounsaturated 1.5 g
CHOLESTEROL 0 mg
SODIUM 36 mg
CARBOHYDRATES 54 g
   Fiber 2 g
   Sugars 40 g
PROTEIN 2 g
CALCIUM 21 mg
POTASSIUM 205 mg
DIETARY EXCHANGES
   1 starch
   1½ fruit
   1 other carbohydrate

Deep-Dish Cherry Pie

Serves 8; 1 slice per serving

This pie is so wonderful, you'll want to eat it straight from the oven—and not just on George Washington's birthday.

Vegetable oil spray
1   cup sugar
½   cup all-purpose flour
½   teaspoon ground cinnamon
2   16-ounce cans sour cherries, drained
⅛   teaspoon almond extract
1   recipe Piecrust (page 270), unbaked

Preheat the oven to 425°F. Spray a 9-inch deep-dish glass pie pan with vegetable oil spray.

In a medium bowl, stir together the sugar, flour, and cinnamon.

In another medium bowl, stir together the cherries and almond extract. Stir into the sugar mixture. Pour into the pie pan.

Top the cherry mixture with the crust. Cut off the excess crust. Crimp the crust around the edge to create a ruffle. Make four to six slits in the crust about ½ inch deep. Cover the rim of the pie with aluminum foil to prevent overbrowning.

Bake for 25 minutes. Remove the foil and bake for 20 minutes, or until the crust is golden. Let the pie cool on a cooling rack.

DEEP-DISH CHERRY	DEEP-DISH BLUEBERRY
PER SERVING	**PER SERVING**
CALORIES 250	**CALORIES** 226
TOTAL FAT 3 g	**TOTAL FAT** 3 g
Saturated 0.5 g	Saturated 0.5 g
Polyunsaturated 1 g	Polyunsaturated 1 g
Monounsaturated 1.5 g	Monounsaturated 1.5 g
CHOLESTEROL 0 mg	**CHOLESTEROL** 0 mg
SODIUM 43 mg	**SODIUM** 36 mg
CARBOHYDRATES 54 g	**CARBOHYDRATES** 48 g
Fiber 2 g	Fiber 2 g
Sugars 39 g	Sugars 31 g
PROTEIN 3 g	**PROTEIN** 3 g
CALCIUM 22 mg	**CALCIUM** 14 mg
POTASSIUM 139 mg	**POTASSIUM** 83 mg
DIETARY EXCHANGES	**DIETARY EXCHANGES**
1½ starch	1½ starch
1 fruit	1 fruit
1 other carbohydrate	½ other carbohydrate

Deep-Dish Blueberry Pie

Substitute 4 cups fresh or frozen blueberries for the cherries, and reduce the sugar to ¾ cup.

Pumpkin Pie

Serves 8; 1 slice per serving

Our version of this old-time favorite is so tasty you'll want to have it year-round.

    Vegetable oil spray
    16-ounce can solid-pack pumpkin (not pumpkin pie mix)
2/3 cup firmly packed light brown sugar
  1 teaspoon ground cinnamon
1/2 teaspoon ground ginger
1/4 teaspoon ground cloves or ground allspice
    13-ounce can fat-free evaporated milk
    Whites of 3 large eggs, beaten until foamy
  1 recipe Piecrust (page 270), unbaked
  1 cup frozen fat-free or light whipped topping, thawed (optional)

Preheat the oven to 400°F. Spray a 9-inch deep-dish glass pie pan with vegetable oil spray.

In a large mixing bowl, stir together the pumpkin, brown sugar, cinnamon, ginger, and cloves.

Add the milk and egg whites. With an electric mixer, beat on medium until thoroughly combined.

Line the pan with the pie dough. Crimp the crust around the edge to create a ruffle. Fill with the pumpkin mixture. Cover the rim of the pie with aluminum foil to prevent overbrowning.

Bake for 25 minutes. Remove the foil from the pie. Bake for 20 minutes, or until a knife inserted near the center of the pie comes out clean. Transfer to a cooling rack.

Lightly spray the pie with vegetable oil spray. Let cool.

To serve, cut the pie into 8 slices. Top each with 2 tablespoons whipped topping.

Lightly spraying the pie with vegetable oil spray provides a sheen to the pie filling.

PER SERVING
CALORIES 215
TOTAL FAT 3 g
   Saturated 0.5 g
   Polyunsaturated 1 g
   Monounsaturated 1.5 g
CHOLESTEROL 2 mg
SODIUM 119 mg
CARBOHYDRATES 41 g
   Fiber 2 g
   Sugars 30 g
PROTEIN 7 g
CALCIUM 175 mg
POTASSIUM 375 mg
DIETARY EXCHANGES
   1 starch
   1/2 skim milk
   1 other carbohydrate

Nectarine Crumble

Sliced almonds provide crunch to the crumbles that top plump slices of sweet, firm-fleshed nectarines in this fragrant dessert.

2 pounds fresh unpeeled nectarines, sliced (about 4 cups), or 2 pounds frozen unsweetened sliced peaches, thawed

¼ cup light brown sugar, packed

2 tablespoons orange juice concentrate

1 teaspoon grated lemon zest

½ teaspoon almond extract

¼ teaspoon ground nutmeg

½ cup uncooked quick-cooking oatmeal

3 tablespoons sliced almonds

2 tablespoons all-purpose flour

1 tablespoon light brown sugar, packed

1 tablespoon light tub margarine

½ teaspoon ground cinnamon

Preheat the oven to 375°F.

In a medium bowl, stir together the nectarines, ¼ cup brown sugar, orange juice concentrate, lemon zest, almond extract, and nutmeg. Pour into an 8-inch square nonstick baking pan.

In a small bowl, using a fork, combine the remaining ingredients until the margarine is distributed throughout. Sprinkle over the nectarine mixture.

Bake for 30 to 35 minutes, or until the fruit is tender and the topping is golden brown.

PER SERVING

CALORIES 131

TOTAL FAT 2.5 g
  Saturated 0 g
  Polyunsaturated 0.5 g
  Monounsaturated 1 g
CHOLESTEROL 0 mg
SODIUM 15 mg
CARBOHYDRATES 27 g
  Fiber 3 g
  Sugars 18 g
PROTEIN 3 g
CALCIUM 26 mg
POTASSIUM 305 mg
DIETARY EXCHANGES
  1 starch
  1 fruit
  ½ fat

Matzo Crumb Piecrust

Makes 1 9-inch piecrust
Serves 8; 1/8 crust per serving

This crust is particularly suited to a pudding or cream pie filling. It turns fat-free pudding made from a mix into a special sweet treat.

1 cup unsalted matzo meal

¼ cup sugar

¼ teaspoon ground cinnamon (optional)

3 tablespoons light stick margarine, melted

Preheat the oven to 350°F.

In a small bowl, stir together the matzo meal and sugar.

Stir in the cinnamon and margarine. Press firmly into a 9-inch pie pan.

Bake for 20 minutes, or until lightly browned.

PER SERVING
CALORIES 108
TOTAL FAT 2.5 g
    Saturated 0.5 g
    Polyunsaturated 0.5 g
    Monounsaturated 0.5 g
CHOLESTEROL 0 mg
SODIUM 28 mg
CARBOHYDRATES 20 g
    Fiber 0 g
    Sugars 7 g
PROTEIN 2 g
CALCIUM 0 mg
POTASSIUM 27 mg
DIETARY EXCHANGES
    1½ starch

Piecrust

Makes 1 9-inch piecrust
Serves 8; 1/8 crust per serving

Remember your grandmother's homemade piecrust? This "grandmother-style" crust has all the same goodness but little of the trans fat.

2/3 cup all-purpose flour

3 tablespoons sugar

2 tablespoons corn oil stick margarine, diced

1 tablespoon plus 1½ teaspoons fat-free milk

1 teaspoon all-purpose flour

Put all the ingredients except 1 teaspoon flour in a food processor. Process until the dough begins to stick together. Form the pie dough into a disk about 4 inches in diameter. Cover with plastic wrap and refrigerate for 15 minutes.

Place a sheet of plastic wrap on a flat surface. Sprinkle with the remaining flour. Put the dough on the floured surface, press lightly, and turn the dough over (this allows some flour to stick to both sides of the dough). Cover the dough with another sheet of plastic wrap. Roll out the dough to a 10-inch circle. Remove the top sheet of plastic wrap. Use the crust according to the recipe directions.

For easiest handling, be sure to use plastic wrap, not wax paper, when rolling out dough.

Baking Unfilled Piecrust

When baking an unfilled crust, or "baking blind," use the weight of dried beans, dried rice, or metal or ceramic pie weights to prevent the crust from puffing up and slipping down the side of the pan. If you don't have any of these, you can nestle a pie pan of equal size into the pan with the uncooked crust, then bake it.

PER SERVING
CALORIES 84
TOTAL FAT 3 g
  Saturated 0.5 g
  Polyunsaturated 0.5 g
  Monounsaturated 1.5 g
CHOLESTEROL 0 mg
SODIUM 35 mg
CARBOHYDRATES 13 g
  Fiber 0 g
  Sugars 5 g
PROTEIN 1 g
CALCIUM 6 mg
POTASSIUM 18 mg
DIETARY EXCHANGES
  1 starch
  ½ fat

Brownies

Serves 12; 1 brownie per serving

For that melt-in-your-mouth flavor, serve these brownies as soon as they're cool.

Vegetable oil spray
1 cup sugar
¾ cup all-purpose flour
½ cup unsweetened cocoa powder
½ teaspoon baking powder
4-ounce jar baby-food prunes
Whites of 3 large eggs
3 tablespoons corn oil stick margarine, melted
1 teaspoon vanilla extract
2 tablespoons confectioners' sugar

Preheat the oven to 350°F. Lightly spray an 8-inch square baking pan with vegetable oil spray.

In a medium bowl, sift together the sugar, flour, cocoa, and baking powder. Stir in the remaining ingredients except the confectioners' sugar. Pour into the baking pan.

Bake for 30 minutes, or until the edges begin to pull away from the sides of the pan. Let cool on a cooling rack. Cut into 12 squares. Sift the confectioners' sugar over all before removing from the pan.

Cook's TIP

You can make these brownies up to 48 hours in advance, but don't add the confectioners' sugar then. The sugar may dissolve into the brownie, giving it a mottled appearance. You can add the sugar up to 4 hours before serving, but a little of it will dissolve.

PER SERVING
CALORIES 153
TOTAL FAT 3.5 g
  Saturated 0.5 g
  Polyunsaturated 0.5 g
  Monounsaturated 1.5 g
CHOLESTEROL 0 mg
SODIUM 65 mg
CARBOHYDRATES 28 g
  Fiber 1 g
  Sugars 19 g
PROTEIN 3 g
CALCIUM 15 mg
POTASSIUM 234 mg
DIETARY EXCHANGES
  2 other carbohydrate
  ½ fat

Peanut Butter Cookies

Serves 48; 2 cookies per serving

You're sure to have a crowd gather when you set out a plate of these freshly baked treats.

Vegetable oil spray

½ cup corn oil stick margarine

½ cup sugar

½ cup firmly packed light brown sugar

Egg substitute equivalent to 1 egg, or 1 large egg

1 cup unsalted peanut butter

½ teaspoon vanilla extract

1½ cups all-purpose flour

1¼ teaspoons baking powder

Preheat the oven to 350°F. Lightly spray two baking sheets with vegetable oil spray.

In a large mixing bowl, cream the margarine and sugars with an electric mixer.

Beat in the egg substitute.

Add the peanut butter and vanilla. Beat until smooth.

In a medium bowl, sift together the flour and baking powder. Gradually stir into the margarine mixture. Beat on medium for 15 to 20 seconds.

Roll the dough into ¾-inch balls and place 1½ to 2 inches apart on the baking sheets. Partially flatten with a fork.

Bake for 15 minutes, or until a wooden toothpick or cake tester inserted in the center comes out clean. Let the cookies cool for 2 to 3 minutes on the baking sheets. Transfer the cookies to cooling racks. Repeat with the remaining dough.

PER SERVING
CALORIES 80
TOTAL FAT 4.5 g
    Saturated 1 g
    Polyunsaturated 1 g
    Monounsaturated 2.5 g
CHOLESTEROL 0 mg
SODIUM 37 mg
CARBOHYDRATES 8 g
    Fiber 0 g
    Sugars 5 g
PROTEIN 2 g
CALCIUM 12 mg
POTASSIUM 51 mg
DIETARY EXCHANGES
    ½ other carbohydrate
    1 fat

Oatmeal Cookies

Serves 16; 2 cookies per serving

Moist, chewy, and delicious, these will become the new "traditional" oatmeal cookies in your household.

	Vegetable oil spray
6	tablespoons light stick margarine
½	cup firmly packed light brown sugar
1	tablespoon light corn syrup
½	teaspoon vanilla extract
1	cup all-purpose flour
¼	teaspoon baking soda
¼	teaspoon ground cinnamon
1	cup uncooked quick-cooking oatmeal
	Flour for rolling dough

Preheat the oven to 375°F. Lightly spray two baking sheets with vegetable oil spray.

In a large mixing bowl, beat the margarine and brown sugar with an electric mixer on medium until creamy, about 2 minutes.

Stir in the corn syrup and vanilla.

In a medium bowl, stir together 1 cup flour, baking soda, and cinnamon. Gradually add to the margarine mixture, stirring after each addition until the dough pulls away from the side of the bowl.

Stir in the oatmeal.

Lightly flour your hands and roll the dough into 1-inch balls. Place 2 inches apart on the baking sheets. Dip a fork in the flour and slightly flatten each cookie to about ½ inch thick.

Bake for 8 to 9 minutes, or until lightly browned. Immediately transfer the cookies from the baking sheets to cooling racks. The cookies can be stored in an airtight container for up to one week.

PER SERVING
CALORIES 97
TOTAL FAT 2.5 g
  Saturated 0.5 g
  Polyunsaturated 0.5 g
  Monounsaturated 0.5 g
CHOLESTEROL 0 mg
SODIUM 52 mg
CARBOHYDRATES 17 g
  Fiber 1 g
  Sugars 8 g
PROTEIN 2 g
CALCIUM 10 mg
POTASSIUM 52 mg
DIETARY EXCHANGES
  1 other carbohydrate
  ½ fat

Gingerbread Cookie Cutouts

Serves 18; 2 4-inch cookies per serving

You'll know the holidays have arrived when the spicy aroma of gingerbread cookies fills your home!

- 3 cups all-purpose flour
- 1 teaspoon baking powder
- 1 teaspoon ground cinnamon
- 1 teaspoon ground ginger
- ½ teaspoon baking soda
- ½ teaspoon salt
- ½ teaspoon ground cloves
- ¾ cup firmly packed light brown sugar
- ½ cup molasses
- ¼ cup canola or corn oil
  Egg substitute equivalent to 1 egg, or 1 large egg
- 2 tablespoons sugar
  Flour for rolling dough
  Vegetable oil spray

In a medium bowl, stir together the flour, baking powder, cinnamon, ginger, baking soda, salt, and cloves.

In a large bowl, stir together the brown sugar, molasses, oil, egg substitute, and sugar. Gradually add the flour mixture to the brown sugar mixture, stirring to form a soft dough. Return the dough to the medium bowl, cover tightly with plastic wrap, and refrigerate for 2 to 12 hours.

Preheat the oven to 375°F. Lightly spray two baking sheets with vegetable oil spray.

Sprinkle flour on a board or pastry cloth. Roll half the cookie dough to ⅛-inch thickness. Dip the edges of the cookie cutters in flour, shaking off the excess. Cut out the cookies, continuing to dip the cookie cutters in flour as needed to keep the dough from sticking. Place the cookies on the baking sheets.

Bake for 5 to 6 minutes, or until the cookies are slightly firm to the touch (the cookies shouldn't brown). Let the cookies cool slightly, then transfer them from the baking sheets to a cooling rack. When the cookies have cooled completely, store them in airtight tins for up to one week.

PER SERVING
CALORIES 172
TOTAL FAT 3.5 g
    Saturated 0.5 g
    Polyunsaturated 1 g
    Monounsaturated 2 g
CHOLESTEROL 0 mg
SODIUM 136 mg
CARBOHYDRATES 33 g
    Fiber 1 g
    Sugars 15 g
PROTEIN 3 g
CALCIUM 46 mg
POTASSIUM 195 mg
DIETARY EXCHANGES
    2 other carbohydrate
    ½ fat

Praline Cookies

Loaded with toasted pecans, these cookies look and taste like pralines. The batter will be creamy, not stiff.

Vegetable oil spray
1/3 cup light stick margarine
1 cup firmly packed light brown sugar
Egg substitute equivalent to 1 egg, or 1 large egg
1 tablespoon vanilla, butter, and nut flavoring or vanilla extract
1 1/2 cups sifted all-purpose flour
3/4 cup chopped dry-roasted pecans

Preheat the oven to 375°F. Lightly spray two baking sheets with vegetable oil spray.

In a large mixing bowl, beat the margarine and brown sugar with an electric mixer on medium for 2 minutes, or until creamy.

Beat in the egg substitute and flavoring.

Stir in the flour and pecans, blending well.

Drop the dough by teaspoonfuls onto the baking sheets.

Bake for 8 to 9 minutes, or until lightly browned. Transfer the cookies from the baking sheets to cooling racks.

PER SERVING
CALORIES 68
TOTAL FAT 2.5 g
  Saturated 0.5 g
  Polyunsaturated 1 g
  Monounsaturated 1 g
CHOLESTEROL 0 mg
SODIUM 17 mg
CARBOHYDRATES 10 g
  Fiber 0 g
  Sugars 6 g
PROTEIN 1 g
CALCIUM 8 mg
POTASSIUM 41 mg
DIETARY EXCHANGES
  1/2 other carbohydrate
  1/2 fat

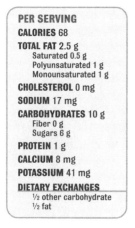

Fudge

This delightful chocolate treat is easy, easy, easy.

Vegetable oil spray
1 cup firmly packed light brown sugar
1 cup sugar
2/3 cup fat-free milk
1/3 cup unsweetened cocoa powder
2 tablespoons light tub margarine
1 teaspoon vanilla extract

Lightly spray an 8-inch square baking pan with vegetable oil spray.

In a medium saucepan, whisk together the sugars, milk, and cocoa powder. Cook over medium-high heat until the mixture reaches 236°F on a candy thermometer, or until a small amount of syrup dropped into cold water forms a soft ball. Remove from the heat.

Add the margarine but don't stir. Let the mixture cool until the bottom of the pan is lukewarm to the touch.

Add the vanilla. Beat with an electric mixer on medium for 5 to 10 minutes, or until the fudge is thick and no longer glossy. Spread in the baking pan. Let cool until firm. Cut into 25 pieces.

FUDGE
PER SERVING
CALORIES 75
TOTAL FAT 0.5 g
   Saturated 0 g
   Polyunsaturated 0 g
   Monounsaturated 0 g
CHOLESTEROL 0 mg
SODIUM 13 mg
CARBOHYDRATES 18 g
   Fiber 0 g
   Sugars 17 g
PROTEIN 0 g
CALCIUM 16 mg
POTASSIUM 99 mg
DIETARY EXCHANGES
   1 other carbohydrate

PEANUT BUTTER FUDGE
PER SERVING
CALORIES 107
TOTAL FAT 3 g
   Saturated 0.5 g
   Polyunsaturated 1 g
   Monounsaturated 1.5 g
CHOLESTEROL 0 mg
SODIUM 24 mg
CARBOHYDRATES 19 g
   Fiber 1 g
   Sugars 17 g
PROTEIN 2 g
CALCIUM 18 mg
POTASSIUM 138 mg
DIETARY EXCHANGES
   1 other carbohydrate
   1/2 fat

Peanut Butter Fudge

After beating the fudge, stir in 1/2 cup reduced-sodium peanut butter just until combined.

Lemon Cream with Raspberries and Gingersnap Topping

Serves 4; ½ cup pudding, 1 tablespoon raspberry mixture, and 2 tablespoons cookie mixture per serving

Terrific all by itself, this lemon cream is even more delicious with a double dose of raspberries plus gingersnaps and lemon zest.

8	reduced-fat gingersnaps, finely crushed
1	teaspoon grated lemon zest
¾	cup boiling water
	0.3-ounce box sugar-free lemon gelatin (small box)
1	cup ice cubes or ⅔ cup cold water
1	cup frozen fat-free or light whipped topping, thawed
2	ounces fat-free or light cream cheese
1	cup fresh or frozen unsweetened raspberries, thawed if frozen
1	tablespoon confectioners' sugar
¼	teaspoon vanilla extract
¼	cup fresh raspberries (optional)

In a small bowl, stir together the gingersnap crumbs and lemon zest. Sprinkle a thin layer into dessert bowls or wine goblets. Set the remaining mixture aside.

Put the boiling water and gelatin in a blender or food processor. Holding down the lid tightly, blend until the gelatin dissolves.

Add the ice cubes or cold water and stir until well blended or the ice has melted.

Add the whipped topping and cream cheese and blend until smooth. Pour into the bowls or goblets. Refrigerate until firm, about 1 hour.

Meanwhile, in another small bowl, gently stir together 1 cup raspberries, confectioners' sugar, and vanilla.

When the gelatin is firm, top with the raspberry mixture, then with the remaining gingersnap mixture. Garnish with the ¼ cup raspberries.

Cook's TIP

Raspberries

Raspberries are quite perishable, so don't count on keeping them in the refrigerator for more than a day or two after you buy them. Remove them from the container as soon as you get them home, and discard any moldy berries to keep the mold from spreading to the other berries. Blot the remaining berries with paper towels. If you aren't going to eat the berries the day of purchase, spread the unrinsed berries in a shallow pan or on a plate, cover them with paper towels, then wrap the container in plastic wrap. For longer storage, first rinse the berries, drain them thoroughly, and pat them dry with paper towels. Then spread them in a single layer on a baking sheet with shallow sides and freeze them. When they are solidly frozen, transfer them to an airtight freezer bag and keep frozen for up to nine months. You don't need to thaw the berries before using them in recipes, but you may need to add a few minutes to the cooking time. Also, frozen berries exude more juice than their fresh counterparts, so when using frozen berries in pies, cobblers, crisps, and similar dishes, use less liquid and more thickener.

PER SERVING
CALORIES 128
TOTAL FAT 1.5 g
    Saturated 0.5 g
    Polyunsaturated 0 g
    Monounsaturated 0.5 g
CHOLESTEROL 3 mg
SODIUM 184 mg
CARBOHYDRATES 22 g
    Fiber 2 g
    Sugars 10 g
PROTEIN 4 g
CALCIUM 50 mg
POTASSIUM 78 mg
DIETARY EXCHANGES
    1 starch
    ½ fruit

Flan Caramel

Serves 6; ½ cup per serving

You can make this flan up to 24 hours ahead of time. For a special treat, serve sliced peaches or nectarines on the caramel topping.

Vegetable oil spray
2½ cups fat-free milk
Egg substitute equivalent to 2 eggs, or whites of 4 large eggs
¼ cup sugar
1 tablespoon dry or sweet sherry
1 teaspoon vanilla extract
Dash of nutmeg
¼ cup plus 2 tablespoons fat-free caramel ice cream topping

Preheat the oven to 325°F. Lightly spray six custard cups with vegetable oil spray.

In a large bowl, whisk together the remaining ingredients except the caramel topping. Pour about ½ cup batter into each custard cup. Place the custard cups in a large pan with a rim, place the pan in the oven, and carefully pour hot water into the large pan to a depth of about 1 inch. Be sure the water doesn't get into the custard cups.

Bake for 50 minutes, or until a wooden toothpick or knife inserted near the center of the custard comes out clean. Remove the custard cups from the pan and let cool completely on a cooling rack. Cover with plastic wrap and refrigerate until serving time. Run a knife around the edge of a custard, place a dessert plate on top, and flip to remove the custard. Repeat with the remaining custards.

In a microwaveable bowl, microwave the caramel topping on 100 percent power (high) for 10 seconds. Spoon 1 tablespoon topping over each serving. Serve immediately.

Egg Whites

If you're using egg whites in a light-colored recipe, such as this one, you can add several drops of yellow food coloring to make it look as though you used whole eggs.

PER SERVING
CALORIES 146
TOTAL FAT 0 g
  Saturated 0 g
  Polyunsaturated 0 g
  Monounsaturated 0 g
CHOLESTEROL 2 mg
SODIUM 140 mg
CARBOHYDRATES 29 g
  Fiber 0 g
  Sugars 24 g
PROTEIN 5 g
CALCIUM 135 mg
POTASSIUM 191 mg
DIETARY EXCHANGES
  ½ skim milk
  1½ other carbohydrate

Spiced Fruit

Serves 8; ¾ cup per serving

This is so good on its own, it's hard to believe it might be even better served over half a cup of fat-free vanilla frozen yogurt.

1   cup firmly packed light brown sugar

½   cup sauterne, dry white wine (regular or nonalcoholic), or apple juice

¼   cup cider vinegar

10 to 15 whole cloves

2   cinnamon sticks (each about 3 inches long)

⅛   teaspoon curry powder

    15-ounce can sliced peaches in fruit juice, drained

    15-ounce can sliced pears in fruit juice, drained

16 to 20 honeydew melon balls, fresh or frozen, or 4 medium kiwifruit, peeled and sliced

8   fresh pineapple spears or 20-ounce can pineapple chunks in their own juice, drained

2   to 4 plums, sliced

In a medium saucepan, stir together the brown sugar, wine, vinegar, cloves, cinnamon, and curry powder. Add the cinnamon sticks. Cook over medium heat for 3 to 5 minutes, or until thoroughly heated, stirring frequently.

Meanwhile, in a large bowl, stir together the remaining ingredients.

Pour the hot syrup over the fruit. Stir well. Let cool at room temperature for 30 minutes. Cover and refrigerate for 8 to 24 hours. Remove the cloves and cinnamon sticks before serving the fruit.

PER SERVING
CALORIES 206
TOTAL FAT 0 g
  Saturated 0 g
  Polyunsaturated 0 g
  Monounsaturated 0 g
CHOLESTEROL 0 mg
SODIUM 28 mg
CARBOHYDRATES 50 g
  Fiber 2 g
  Sugars 45 g
PROTEIN 1 g
CALCIUM 33 mg
POTASSIUM 323 mg
DIETARY EXCHANGES
  1½ fruit
  2 other carbohydrate

Ice Cream with Hot Tropical Fruit

Serves 4; ½ cup ice cream and ¼ cup banana mixture per serving

Bananas Foster goes tropical with the addition of pineapple and toasted coconut.

2 tablespoons sweetened flaked coconut

2 tablespoons light tub margarine

2 medium bananas, sliced

4 ounces canned pineapple chunks, packed in their own juice, drained and halved

2 tablespoons firmly packed light or dark brown sugar

½ teaspoon ground cinnamon

½ teaspoon vanilla extract

2 cups fat-free or low-fat vanilla ice cream or frozen yogurt

Heat a large nonstick skillet over medium-high heat. Toast the coconut for 1 to 2 minutes, or until it begins to brown on the edges, stirring constantly. Transfer to a plate. Set aside.

Return the skillet to the heat. Melt the margarine and swirl to coat the bottom. Gently stir in the bananas, pineapple, brown sugar, and cinnamon. Cook for 2 minutes, or until the bananas are soft and glossy, stirring gently and constantly. Remove from the heat.

Stir in the vanilla.

To serve, spoon the ice cream into dessert bowls. Spoon the banana mixture over each serving. Sprinkle with the coconut.

PER SERVING

CALORIES 229
TOTAL FAT 3 g
  Saturated 0.5 g
  Polyunsaturated 0.5 g
  Monounsaturated 1.5 g
CHOLESTEROL 0 mg
SODIUM 120 mg
CARBOHYDRATES 49 g
  Fiber 2 g
  Sugars 34 g
PROTEIN 5 g
CALCIUM 32 mg
POTASSIUM 310 mg
DIETARY EXCHANGES
  1½ fruit
  2 other carbohydrate
  ½ fat

Strawberry Banana Sorbet

Serves 6; ½ cup per serving

When the bananas on your counter start to freckle, it's time to make sorbet!

- 1 pound fresh strawberries, stemmed and halved, or 1 pound frozen unsweetened strawberries, slightly thawed
- 2 large bananas, cut into ½-inch slices
- ¼ cup light brown sugar, packed
- 2 tablespoons pineapple juice
- 1 teaspoon grated lemon zest
- 2 kiwifruit, peeled, sliced, and mashed with a fork

Put the strawberries and bananas in a large airtight plastic bag. Place the bag in the freezer so the fruit is in a single layer. Freeze for 2 to 3 hours, or until firm (the fruit will still be very slightly soft).

In a food processor or blender, process all the ingredients except the kiwifruit until smooth. Stir in the kiwifruit.

Serve the sorbet immediately (it will be slightly soft), or return it to the freezer for 1 to 2 hours, or until it reaches the desired texture. If you opt to freeze the sorbet for the longer time (or up to one month), remove it from the freezer 5 to 10 minutes before serving to soften slightly.

Cook's TIP

Kiwifruit

When kiwifruit seeds are chopped in a food processor or blender, they impart a bitter flavor. That is why it is best to mash kiwifruit with a fork.

PER SERVING
CALORIES 117
TOTAL FAT 0.5 g
    Saturated 0 g
    Polyunsaturated 0 g
    Monounsaturated 0 g
CHOLESTEROL 0 mg
SODIUM 6 mg
CARBOHYDRATES 30 g
    Fiber 4 g
    Sugars 21 g
PROTEIN 1 g
CALCIUM 31 mg
POTASSIUM 396 mg
DIETARY EXCHANGES
    2 fruit

Frozen Mini Chocolate Mousse Soufflés

Serves 8; ½ cup per serving

Fear of falling? Not with these frosty, airy treats.

14-ounce can fat-free sweetened condensed milk
¼ cup unsweetened cocoa powder
1 teaspoon vanilla extract
½ cup warm water
2 tablespoons plus 2 teaspoons powdered egg whites (pasteurized dried egg whites)
1 cup frozen fat-free or light whipped topping, thawed

In a medium bowl, whisk together the condensed milk, cocoa powder, and vanilla until the cocoa powder is incorporated.

In a large mixing bowl, whisk together the water and powdered egg whites. Let stand for 2 to 3 minutes, or until the egg whites are rehydrated. Beat with an electric mixer on medium-low until foamy, about 30 seconds. Beat on medium-high for 2 to 3 minutes, or until the mixture forms stiff peaks.

Pour the milk mixture over the egg whites. Fold in with a rubber scraper.

Fold in the whipped topping. Ladle the mixture into 5-ounce glass or ceramic custard cups. Cover with plastic wrap. Place the custard cups on a tray if desired. Freeze for 4 hours, or until the mixture is firm. Will keep in the freezer for up to one month.

PER SERVING
CALORIES 176
TOTAL FAT 0.5 g
   Saturated 0 g
   Polyunsaturated 0 g
   Monounsaturated 0 g
CHOLESTEROL 3 mg
SODIUM 85 mg
CARBOHYDRATES 35 g
   Fiber 1 g
   Sugars 32 g
PROTEIN 6 g
CALCIUM 129 mg
POTASSIUM 346 mg
DIETARY EXCHANGES
   ½ skim milk
   2 other carbohydrate

Appendix A: Shopping

Shopping for low-sodium foods is easier than you might think, thanks to the many familiar items now available in no-salt or low-salt varieties. You will find some, such as no-salt-added tomato paste and sauce, in the usual section of the grocery store. Look for other unsalted foods in the special diet section. If the items you want are not in stock, ask your grocer to order them for you.

As you make your shopping list, use the chart on page xv as a guide, and be sure to include a wide variety of foods. Check the nutrition labels for calories, saturated and trans fats, and cholesterol, as well as for sodium, as you choose among the many different products available.

GRAINS AND GRAIN PRODUCTS

Whole grains and whole-grain or enriched breads and pastas are major sources of energy and fiber. They provide essential nutrients and relatively few calories. Experiment with different kinds of bread, such as whole or cracked wheat, rye, and pumpernickel. Steer clear of the salty or high-fat sauces and condiments that often accompany pasta dishes.

Check the labels on crackers and other packaged products for sodium and saturated and trans fats. Look for low-sodium crackers, melba toast, and pretzels when you want something crunchy. Try Scandinavian-style rye crackers and other whole-grain crackers that often are made with little or no salt and without fats or oils.

Be wary of prepared mixes and commercially baked goods such as muffins, biscuits, sweet rolls, cakes, cookies, and pastries. They usually contain significant amounts of sodium, saturated fat, trans fat, and cholesterol. Use the recipes in this book to bake your own, or adjust your favorite recipes by omitting the salt and using the ingredient substitutions listed on page 312.

Whole-grain cereals are good choices for a low-sodium diet. (One notable exception, however, is granola.) Be sure to read the labels and choose those cereals that are lowest in sodium and saturated and trans fats. Hot cereals, brown or white rice, and pastas contain almost no sodium. Just remember to leave the salt out of the cooking water when you prepare these foods.

FRUITS AND VEGETABLES

The Dietary Approaches to Stop Hypertension (DASH) emphasizes the benefits of vegetables and fruits, which are important sources of potassium, magnesium, and fiber. These food groups tend to be low in sodium and calories, have no cholesterol and saturated or trans fats, and are usually high in vitamins. The exceptions include coconut, avocados, and olives. Coconut is high in saturated fat. Avocados are high in healthful monounsaturated fat but are also high in calories. Green olives are high in sodium, and black olives are moderately high in sodium.

Always read the labels on frozen and processed vegetables. Many of these foods contain added salt, butter, or sauces. Also note that frozen and processed fruits may contain added sugar. Fresh fruits or those canned in water are lower in calories than fruits canned in juice or syrup.

Stay away from vegetables packed in brine, such as pickles and sauerkraut, because they're loaded with sodium. It's simple and fun to make your own no-salt-added pickles with our recipes for Easy Dill Pickles or Sweet Bread-and-Butter Pickles (pages 228 and 230).

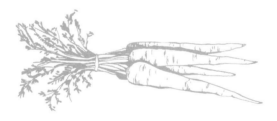

DAIRY PRODUCTS

Fat-free milk and low-sodium, fat-free or low-fat milk products are an important part of a balanced diet. Most milk and milk products do not contain added salt, but watch out for the saturated fat and cholesterol found in whole milk and whole-milk products. Try to make your dairy selections from the wide variety of fat-free and low-fat dairy products on the market instead.

You may be surprised at how much saturated fat and cholesterol you can eliminate from your diet by using fat-free or low-fat milk products. For example, a 2-tablespoon serving of regular sour cream contains about 3.5 grams of saturated fat and 20 milligrams of cholesterol. The same amount of light sour cream has just 1 gram of saturated fat and 10 milligrams of cholesterol. Fat-free sour cream has no saturated fat and no cholesterol.

You can replace whole-milk products with these alternatives:

- Fat-free milk, fat-free evaporated milk, nonfat dry milk
- Cottage cheese that has no salt added
- Cheese made from fat-free or part-skim milk with no salt added
- Fat-free or low-fat yogurt or frozen yogurt, ice milk, and sherbets
- Nondairy whipped toppings and creamers or whiteners

MEATS, POULTRY, AND SEAFOOD

Although a balanced diet requires some protein every day, most Americans eat far more than the recommended daily maximum of 6 ounces (cooked weight) of lean meat, poultry, and seafood. When buying meats, poultry, and seafood, keep your sodium intake to a minimum by choosing only unsalted fresh or frozen lean products.

The best meats are lean cuts with all visible fat trimmed and little or no marbled fat. Some of the leanest cuts are round steak, sirloin tip, tenderloin, and extra-lean ground beef. Look for lean pork, such as low-sodium fresh center-cut ham, tenderloin, and loin chops. Leg of lamb is the leanest cut, and all cuts of veal except cutlets are lean.

In general, avoid the following meats, which usually contain large amounts of things you want to limit (sodium, saturated fat, and cholesterol): luncheon meats; frankfurters; sausage; spareribs; corned beef; salt pork; liver and other organ meats; smoked, cured, or dried meats, such as ham and bacon; and canned meat or poultry, unless packed without salt.

Fresh poultry cooked without skin is an excellent protein choice. When preparing whole chickens and turkeys, however, roast them with the skin on to prevent the meat from drying out. To reduce saturated fat, remove the skin before eating the poultry. Stay away from self-basting turkeys because commercial basting fats are highly saturated. Even when the turkey is basted in broth, the broth is usually high in sodium. It's better to baste your own turkey with an unsalted broth or cook it in an oven-cooking bag, which produces a more healthful, self-basted turkey.

Seafood is a versatile low-sodium favorite. Fish contains less saturated fat and cholesterol than meat and poultry. Research indicates that eating fish rich in omega-3 fatty acids reduces the risk for coronary events such as heart attack. Some fish high in omega-3 fatty acids are Atlantic and coho salmon, tuna, mackerel, and lake and brook trout. We recommend that you eat at least two servings of oily fish each week. However, some fish contain high levels of mercury, PCBs (polychlorinated biphenyls), dioxins, and other environmental contaminants. Women who are pregnant, are planning to become pregnant, or are nursing, as well as young children, should avoid eating potentially contaminated fish.

Shrimp, lobster, crab, crayfish, and most other shellfish are very low in saturated fat. However, ounce for ounce, some varieties contain more sodium and cholesterol than poultry, meat, or fish. Even these, however, are acceptable if you eat them occasionally and stay within the recommended guidelines of 300 milligrams of cholesterol per day.

EGGS

One large egg yolk contains almost the entire daily recommended amount of cholesterol (about 212 milligrams), so it's a good idea to limit your egg yolk consumption. On the other hand, egg whites contain no cholesterol and are an excellent source of protein. You can often use egg whites in place of whole eggs. In fact, in most recipes, two egg whites will substitute nicely for a whole egg. Be sure to eat only cooked eggs and egg whites—not raw—to help avoid salmonella.

NUTS, SEEDS, AND DRIED BEANS

Nuts and seeds are tasty snacks and are good sources of potassium, magnesium, fiber, and protein. Be sure to choose the kinds available in their natural state: unsalted. Remember that although the fat in nuts and seeds is mostly unsaturated, there's lots of it, so the calorie count is high. Also, some nuts such as macadamia and Brazil nuts, are quite high in saturated fat. Legumes such as dried beans and peas are rich in fiber and provide plant proteins. Good examples are lentils and kidney beans.

FATS AND OILS

Fat in food is made up mostly of two types: saturated and unsaturated. Unsaturated fat may be either polyunsaturated or monounsaturated. Some fats are a concentrated source of saturated fat, and others are higher in polyunsaturated or monounsaturated fat.

Saturated and Trans Fats

Fats and oils high in saturated fat tend to become hard at room temperature. These include animal fats, such as butter, cheese, and whole milk, and some plant sources, such as coconut, cocoa butter, and coconut, palm, and palm kernel oils. Trans fat is found in products that contain hydrogenated oil or fat, such as margarines and shortenings. Processed foods such as crackers and other snack foods are often high in trans fat.

A diet high in saturated and trans fats raises blood levels of bad LDL and lowers good HDL. When shopping, choose products with the least amount of saturated and trans fats. For instance, look for liquid or tub margarines or for stick margarines that have a liquid oil listed as the first ingredient.

Monounsaturated and Polyunsaturated Fats

Oils that stay liquid at room temperature are high in unsaturated fats. They include corn, safflower, soybean, sunflower, olive, and canola oils. None contain sodium and all are cholesterol free and low in saturated fat.

Polyunsaturated and monounsaturated are the kinds of fats you should include in your daily diet in salad dressings, margarines, or cooking oils. Keep in mind that mayonnaise and most margarines do contain some salt. Most commercial salad dressings contain large amounts of salt and should be avoided. Instead, make your own low-salt dressings using our recipes on pages 57 through 64.

Use the following chart to identify recommended fats and oils.

RECOMMENDED FATS	FATS FOR OCCASIONAL USE ONLY
Canola oil	Vegetable shortening
Olive oil	Regular stick margarine
Safflower oil	Butter
Sunflower oil	Bacon
Corn oil	Chicken or turkey fat, meat fat
Sesame oil	
Soybean oil	
Polyunsaturated margarine	

BEVERAGES

When you're thirsty, reach for water and fat-free milk. The sodium content of tap water varies widely from one location to another. If your water supply is high in sodium, use low-sodium bottled water for drinking and for preparing drinks such as tea and coffee. Fruit juices and low-sodium vegetable juices count as one daily serving of fruit or vegetables.

If you're trying to lose weight, steer clear of sugared carbonated beverages, fruit drinks, beer, wine, and other alcoholic drinks. Some diet soft drinks and mineral waters are high in sodium. Be sure to read the nutrition labels as you shop.

If you drink alcohol, limit your intake to two drinks per day if you're a man and one if you're a woman. Apart from the effect of its calories on your weight, alcohol can also raise blood pressure.

READ NUTRITION LABELS

To make the most of your low-sodium eating plan, learn to read and compare nutrition labels. As you shop, check for sodium, calories, saturated fat, trans fat, and cholesterol content. Choose the products lowest in these values that you can find.

The nutrition label also gives you the number of calories and the amount of carbohydrates, fiber, sugar, and protein per serving. In addition, the label tells you what percentage of the U.S. Recommended Daily Allowances (RDA) for vitamins A and C, calcium, and iron are in a serving. For example, if a serving contains 100 percent of the RDA for iron, you don't need to eat any other foods with iron that day.

SORTING OUT SODIUM

Food labels use certain names or blurbs to describe the sodium content of the food. Each has a meaning defined by the U.S. Food and Drug Administration. Knowing what each means can help you make the best choice.

- "Sodium Free" means 5 mg sodium or less per serving.
- "Very Low Sodium" means 35 mg sodium or less per serving.
- "Low Sodium" means 140 mg sodium or less per serving.
- "Reduced Sodium" means the usual sodium level is reduced by 25 percent.
- "Unsalted" or "No Salt Added" means no salt was added during processing.

These terms refer only to sodium content and do not mean the product has less fat or saturated fat. It's important to read labels carefully since some foods are low in sodium but high in fat.

AMERICAN HEART ASSOCIATION FOOD CERTIFICATION PROGRAM

To help consumers with food choices, the American Heart Association introduced its Food Certification Program in 1995. The heart-check mark is an easy, reliable tool that grocery shoppers can use to quickly identify heart-healthy products. The simple red heart with a white check mark on a food package is your assurance that the product meets American Heart Association food criteria for saturated fat and cholesterol for healthy people over age 2. For a complete list of certified products, visit heartcheckmark.org. While there, use our online tools to create a heart-healthy grocery list to take with you to the store.

American Heart Association

Meets American Heart Association food criteria for saturated fat and cholesterol for healthy people over age 2.

Appendix B: Cooking with Less Salt

The recipes in this book will prove that food cooked with little or no added salt can be delicious, appealing, and full of flavor. You'll learn to use new combinations of spices, herbs, and wines. You'll see how easy it is to season for flavor, not the taste of salt. You'll be able to make your own low-sodium versions of mustard, horseradish, chili sauce, pickles, and other foods that can spice up a diet.

BE SAVVY ABOUT SEASONING

One source of sodium is salt added during food preparation (at home or in restaurants) and at the table. You were not born with the taste for salt—you acquired it. You can decrease your taste for salt (and sodium) by using little or none in food preparation, by not adding it at the table, and by avoiding processed foods containing large amounts of sodium. It usually takes about a month of eating less salt and high-sodium foods to reduce your desire to salt your food.

Replace salt with herbs and spices or some of the salt-free seasoning mixes on the market. Prepare your own salt-free seasoning blends using the recipes on pages 223–227. Add pepper, garlic, onion, and/or lemon to foods to give them a more distinct flavor and help replace the taste of salt.

Herb and spice blends, such as chili powder, aren't required to have a nutrition label. You can, however, check the ingredients list to see whether the word "salt" or "sodium" or any related word (such as "monosodium gluta-mate," or MSG) is listed as one of the first three ingredients. If so, find an alternative.

Most salt substitutes are potassium chloride. Adding a small amount of salt substitute to food after cooking will make the food taste salty. However, before using any salt substitute, check with your healthcare provider. Products labeled "lite" salt are usually part sodium chloride (salt) and part potassium chloride. Because they add sodium to food, we don't recommend using them.

Any seasoning product that uses "salt" as part of the name is high in sodium. Examples are garlic salt, onion salt, and celery salt. Garlic powder, onion powder, and celery seeds or flakes are low in sodium, however, and make an easy substitution possible if these are flavors you love.

HIGH-SODIUM CONDIMENTS AND FOODS

Many dishes you enjoy are likely to contain high-sodium seasonings and other salty ingredients. Read nutrition labels to find the lowest-sodium versions when shopping for these common products: commercial soups, bouillon cubes and powders, relishes, pickles, salad dressings, flour tortillas, canned beans and vegetables, soy sauce, Worcestershire sauce, steak sauce, ketchup, chili sauce, and flavored seasoning salts. This book includes recipes for some of these favorites so you can make your own.

You can also use the Ingredient Substitutions on pages 312 and 313 for ideas on how the reduce the sodium in the recipes you love. For example, to tenderize meats, marinate them rather than using high-sodium meat tenderizer. Instead of using seasoned bread crumbs, add salt-free herbs to unseasoned bread crumbs. Cooking wine is very high in sodium; use regular or nonalcoholic wine for better flavor without the salt.

For some high-sodium foods, such as green olives, we recommend using small amounts. Another way to remove sodium is to rinse foods such as canned beans, capers, and bottled roasted bell peppers.

COOKING TECHNIQUES

All cooking methods are not created equal. Some are better than others for preserving basic nutrients and keeping added fat and sodium to a minimum. Try to avoid methods that add fat or allow food to cook in its own fat, such as deep-fat frying or pan frying. Instead, use the following techniques to enhance flavor and help protect your heart.

Roasting and Baking

Roasting and baking use slow, dry heat to cook foods. For roasting, trim as much fat as you can from the meat, leaving a thin covering of fat across the top. Place the meat with the fat side up on a rack to be sure the meat does not sit in the drippings. For basting, use low-sodium, fat-free liquids such as table wine, no-salt-added tomato juice, or fresh lemon juice. You don't need a rack for baking, which is another excellent way to prepare poultry, fish, and meat. Foods can be baked in covered cookware with a little additional liquid to add flavor and keep food moist.

Braising or Stewing

This slow-cooking method is a good way to tenderize tougher cuts of meat. Because the fat cooks out of the meat into the liquid, it's a good idea to prepare your recipe a day ahead and refrigerate it. You can then remove the chilled fat easily before reheating. Braising is also an excellent way to cook vegetables.

Grilling or Broiling

Placing food on a rack and cooking with either of these methods allows the fat to drip away from meat or poultry. It's also a tasty way to cook fish steaks or whole fish. For extra flavor, try marinating food before putting it over the coals or under the broiler. Skewered vegetables also taste great browned over an open flame.

Steaming

Cooking food in a basket over simmering water leaves the natural flavor, color, and nutritional value of vegetables intact. Try adding herbs to the steaming water or using low-sodium broth instead of water to add even more flavor to the finished dish.

Poaching

To poach chicken or fish, immerse it in a pan of simmering liquid on top of the stove. This method works especially well when you serve the food with a sauce made of pureed vegetables and herbs.

Stir-Frying

The constant movement of stir-frying keeps foods from sticking and burning as they cook, even over high temperature. Try stir-frying vegetables and diced poultry or seafood with a tiny bit of peanut oil, which has a high smoking point. Be sure to use the low-sodium version when your recipe calls for soy sauce.

Microwave Cooking

This is a fast, easy cooking method that requires no added fat because foods don't tend to stick in the moist heat of the microwave. In fact, you can drain food of fat as it cooks by placing it in the microwave between two paper towels. If you are adapting a recipe for the microwave, reduce the liquid used by about one-third because less evaporates in microwave cooking.

LOW-SALT FLAVOR TIPS

Spicing up low-salt cooking is easy when you know a few good tricks. The following ideas will help you enhance the flavor of a variety of foods without using salt.

- Dry-roast seeds, nuts, and whole spices to bring out their full flavor. Use a skillet over moderate heat or a baking sheet in a 350°F oven, stirring frequently to toast evenly and prevent burning.
- Buy the best and the freshest whole spices and grind them in a spice grinder. You'll taste a big difference compared to dried spices. In most recipes, fresh herbs provide more flavor than dried. Chop and add them at the last minute for a more "alive" taste.
- If you buy spices and herbs already ground, buy them in small bottles. You'll need to replenish your supply more often but they'll be fresher.
- Use dry mustard or no-salt-added mustard (such as Hot Mustard, page 221) instead of high-sodium prepared mustard. You can also try honey mustard, which is very low in sodium. Check the labels when new products appear; some are low in sodium without saying so on the front.

- For a little bite, add fresh hot chile peppers to your dishes. Using plastic gloves, discard the membrane and seeds before finely chopping the peppers. Raw peppers are very low in sodium and have a lot more flavor than the pickled kind. A small amount can go a long way!

- Fill a salt shaker with a combination of fresh herbs and spices to use in place of salt. Try our favorites on pages 298 and 299.

- Use a food processor to grate fresh horseradish, which packs more punch than the salted, bottled kind. (See the recipe for Horseradish, page 222.)

- Experience the flavor of fresh ginger. Peel it, then grate the gingerroot using a ginger grater, microplane grater, or flat, sheet-type grater.

- Use citrus zest. The zest is the part of the peel without the white pith; it holds the true flavor of the fruit. Grate it with either a microplane grater or a flat, sheet-type grater. You can also remove the zest with a vegetable peeler and cut it into thin strips.

- Vinegar or citrus juice sprinkled on foods is a flavor enhancer, but add it at the last minute. Vinegar is wonderful on vegetables such as greens; citrus juice, on fruits such as cantaloupe. Either is great on fish.

- Some vegetables and fruits, such as mushrooms, tomatoes, chiles, cherries, cranberries, and currants, impart a more intense flavor when dried than when fresh. If you reconstitute them in water, you will have a natural "broth" to work with as a bonus.

- Roast vegetables in a hot oven to caramelize their natural sugars.

HERB, SPICE, and SEASONING GUIDE

When preparing foods, try these suggestions to add flavor instead of salt.

BAKED GOODS

Breads	Anise, caraway, cardamom, fennel, poppy seeds, sesame seeds
Desserts	Anise, caraway, cardamom, cinnamon, cloves, coriander, fennel, ginger, mace, mint, nutmeg, poppy seeds, sesame seeds

DIPS

Caraway, dill, garlic, oregano, fresh parsley

EGGS

Basil, chervil, chili powder, cumin, curry, fennel, marjoram, mustard, oregano, parsley, poppy seeds, rosemary, saffron, savory, sesame seeds, tarragon, thyme, turmeric, watercress

MEATS, POULTRY, and SEAFOOD

Beef	Allspice, bay leaf, cayenne, cumin, curry powder, garlic, green bell pepper, marjoram, fresh mushrooms, dry mustard, nutmeg, onion, rosemary, sage, thyme, red wine
Pork	Apple, applesauce, cinnamon, cloves, fennel, garlic, ginger, mint, onion, sage, savory, red wine
Poultry	Basil, bay leaf, cinnamon, curry powder, garlic, green bell pepper, fresh lemon juice, mace, marjoram, fresh mushrooms, onion, paprika, fresh parsley, lemon pepper, poultry seasoning, rosemary, saffron, sage, savory, sesame, thyme, tarragon, white wine
Seafood	Allspice, basil, bay leaf, cayenne, curry powder, cumin, fennel, garlic, green bell pepper, fresh lemon juice, mace, marjoram, mint, fresh mushrooms, Dijon mustard, dry mustard powder, green onion, paprika, saffron, sage, sesame, tarragon, thyme, turmeric, white wine

SALADS

Basil, chervil, coriander, dill, fresh lemon juice, mint, mustard, oregano, parsley, rosemary, sage, savory, sesame seeds, turmeric, vinegar, watercress

SOUPS and STEWS

Bean Soup	Dry mustard powder
Chowders	Bay leaf, peppercorns
Pea Soup	Bay leaf, coriander, fresh parsley
Stews	Basil, bay leaf, cayenne, chervil, chili powder, cinnamon, cumin, curry, fennel, garlic, ginger, marjoram, nutmeg, onion, parsley, saffron
Vegetable Soup	Onion, vinegar

VEGETABLES

Asparagus	Garlic, fresh lemon juice, onion, vinegar
Beans	Caraway, cloves, cumin, mint, savory, tarragon, thyme
Beets	Anise, caraway, fennel, ginger, savory
Carrots	Anise, cinnamon, cloves, mint, sage, tarragon
Corn	Allspice, cumin, green bell pepper, pimiento, fresh tomato
Cucumbers	Chives, dill, garlic, vinegar
Green Beans	Dill, fresh lemon juice, marjoram, nutmeg, pimiento
Greens	Garlic, fresh lemon juice, onion, vinegar
Peas	Allspice, green bell pepper, mint, fresh mushrooms, onions, fresh parsley, sage, savory
Potatoes	Chives, dill, green bell pepper, onion, pimiento, saffron
Squash	Allspice, brown sugar, cinnamon, cloves, fennel, ginger, mace, nutmeg, onion, savory
Tomatoes	Allspice, basil, garlic, marjoram, onion, oregano, sage, savory, tarragon, thyme

HEART-HEALTHY COOKING TIPS

These techniques will help you cut back on saturated fat and calories while maintaining taste and texture.

- Use a nonstick skillet so you can cook with less oil, or try vegetable oil spray in your pan instead of butter or margarine.
- Trim all visible fat from meat before cooking.
- Buy only lean ground beef and pork (no more than 10 percent fat).
- When figuring serving sizes, remember that meat loses about 25 percent of its weight during cooking. (For example, 4 ounces of raw meat will be about 3 ounces cooked.)
- After you roast meat or poultry, chill the drippings in the refrigerator. Once they are cooled, the fat will rise to the top and harden. You can then remove it easily and save the liquid to use in stews, sauces, and soups.
- Except when roasting whole chickens or other poultry, make a habit of discarding the skin and removing all visible fat before cooking the poultry. Raw skin will be easier to remove if you use paper towels or a clean cloth to take hold of it. To help prevent the spread of bacteria, scrub the cutting surface and utensils well with hot sudsy water after preparing poultry.
- Cut down on dietary cholesterol by using more vegetables and less poultry or meats in soups, stews, and casseroles. Finely chopped vegetables are great for stretching ground poultry or meat.
- Seal in natural juices by wrapping foods in aluminum foil before cooking. Or try wrapping foods in edible pouches made of large steamed lettuce or cabbage leaves and baking them with the seam side down.
- Buy low-sodium canned tuna and canned salmon packed in spring water.

Appendix C: Dining Out

Dining out on a low-sodium diet can be a challenge, but here are some suggestions to make it easier. Start by choosing a restaurant that offers a wide variety of foods. It is more likely to offer more lower-sodium selections. Most restaurant food has salt and often monosodium glutamate (MSG) added to it. This is especially true if foods are prepared ahead of time, frozen, and reheated before serving. When you choose a restaurant that prepares food as it is ordered, you can request that the kitchen staff leave the salt and MSG out of your portion. Naturally, you'll want to avoid using salt at the table. Also remember to avoid high-sodium condiments, such as ketchup, mustard, soy sauce, steak sauce, and salad dressing. A single restaurant meal may contain anywhere from 1,000 to 4,000 milligrams of sodium.

DINING TIPS

- Be aware of those foods that have salt added during preparation; either avoid them or select only one.
- Remove breading and toppings from your food.
- Request that sauces are served on the side.
- Avoid table salt and high-sodium condiments and garnishes, such as pickles and olives.
- Avoid salad and other foods containing cheese and cottage cheese.
- Squeeze fresh lemon on your salads, or use oil and vinegar (in separate bottles, not Italian dressing). If these are not available, ask for your salad dressing on the side.
- Compensate for high-sodium foods eaten out by using very low sodium foods, such as unsalted margarine, unsalted bread, and unsalted cereal, at home.

If you eat out very often, you'll want to keep track of the sodium in restaurant food. To see how much you can decrease the sodium you are likely to consume when you dine out, compare the sodium values on page 302 for some typical restaurant choices with the suggested alternatives.

TYPICAL MENU ITEM	SODIUM (mg)	SUGGESTED ALTERNATIVE	SODIUM (mg)
Baked fish with breading (5 ounces)	1,002	Baked fish, breading removed (5 ounces)	575
Baked potato with butter, cheese, sour cream, bacon bits	325	Baked potato with margarine, chives	60
Blue cheese dressing (2 tablespoons)	335	Oil and vinegar dressing (2 tablespoons, using 2 teaspoons oil)	0
Apple pie (1 slice)	400	Sherbet (½ cup)	45
Chocolate cake with frosting (1 slice)	300	Melon wedge	10

CHOOSING FAST FOOD

Finding healthful fast food can be a real undertaking. Sodium, saturated fat, trans fat, cholesterol, and calories can be high in fast foods. To make the wisest choices, read the nutrition facts that most restaurants provide. In general, the less preparation that has gone into a food item, the less sodium it will contain.

Many fast-food restaurants now offer a salad bar. Here you usually have a lot of good choices.

- Choose fresh greens and other fresh vegetables.
- Select fruit salads when available.
- Avoid the pickled items, such as olives and peppers, and the obviously salted items, such as ham, cheese, and bacon.
- Limit any prepared salads, such as potato salad and pasta salad, which frequently contain lots of mayonnaise and salt.

A plain baked potato is another good selection. Add a tablespoon of sour cream—lower in fat and sodium than soft margarine—and as many chives as you want. Even if you do shake a little salt on the potato, you'll still be getting a lot less sodium than if you added cheese, bacon, and more margarine.

Most fast-food restaurants serve a green salad with chicken. It can be a good choice if you order the chicken grilled, not fried or "crispy," skip the cheese, and have the dressing on the side. When you're ordering at a deli counter, be aware that many of the precooked meats are high in sodium and sodium-containing preservatives.

PORTION CONTROL

If you're in the position of having to eat something that doesn't fit into your eating plan, think *small*! Portion control is the most effective way to cut down on excess sodium, as well as calories, saturated and trans fats, and cholesterol.

- Have one slice of mushroom or vegetarian pizza.
- Choose a small burger without cheese. Add lettuce, tomato, and onion. Have one spread—mustard, mayonnaise, or ketchup—on the side. Ketchup—with less sodium than mustard and less fat than mayonnaise —is probably your best bet. Beware of "special" sauces unless you know what they contain.
- Split a small order of French fries with a friend.

If you follow a few simple rules and keep these tips in mind, you'll be able to enjoy eating out without jeopardizing your good health.

Appendix D:
Heart Disease and Stroke

Recent research has identified many of the possible causes of heart attack and stroke—and what can be done to lessen your risk. It's reassuring to know that you can do a number of things to take control of your individual risks.

You can help prevent cardiovascular diseases if you:

- Follow a heart-healthful diet.
- Are physically active each day.
- Achieve and maintain a normal blood pressure level.
- Achieve and maintain a healthful body weight.
- Achieve and maintain recommended blood cholesterol levels.
- Achieve and maintain a normal fasting blood glucose level.
- Don't use tobacco and avoid secondhand smoke.

More and more Americans are taking charge of their health. Millions are watching what they eat by counting calories; cutting down on saturated fat, trans fat, and cholesterol in their diets; and helping control their high blood pressure by reducing the salt in their diets. Millions are walking, running, and working out at health centers. Millions more have stopped smoking. All these lifestyle changes work together to promote good health and prevent disease.

RISK FACTORS

In addition to high blood pressure (see page xi), certain risk factors increase the chance that you may develop cardiovascular disease, especially heart disease and stroke. You have no control over some, such as aging, being male, or belonging to your family or your race. However, other risk factors can be controlled or treated: high blood cholesterol, physical inactivity, obesity or overweight, diabetes, and tobacco smoke. No matter what your individual situation, you may be able to reduce your personal risk of disease by making healthful choices for a healthful lifestyle.

High Blood Cholesterol

A high level of cholesterol in the blood is a risk factor for heart disease. High blood cholesterol contributes to atherosclerosis, the process by which cholesterol and other elements in blood are deposited along the inner linings of arteries to form plaque. Over time, plaque builds up and narrows the inside of the artery. If the plaque ruptures and the narrowed artery becomes entirely blocked, blood cannot carry life-sustaining oxygen to the body's cells. If the blocked artery is in the heart itself, the result is a heart attack. If the blocked artery is in the neck or head, the result is a stroke. Research shows that lowering elevated blood cholesterol levels helps reduce the risk of heart disease.

TOTAL BLOOD CHOLESTEROL LEVELS		
DESIRABLE	BORDERLINE-HIGH	HIGH
Total less than 200 mg/dL	200 to 239 mg/dL	240 mg/dL and above

These levels apply to adults 20 years or older.
Mg/dL indicates milligrams of cholesterol per deciliter of blood.

Eating foods high in saturated fat tends to raise your blood cholesterol level. Saturated fat is found in animal products and in some plant products. A diet low in saturated fat and cholesterol will help reduce blood cholesterol levels. The American Heart Association recommends that your diet should include less than 10 percent of calories from saturated fat and less than 300 milligrams of cholesterol per day.

Replace the saturated fat in your diet with the unsaturated fats—polyunsaturated and monounsaturated. Both types of unsaturated fat help lower blood cholesterol when consumed as part of a diet low in saturated fats. Another recommendation for controlling blood cholesterol is to achieve and maintain your ideal body weight. Eating foods that contain soluble fiber also may help lower blood cholesterol.

Physical Inactivity and Obesity

Being inactive, overweight, or obese can increase your risk of developing cardiovascular disease. If you are overweight or obese, take steps to lose weight. Increase the amount of activity in your life by taking a brisk walk, climbing the stairs, or doing whatever works for you to get moving more often. Try to get a total of at least 30 minutes of physical activity on most, if not all, days. Studies have shown that being active and losing weight can reduce blood pressure, prevent or delay the onset of type 2 diabetes, and help reduce the risk for heart attack and stroke.

Smoking

Smoking tobacco products acts with other risk factors to greatly increase your risk for coronary heart disease. In fact, if you smoke cigarettes, your risk of heart attack is more than twice that of a nonsmoker. Secondhand, or passive, smoke (constant exposure to other people's smoke) increases the risk of heart disease even for nonsmokers.

Diabetes

Diabetes seriously increases the risk of heart disease and stroke, even when blood sugar levels are under control. Studies also report an association between high blood pressure and insulin resistance. If you have diabetes, it's important to work with your healthcare provider to manage it and control any other risk factors you can. If you have both diabetes and hypertension—a common combination—you are at twice the risk for developing cardiovascular disease as you would be with only one of the conditions.

MEDICATIONS FOR HIGH BLOOD PRESSURE

If you have been given medication to control your blood pressure, you may think that taking a pill is all you need to do. Research confirms, however, that lifestyle changes in diet and physical activity level are the best ways to maximize the effectiveness of your treatment. In addition, medication can work only if you take it regularly. Even after your blood pressure reaches a more healthful level, you may need to follow a drug regimen over your lifetime to keep a normal blood pressure. However, coping with the inconvenience of medication is still much better than suffering a stroke or heart attack.

Several types of drug are available, and they work in different ways to lower blood pressure. In some cases, it is most effective to use a combination of medications.

Some types of medication include:

- Diuretics, which rid the body of excess sodium and water
- Beta-blockers, which slow the heart rate and the heart's output of blood
- Vasodilators, ACE inhibitors, and calcium channel blockers, which relax and open up narrowed blood vessels

Be sure to take medications exactly as prescribed. If you experience side effects from the treatment, tell your healthcare provider, but don't stop taking your medication. These tips will make it easier to keep track of when and how.

- Take medications at the same time every day, such as with meals or when you brush your teeth.
- Keep a weekly pill box with separate compartments for each day or time of day.
- Use a calendar to mark down when you take a pill.
- Leave a note for yourself as a reminder.

WARNING SIGNS OF HEART ATTACK AND STROKE

When heart attack and stroke do occur, every second counts. If you have any of the symptoms listed below, or think anyone else is experiencing them, immediately call 911. Not all these signs occur in every heart attack or stroke. Today, heart attack and stroke victims can benefit from new medications and treatments unavailable to patients in years past. For example, clot-busting drugs can stop some heart attacks and strokes in progress, reducing disability and saving lives.

Heart Attack

It's important to reduce your risk factors and know the following warning signs and how to respond quickly and properly if they occur.

- Chest discomfort. Most heart attacks involve discomfort in the center of the chest that lasts more than a few minutes or that goes away and comes back. It can feel like uncomfortable pressure, squeezing, fullness, or pain.
- Discomfort in other areas of the upper body. Symptoms can include pain or discomfort in one or both arms, the back, neck, jaw, or stomach.
- Shortness of breath. This may occur with or without chest discomfort.
- Other signs. These may include breaking out in a cold sweat, nausea, or lightheadedness.

Stroke

High blood pressure is strongly linked with the risk of stroke. Stroke is a medical emergency. Know the warning signs of stroke listed below, and encourage the people around you to learn them and be able to act quickly if they or someone they know experiences any of the warning signs. We can't overemphasize it: Every second counts.

- Sudden numbness or weakness of the face, arm, or leg, especially on one side of the body.
- Sudden confusion, trouble speaking or understanding.
- Sudden trouble seeing in one or both eyes.
- Sudden trouble walking, dizziness, loss of balance or coordination.
- Sudden, severe headache with no known cause.

Most people who are treated successfully for high blood pressure live a longer and healthier life. Call 1-800-AHA-USA1 (1-800-242-8721) or visit americanheart.org to learn more about high blood pressure, cardiovascular disease, and living a healthful lifestyle.

Appendix E: Handy Reference Lists

Common Foods High in Sodium

Several of these items are also available as unsalted or low-sodium products.
Be aware which variety you are selecting when you shop.

Anchovies

Bacon

Barbecue sauce

Bologna

Bouillon cubes or granules

Breads and bread products

Buttermilk

Celery salt

Cereal, dry

Cheese

Chips, potato and corn

Crackers

Frankfurters

Frozen dinners and entrées

Garlic salt

Ham, processed or cured

Ketchup

Kosher processed meat

Meat, canned or frozen in sauce

Meat, processed or cured

Monosodium glutamate (MSG)

Mustard

Nuts, salted

Olives, green

Onion salt

Pastrami

Pepperoni

Pickles

Pizza

Salami

Salt

Sauerkraut

Sausage

Seasoned salt

Seeds, salted

Soup, canned

Soy sauce

Steak sauce

Tomato juice

Wieners—beef, pork, and turkey

Worcestershire sauce

Good Sources of Potassium

Potassium is considered to be an important component of a dietary approach to lowering blood pressure. The list below is a handy reference if you're looking for ways to add more potassium to your daily diet. Foods under each heading are listed in descending order by the amount of potassium they contain.

400 mg or more

Potato, cooked, 1 medium

Beet greens, cooked, ½ cup

Prunes, dried, 10 medium

Yogurt, plain, fat-free, 8 ounces

Prune juice, ¾ cup

Apricots, dried, ¼ cup

Molasses, blackstrap,
1 tablespoon

Halibut, cooked, 3 ounces

Soybeans, green, cooked, ½ cup

Lima beans, frozen, ½ cup

Tomato sauce, no-salt-added, ½ cup

Cantaloupe, cubed, 1 cup

Banana, 1 medium

Spinach, cooked, ½ cup

Tomato juice, no-salt-added, ¾ cup

200 to 399 mg

Carrot juice, ¾ cup

Honeydew melon, cubed, 1 cup

Milk, fat-free, 1 cup

Nectarine, 1 medium

Orange juice, ¾ cup

Port tenderloin, lean, cooked,
3 ounces

Buttermilk, low-fat, cultured,
1 cup

Lentils, cooked, ½ cup

Sweet potato, cooked, 1 medium

White beans, cooked, ½ cup

Beef, lean, cooked, 3 ounces

Grapefruit juice, ¾ cup

Flounder, cooked, 3 ounces

Salmon, pink, no-salt-added, canned,
3 ounces

Tomatoes, canned, no-salt added,
½ cup

Tuna, light, packed in water,
no-salt-added

Orange, 1 medium

Beets, cooked, ½ cup

Strawberries, fresh, sliced, 1 cup

Turkey, light meat without skin,
cooked, 3 ounces

Carrot, raw, 1 large

Red beans, cooked, ½ cup

Apple juice, ¾ cup

Chicken, cooked, 3 ounces

Ingredient Substitutions

There's no need to toss out old family recipes and holiday treats because you're watching your sodium intake. You can keep enjoying many of your favorite recipes if you make a few simple ingredient substitutions, such as those listed below. You will reduce enough of the sodium and saturated fat to make almost any recipe fit right into your heart-healthy eating plan.

IF YOUR RECIPE CALLS FOR	USE
Broth or bouillon	Chicken Broth (page 19); Beef Broth (page 18); Vegetable Broth (page 20); very low sodium bouillon granules or cubes; or commercially prepared low-sodium broth.
Butter, melted butter, or shortening	Unsaturated, unsalted margarine or oil. When possible, use fat-free or light tub or fat-free spray margarine. However, if the type of fat is critical to the recipe, especially in baked goods, you may need to use a stick margarine (see page xix).
Butter for sautéing	See vegetable oil.
Cream	Fat-free half-and-half; polyunsaturated nondairy coffee cream; undiluted fat-free evaporated milk.
Eggs	Cholesterol-free egg substitutes or egg whites (for 1 whole egg, substitute 2 egg whites).
Evaporated milk	Fat-free evaporated milk.
Flavored salts, such as onion salt, garlic salt, and celery salt	Onion powder, garlic powder, celery seeds or flakes. Use about one-fourth the amount of flavored salt indicated in the recipe.
Ice cream	Fat-free or low-fat ice cream; fat-free or low-fat frozen yogurt; sorbet; sherbet.
Oil in baking	Unsweetened applesauce.

IF YOUR RECIPE CALLS FOR	USE
Salt	Seasoning blends, pages 223–227.
Tomato juice	No-salt-added tomato juice; 6-ounce can no-salt-added tomato paste diluted with 3 cans of water.
Tomato sauce	No-salt-added tomato sauce; 6-ounce can no-salt-added tomato paste diluted with 1 can of water.
Unsweetened baking chocolate	3 tablespoons cocoa powder plus 1 tablespoon polyunsaturated oil or unsaturated, unsalted margarine for every 1-ounce square of chocolate.
Whipping cream	Fat-free evaporated milk (thoroughly chilled before whipping).
Whole milk	Fat-free milk.

Ingredient Equivalents

INGREDIENT	MEASUREMENT
Almonds	1 ounce = ¼ cup slivers
Apple	1 medium = ¾ cup chopped, 1 cup sliced
Basil leaves, fresh	⅔ ounce = ½ cup chopped, stems removed
Bell pepper, any color	1 medium = 1 cup chopped or sliced
Carrot	1 medium = ⅓ to ½ cup chopped or sliced, ½ cup shredded
Celery	1 medium rib = ½ cup chopped or sliced
Cheese, hard, such as Parmesan	4 ounces = 1 cup grated 3½ ounces = 1 cup shredded
Cheese, semihard, such as Cheddar	4 ounces = 1 cup grated
Cheese, soft, such as blue, feta, or goat	1 ounce, crumbled = ¼ cup
Cucumber	1 medium = 1 cup sliced
Lemon juice	1 medium = 3 tablespoons
Lemon zest	1 medium = 2 to 3 teaspoons
Lime juice	1 medium = 1½ to 2 tablespoons
Lime zest	1 medium = 1 teaspoon
Mushrooms (button)	1 pound = 5 cups sliced or 6 cups chopped
Onions, green	8 to 9 medium = 1 cup sliced (green and white parts)
Onions, white or yellow	1 large = 1 cup chopped; 1 medium = ⅔ cup chopped; 1 small = ⅓ cup chopped
Orange juice	1 medium = ⅓ to ½ cup
Orange zest	1 medium = 1½ to 2 tablespoons
Strawberries	1 pint = 2 cups sliced or chopped
Tomatoes	2 large, 3 medium, or 3 small = 1½ to 2 cups chopped
Walnuts	1 ounce = ½ cup chopped

Appendix F:
American Heart Association National Center and Affiliates

For more information about our programs and services, call 1-800-AHA-USA1 (1-800-242-8721) or contact us online at www.americanheart.org. For information about the American Stroke Association, a division of the American Heart Association, call 1-888-4STROKE (1-888-478-7653).

National Center

American Heart Association
7272 Greenville Avenue
Dallas, TX 75231-4596
214-373-6300

AFFILIATES

GREATER MIDWEST AFFILIATE
Illinois, Indiana, Michigan, Minnesota,
North Dakota, South Dakota, Wisconsin
Chicago, IL

GREATER RIVERS AFFILIATE
Delaware, Kentucky, Ohio, Pennsylvania,
West Virginia
Columbus, OH

GREATER SOUTHEAST AFFILIATE
Alabama, Florida, Georgia, Louisiana,
Mississippi, Puerto Rico, Tennessee
Marietta, GA

HEARTLAND AFFILIATE
Arkansas, Iowa, Kansas, Missouri,
Nebraska, Oklahoma
Topeka, KS

HERITAGE AFFILIATE
Connecticut, Long Island, New Jersey,
New York, Bronx, Queens, Richmond/
Staten Island
New York City, NY

MID-ATLANTIC AFFILIATE
Washington, D.C.; Maryland;
North Carolina; South Carolina; Virginia
Glen Allen, VA

NORTHEAST AFFILIATE
Maine, Massachusetts, New Hampshire,
New York State (excluding Heritage's
designated areas), Rhode Island, Vermont
Framingham, MA

PACIFIC/MOUNTAIN AFFILIATE
Alaska, Arizona, Colorado, Hawaii,
Idaho, Montana, New Mexico, Oregon,
Washington, Wyoming
Seattle, WA

TEXAS AFFILIATE
Austin, TX

WESTERN STATES AFFILIATE
California, Nevada, Utah
Los Angeles, CA

Index

D